Mathematics

Class 12 (CBSE & CUET Exam 2025-26)
Part-1

Concept-clearing notes and
formulae with examples

By Pavitra Gupta
B.E.

Preface

This is the paperback printed version of my digital book 'MATHEMATICS for class 12 (CBSE & CUET): Concept-clearing notes and formulae with examples Part-1'.

It contains seven chapters 1 to 7. In continuation of it, Part-2 book contains chapters 8 to 14. Both these parts, together, complete the syllabus prescribed by CBSE for class 12 Mathematics and the syllabus of the CUET entrance test for undergraduate programmes. Some topics, which are marked by an asterisk (*) in this book, are not in the CBSE syllabus for session 2025-26 (released in April 2025). However, these topics have been covered for CUET, state boards or other exams.

It's my endeavour to keep the content as simple as possible to make it easy to understand. The books contain complete list of formulae. Concepts have been explained with easy examples. For the students to remember the formulae easily, a formula is written first and then it is explained, if needed, with the help of well labelled figure. After that, an example is given to know how to apply it.

These books are written just like a student makes notes in the class to remember the things easily. It makes the books very helpful to learn and remember all concepts even though they do not contain questions for practice. Also, they become very useful while revising for exams.

I hope the students will be able to understand each and every concept comfortably through these books.

Pavitra Gupta

Table of Contents

---

*Asterisk (*) marked article (if any) is **not** in CBSE 2025-26 syllabus.*

---

*Asterisk (*) marked article (if any) is **not** in CBSE 2025-26 syllabus.*

*Asterisk (*) marked article (if any) is **not** in CBSE 2025-26 syllabus.*

*Asterisk (*) marked article (if any) is **not** in CBSE 2025-26 syllabus.*

*Asterisk (*) marked article (if any) is **not** in CBSE 2025-26 syllabus.*

Chapter-1   Relations and Functions

1 Ordered pair

Two elements grouped together in a particular order, represent an ordered pair.

- If a and b are two elements , then (a, b) or (b, a) represent an ordered pair.
- Two ordered pairs are equal if and only if first element of one pair is equal to the first of the other and second element is equal to the second of the other.

  i.e., If $(a, b) = (c, d)$, then $a = c$ and $b = d$.

  Also, if $a = c$ and $b = d$, then $(a, b) = (c, d)$
- **For different elements a & b :$(a, b) \neq (b, a)$**

2 Ordered triplet

Three elements grouped together in a particular order, represent an ordered triplet.

- If a, b and c are three elements , then (a, b, c) represent an ordered triplet.
- Two ordered triplets are equal if and only if their corresponding first, second and third elements are equal.

3 Cartesian Product

The set of all ordered pairs of elements of 2 non-empty sets A *and* B **such that first element of every pair belongs to set A and second element belongs to B** *is called as Cartesian Product* A $\times$ B.

i.e., $A \times B = \{ (a,b) : a \in A, b \in B \}$

Also, $B \times A = \{ (b,a) : a \in A, b \in B \}$

<u>**Example**</u>

If $A = \{ 1,2,3 \}$ and $B = \{ a,b \}$,

then $A \times B = \{(1,a),(1,b),(2,a),(2,b),(3,a),(3,b)\}$

and $B \times A = \{(a,1),(a,2),(a,3),(b,1),(b,2),(b,3)\}$

- If either of the sets A or B is empty , then A x B is also empty.

  i.e., **If $A = \phi$ or $B = \phi$, then $A \times B = \phi$**
- For different sets A and B,

  $$A \times B \neq B \times A \qquad (\because (a, b) \neq (b, a) \text{ for } a \neq b)$$
- If there are p elements in set A and q elements in set B, then there will be pq elements in $A \times B$.

i.e., if $n(A) = p$ and $n(B) = q$, then $n(A \times B) = pq$.

Example
If $A = \{\,1,2,3\,\}$ and $B = \{\,a,b\,\}$,
then $A \times B = \{(1,a),(1,b),(2,a),(2,b),(3,a),(3,b)\}$
Here, $n(A) = 3$ and $n(B) = 2$
$\therefore \quad n(A \times B) = 3 \times 2 = 6.$

- Cartesian product of three sets:
  $A \times B \times C = \{\,(a,b,c) : a \in A,\, b \in B,\, c \in C\,\}$
- We can also have Cartesian product of a set with itself.
  $$A \times A = \{\,(a,b) : a \in A,\, b \in A\,\}$$
  Also, $A \times A \times A = \{\,(a,b,c) : a \in A,\, b \in A,\, c \in A\,\}$

Example
If $A = \{\,1,2\,\}$,
then $A \times A = \{(1,1),(1,2),(2,1),(2,2)\,\}$
And $A \times A \times A = \{(1,1,1),(1,1,2),(1,2,1),(1,2,2),(2,1,1),$
$$(2,1,2)\,,(2,2,1),(2,2,2),\,\}$$

4 Relation

Any subset of $A \times B$ *is a relation from set* A *to set* B.

- A relation can be represented in *Roster form* or in *Set-builder form*.

Example
If $A = \{\,1,2,3\,\}$ and $B = \{\,a,b\,\}$,
then $A \times B = \{(1,a),(1,b),(2,a),(2,b),(3,a),(3,b)\}$
Suppose we have: $R_1 = \{(1,a),(1,b),(2,a)\}$
$$R_2 = \{(1,a),(3,a)\}$$
$$R_3 = \{(1,a),(2,b),(3,a)\}$$
$$R_4 = \{\} = \emptyset$$
$$R_5 =$$
$\{(1,a),(1,b),(2,a),(2,b),(3,a),(3,b)\} = A \times B$

$\because\ R_1,R_2,R_3,R_4,R_5$, are all subsets of $A \times B$

$\therefore$ these are relations.

$\rightarrow$ All these relations are represented in **Roster form**

Example
For $A = \{\,1,2,3\,\}$ and $B = \{\,4,5,6\,\}$
Relation defined as : $R = \{\,(x,y) : x \in A\,,\, y \in B \text{ and } y = 2x\}$
is in set-builder form.
Its roster form will be $R = \{(2,4),(3,6)\}$

- In every ordered pair of a relation, first element is said to be related with the second element.
- If $a \in A$ is related to $b \in B$ under the relation R, we write it as $(a,b) \in$ R or a R b.
- Second element of an ordered pair is called as the *image* of the first element and the first element is called *pre image* of second element.

  i.e., if $(a,b) \in$ R , then **b is image of a** and **a is pre image of b**.
- The total number of relations that can be defined from set A to set B is the number of possible subsets of $A \times B$.

  i.e., If $n(A) = p$ and $n(B) = q,$ then $n(A \times B) = pq$

  So, no. of possible subsets $= 2^{pq}$

  $\therefore$ **The total number of relations $= 2^{pq}$.**

Example

A = { *1,2,3* } *and* B = { *a,b* }

and relations R *from* A *to* B *is defined as :* R = {*(1,a),(2,b)*}

Here, *(1,a)* $\in$ R , which means

   (i) *1* $\in$ A is related to $a \in$ B

   (ii) a is image of *1*

   (iii) *1* is pre-image of a.

Similarly, *(2,b)* $\in$ R , which means

   (i) *2* $\in$ A is related to $b \in$ B

   (ii) b is image of *2*

   (iii) *2* is pre-image of b.

$\rightarrow$ Here, $n(A) = 3$ and $n(B) = 2 \Rightarrow n(A \times B) = 3 \times 2 = 6$

$\therefore$ **The total number of relations $= 2^6 = 64$.**

- A relation from set A to set A is also stated as relation on set A. i.e. a relation which is a subset of $A \times A$ is said to be a relation on set A.

4.1 Domain

The set of first elements of all the ordered pairs in a relation R *from set* A *to set* B *is called the domain of the relation* R.

- Domain $\subseteq$ A.

4.2 Range

The set of second elements of all the ordered pairs in a relation R *from set A to set* B *is called the range of the relation* R.

- Range $\subseteq$ B.

4.3 Codomain

For a relation R *from set* A *to set* B, *the set* B *is called the codomain of the relation* R.

- Codomain = B
- Range $\subseteq$ Codomain.

Example

A = { *1,2,3* }   and   B = { *a,b* }

(i) For relation R_1 = {*(1,a),(1,b),(2,a)*}

Domain = { *1,2* } $\subset$ A, Range = { *a,b* } $\subset$ B and
Codomain = { *a,b* } =B

(ii) For relation R_2 = {*(1,a),(3,a)*}

Domain = { *1,3* } $\subset$ A , Range = { *a* } $\subset$ B and
Codomain = { *a,b* } =B

4.4 Arrow Diagram

An arrow diagram is a visual representation of a relation R *from set* A *to set* B *in which an arrow is drawn from an element in set* A *to its image in set* B *under the given relation.*

Example

If relation R : A $\rightarrow$ B is defined as R = {*(1, b), (2, d), (4, c)*} where A = {1,2,3,4,5} and B = {*a, b, c, d, e, f,* } , then its arrow diagram is as shown below.

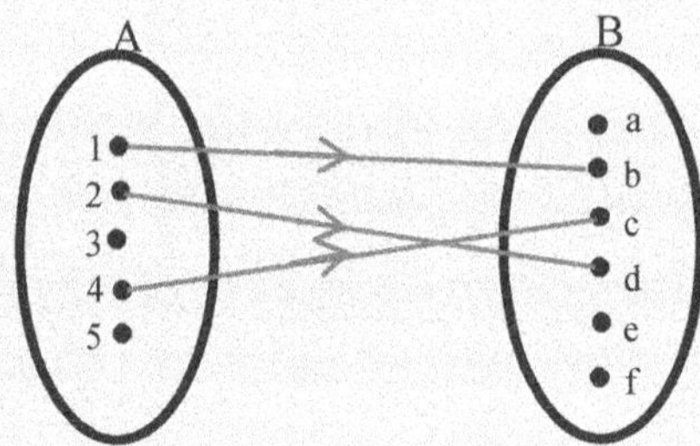

5   Types of Relations

We define the following types of relations on set A (i.e., a relation from set A to set A):

5.1 Empty Relation

If no element in set A *is related to any element of* A, *the relation* R *in set* A *is called as empty relation.*

- Empty relation is denoted by ϕ . (**Note that** $\phi \subset A \times A$)

5.2 Universal Relation

If every element of set A *is related to every element (to itself also) of* A*, the relation* R *in set* A *is called as universal relation.*

- A × A is universal relation

- Empty and Universal relations are both *Trivial Relations.*

5.3 Reflexive Relation

If every element of set A *is related to itself in the relation* R *, then the relation is called reflexive relation in set* A.

i.e. if **$(a,a) \in R$ for every** $a \in A$, then R is reflexive relation in set A.

5.3.1 Procedure to check reflexive relation in roster form

Given: Relation R in roster form in set A.

For each element in set A, check whether the pair formed by this element with itself is present in the relation or not.

- If every element in set A has a pair with itself in the relation , then the relation is reflexive.
- If there is one or more element in set A which does not form pair with itself in the relation , then it is not reflexive.

<u>**Example**</u>

Consider a relation R = {(1,1), (2,2), (3,3), (1,3)} *in set* A = {1,2,3}.

Here, we observe that every element of set A, i.e., 1, 2, and 3, forms a pair with itself in relation R.

i.e., $(1,1) \in R$, $(2,2) \in R$, $(3,3) \in R$

So, we write:

∵ **$(a,a) \in R$ for every** $a \in A$

∴ R is **reflexive** relation in set A.

<u>**Example**</u>

Consider a relation R = {(1,1), (3,3), (1,3)} *in set* A = {1,2,3}.

Here, we observe that the element $2 \in A$

But it doesn't form a pair with itself in relation R.

i.e., $(2,2) \notin R$

So, we write:

∵ **$2 \in A$, but $(2,2) \notin R$**

∴ R is **not reflexive** relation in set A.

5.3.2 Procedure to prove reflexive relation in set-builder form

Given: a relation R in set-bulider form on set A such as :
$$R = \{(x,y) : x,y \in A \text{ and } \text{- some } \textbf{mathematical}$$
$$\textbf{expression/ word statement } \text{in } x \ \& \ y\}$$

Step-1 Let $a \in A$

Step-2 Check whether the expression or statement given in R holds for (a,a).

If it holds, we can write

$(a,a) \in R$ for every $a \in A$

Hence relation R is reflexive.

<u>**Example**</u>

Consider a relation $R = \{(x,y) : x - y \text{ is an integer}\}$ *in set of integers* **Z**.

Step-1: Let $a \in \mathbf{Z}$ i.e., a is an integer.

Step-2: for $(a,a) \in R$, $a - a$ should be an integer as per the given statement in relation R.

Now $a - a = 0 \in \mathbf{Z}$,   for every $a \in \mathbf{Z}$

(**i.e.,** $a - a$ is an integer for all $a \in \mathbf{Z}$)

$\therefore$ $(a,a) \in R$ for every $a \in \mathbf{Z}$

Hence R is a **reflexive** relation.

5.4 Symmetric Relation

If $(a,b) \in R$ **implies** $(b,a) \in R$ **for every** $(a,b) \in R$ where $a,b \in A$, then R is *symmetric relation* in set A.

5.4.1 Procedure to check symmetric relation in roster form

Given: a relation R in roster form in set A.

For each pair in the relation, check whether the pair formed by reversing the order is present in the relation or not.

- If reversed ordered pair of every pair is present in the relation , then it is symmetric relation.
- If reversed pairs of one or more pairs do not exist in the relation , then it is not symmetric.

<u>**Example**</u>

Consider a relation $R = \{(1,1), (3,3), (1,3), (3,1)\}$
in set $A = \{1,2,3\}$.

Here, we observe that for every ordered pair in R there exists its reverse ordered pair also in R .

i.e., $(1,1) \in R$, and its reverse ordered pair $(1,1) \in R$

$$(3,3) \in R, \text{ and its reverse ordered pair } (3,3) \in R$$
$$(1,3) \in R, \text{ and its reverse ordered pair } (3,1) \in R$$
$$(3,1) \in R, \text{ and its reverse ordered pair } (1,3) \in R$$

So, we write: **$(a,b) \in R \Rightarrow (b,a) \in R$ for every $(a,b) \in R$**

$\therefore$ R is **symmetric** relation in set A.

Example

Consider a relation $R = \{(1,1), (3,3), (1,3)\}$ *in set* $A = \{1,2,3\}$.

Here, we observe that the element $(1,3) \in R$, but $(3,1) \notin R$

So, we write:

$\because$ $(1,3) \in R$, but $(3,1) \notin R$

$\therefore$ R is **not symmetric** relation in set A.

5.4.2 Procedure to prove symmetric relation in set-builder form

Given: a relation R in set-bulider form on set A such as :

$$R = \{(x,y) : x,y \in A \text{ and } \text{"-- some \textbf{mathematical}}$$
$$\textbf{expression /word statement} \text{ in } x \,\&\, y \text{ --"}\}$$

Step-1 Let $a \in A$ and $b \in A$ such that $(a,b) \in R$

Step-2 $(a,b) \in R \Rightarrow$ **mathematical expression /word**
$$\textbf{statement} \text{ holds for } (a,b)$$

$\Rightarrow$ we will be able to find that it holds for (b,a) also

$\Rightarrow (b,a) \in R$

This will be true for every $(a,b) \in R$

Step-3 We write $(a,b) \in R \Rightarrow (b,a) \in R$ for every $(a,b) \in R$

Hence relation R is symmetric.

Example

Consider a relation $R = \{(x,y) : x - y$ is an integer$\}$ *in set of*
integers **Z**.

Step-1: Let $a \in \mathbf{Z}$ and $b \in \mathbf{Z}$ such that $(a,b) \in R$

Step-2: Now $(a,b) \in R \Rightarrow a - b$ is an integer (as per the
$$\text{given statement in relation R)}$$

$\Rightarrow -(a-b)$ is also an integer
$$\text{(just sign is reversed)}$$

$\Rightarrow b - a$ is an integer

$\Rightarrow (b,a) \in R$

This is true for every $(a,b) \in R$

Step-3: $\therefore$ **$(a,b) \in R \Rightarrow (b,a) \in R$ for every $(a,b) \in R$**

Hence relation R is **symmetric**.

5.5   Transitive Relation

If $(a,b) \in R$ and $(b,c) \in R$ implies $(a,c) \in R$

for every $(a,b) \in R$ **and** $(b,c) \in R$ where $a, b, c \in A$,

then R is *transitive relation* in set A.

5.5.1   Procedure to check transitive relation in roster form

Given: a relation R in roster form in set A.

Step-1 Find all such two ordered pairs in R where the image in first pair is pre-image in second pair.

Step-2 For each of two such pairs, check whether the pair formed by pre-image of first and image of second exists in the relation R or not.

- If every pair, so formed, exists in the relation , then it is a transitive relation.
- If one or more such pairs do not exist in the relation, then it is not transitive.

<u>**Example**</u>

Consider a relation $R = \{(1,1), (1,3), (3,2), (1,2)\}$
in set $A = \{1,2,3\}$.

Here, we find ordered pairs $(1,3) \in R$ and $(3,2) \in R$ such that in first pair 3 is an image and in second pair 3 is pre-image.

Now taking pre-image of first pair and image of second pair, we get the pair $(1,2)$ and $(1,2) \in R$

So, $(1,3) \in R$ and $(3,2) \in R \Rightarrow (1,2) \in R$

Similarly, we find other such pairs:

$(1,1) \in R$ and $(1,3) \in R \Rightarrow (1,3) \in R$

$(1,1) \in R$ and $(1,2) \in R \Rightarrow (1,2) \in R$.

We have checked for every such two ordered pairs in R.

So, we write:

$\because$ If $(a,b) \in R$ and $(b,c) \in R \Rightarrow (a,c) \in R$

for every $(a,b) \in R$ **and** $(b,c) \in R$

$\therefore$ R is **transitive** relation in set A.

<u>**Example**</u>

Consider a relation $R = \{(1,1), (3,3), (1,2), (2,3)\}$
in set $A = \{1,2,3\}$.

Here, observe that elements $(1,2) \in R$ and $(2,3) \in R$, but $(1,3) \notin R$

So, we write: **(1,2) $\in$ R and (2,3) $\in$ R , but (1,3) $\notin$ R**

$\therefore$ R is **not transitive** relation in set A.

5.5.2 Procedure to prove transitive relation in set-builder form

Given: a relation R in set-bulider form on set A such as :

$$R = \{(x,y) : x,y \in A \text{ and } -- \textbf{some mathematical expression / word statement} \text{ in } x \text{ \& } y --\}$$

Step-1 Let $a \in A$, $b \in A$ and $c \in A$

such that $(a,b) \in R$ and $(b,c) \in R$

Step-2 Now $(a,b) \in R$ and $(b,c) \in R$

$\Rightarrow$ mathematical expression / word statement holds for both pairs (a,b) & (b,c)

$\Rightarrow$ we will be able to find that it holds for (a,c) also

$\Rightarrow (a,c) \in R$

This will be true for every $(a,b) \in R$ and $(b,c) \in R$

Step-3 We write $(a,b) \in R$ and $(b,c) \in R \Rightarrow (a,c) \in R$

for every $(a,b) \in R$ and $(b,c) \in R$

Hence relation R is transitive.

<u>Example</u>

Consider a relation $R = \{(x,y) : x - y$ *is an integer*$\}$ *in set of integers* **Z**.

Step-1: Let $a \in Z$, $b \in Z$ and $c \in Z$

such that $(a,b) \in R$ and $(b,c) \in R$

Step-2: Now $(a,b) \in R$ and $(b,c) \in R$

$\Rightarrow a - b$ & $b - c$ are integers

(as per the given statement in relation R)

$\Rightarrow a - b = m$ & $b - c = n$ where m & n are integers

$\Rightarrow (a - b) + (b - c) = m + n$ where $m+n$ will be integer

$\Rightarrow a - c = m + n$ where $m+n$ is an integer

$\Rightarrow a - c$ is an integer

$\Rightarrow (a,c) \in R$

This is true for every $(a,b) \in R$ and $(b,c) \in R$

Step-3: $\therefore (a,b) \in R$ and $(b,c) \in R \Rightarrow (a,c) \in R$

for every $(a,b) \in R$ and $(b,c) \in R$

Hence relation R is **transitive**.

5.6 Equivalence Relation

If relation R in set A is reflexive, symmetric and transitive, then it is an equivalence relation.

---

6   Equivalence Class

If R *is an equivalence relation in set* A *, then* A *can be divided into* **mutually disjoint sets A_1, A_2, A_3,..., A_n , which are called partitions** *of* A *such that*

(i) $A_1 \cup A_2 \cup A_3 \cup ... \cup A_n = A$ and $A_i \cap A_j = \phi$ for all $i \neq j$

(ii) All elements of A_i are related to one another, for all $i = 1, 2, ..., n$

(iii) No element of A_i is related to any element of A_j, for all $i \neq j$

The partitions or the subsets A_i are called equivalence classes.

- Any equivalence class A_i can be denoted by only one element of A_i , enclosed in square brackets.

   i.e. if $a \in A_i$, then equivalence class A_i can be denoted as $[a]$

Example

If A = { *1,2,3* } ,

then relation R = {*(1,1),(2,2),(3,3),(1,2),(2,1)*} is equivalence relation.

∴ A can be divided into mutually disjoint sets

$A_1 = \{1,2\}$ and $A_2 = \{3\}$ such that

(i) $A_1 \cap A_2 = \phi$ and $A_1 \cup A_2 = A$

(ii) All elements of A_1 are related to one another.

   i.e., *(1,1),(2,2),(1,2),(2,1)* $\in$ R

(iii) All elements of A_2 are related to one another.

   i.e., *(3,3)* $\in$ R

(iv) No element of A_1 is related to any element of A_2.

   Here, A_1 and A_2 are called equivalence classes.

We can denote A_1 by any one of its elements in square brackets

i.e., [1] or [2]

And A_2 by [3]

7   Function

If every element of set A *has one and only one image in set* B *under the given relation , then the relation is known as a function from set* A *to set* B.

- If f is a function from A to B , we write it as $f: A \rightarrow B$.
- We say that the function $f: A \rightarrow B$ maps every element of set A to set B.

- **If $(a, b) \in f$, then** $f(a) = b$, where b is called the *image* of a under f, and a is called the *pre-image* of b under f and we say that the element, $a \in A$, is mapped to element, $b \in B$
- **For a function f : A $\rightarrow$ B , it is necessary for an element of set A to have an image in set B, and also it can't have more than one image.**
- Every function is relation, but every relation is not function.
- For a function $f : A \rightarrow B$, **Domain = A** , but **Range $\subseteq$ B**

Example

A relation $f : A \rightarrow B$ is defined as $f = \{(a,4), (b,5), (c,5)\}$ where A = $\{a,b,c\}$ *and* B = $\{4,5,6,7\}$.

This relation $f : A \rightarrow B$ can also be written as

$$f(a) = 4, \quad f(b) = 5, \quad f(c) = 5 .$$

Here we observe that each element of set A i.e., 'a', 'b', and 'c' have exactly one image.

'a' has exactly one image '4', 'b' has exactly one image '5', and 'c' has exactly one image '5'.

$\therefore$ This is a function.

Its **Domain** = $\{a,b,c\}$ = A and **Range** = $\{4,5\} \subset$ B

Example

A relation $f : A \rightarrow B$ is defined as $f = \{(a,4), (b,5)\}$ where A = $\{a,b,c\}$ *and* B = $\{4,5,6,7\}$.

This relation $f : A \rightarrow B$ can also be written as

$$f(a) = 4, \quad f(b) = 5 .$$

Here we observe that the element 'c' of set A doesn't have any image.

But in a function each element must have an image.

$\therefore$ This is *not* a function.

Example

A relation $f : A \rightarrow B$ is defined as $f = \{(a,4), (b,5), (c,5), (c,6)\}$ where A = $\{a,b,c\}$ *and* B = $\{4,5,6,7\}$.

This relation $f : A \rightarrow B$ can also be written as

$$f(a) = 4, \quad f(b) = 5, \quad f(c) = 5, \quad f(c) = 6 .$$

Here we observe that the element 'c' of set A has two images '5' and '6'.

But in a function each element must have exactly one image.

$\therefore$ This is *not* a function.

- A function can be represented by an expression.

  e.g. $f : N \to N$ expressed as $f(x) = 2x + 1$

7.1 Real Valued Function

If the range of a function is set of real numbers or one of its subsets, then the function is known as a real valued function.

i.e., If Range $\subseteq$ **R**, then function is a real valued function where **R** is set of real numbers.

Example

If a function is $f = \{(a,1),(b,2),(c,1)\}$,

then its range = $\{ 1,2 \}$ is a subset of real numbers.

$\therefore$ It is a real valued function.

Example

If a function is $f = \{(1,a),(2,a),(3,b)\}$,

then its range = $\{ a,b \}$ is not a subset of real numbers.

$\therefore$ It is **not** a real valued function.

7.2 Real Function

If the domain and range of a function are both sets of real numbers or the subsets of real numbers, then the function is known as a real function.

i.e., If Domain $\subseteq$ **R** and Range $\subseteq$ **R**, then function is a real function where **R** is set of real numbers.

Example

If a function is $f = \{(4,1),(5,3),(6,1)\}$,

then its domain = $\{ 4,5,6 \}$ and range = $\{ 1,3 \}$ are both subsets of real numbers.

$\therefore$ It is a real function.

8 Types of Functions

8.1 One-one (or injective) function

The function $f : A \to B$ is said to be one-one or injective function **if distinct elements of set A have distinct images** *in set* B *under the function f.*

Otherwise, it is *many-one function.*

Example

A function $f : A \to B$ is defined as $f = \{(1,4), (2,5), (3,6)\}$

where A = $\{1,2,3\}$ and B = $\{4,5,6,7\}$.

This function $f : A \to B$ can also be written as

$$f(1) = 4, \quad f(2) = 5, \quad f(3) = 6 .$$

Here, we observe that different elements of set A i.e., '1', '2', and '3' have different images '4', '5', and '6' respectively.

$\therefore$ This is a one-one function.

<u>**Example**</u>

A function $f : A \to B$ *is defined as* $f = \{(1,4), (2,5), (3,5)\}$
where $A = \{1,2,3\}$ *and* $B = \{4,5,6,7\}$.

This function $f : A \to B$ can also be written as
$$f(1) = 4, \quad f(2) = 5, \quad f(3) = 5$$
Here, we observe that different elements '2' and '3' of set A have same image '5'.

$\therefore$ This is *not* a one-one function. It is a **many-one** function.

- Injective (or one-one) function in arrow diagram:

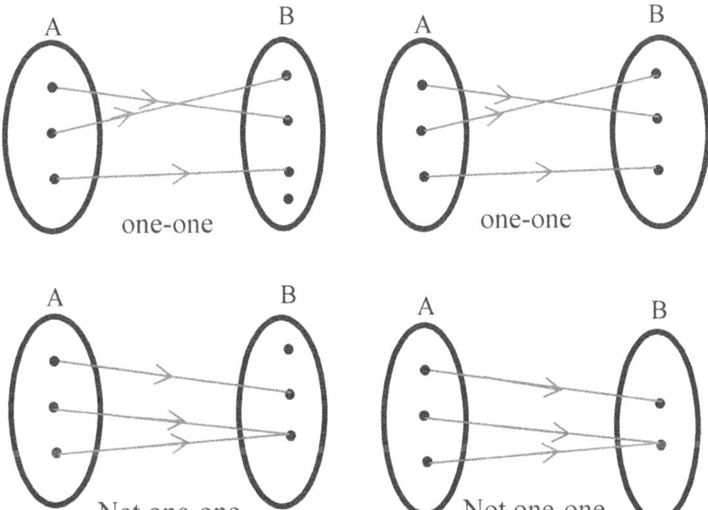

- We can prove that a function is one-one by any of the following two methods:

   Method-1: If $f(x_1) = f(x_2)$ **implies** $x_1 = x_2$ for every $x_1, x_2 \in A$, then $f : A \to B$ is one-one function.

   Method-2: If $x_1 \neq x_2$ **implies** $f(x_1) \neq f(x_2)$ for every $x_1, x_2 \in A$, then $f : A \to B$ is one-one function.

- If a function is not one-one, then it will be many-one.

8.1.1 Procedure to prove one-one function

Given: Function $f : A \to B$ and $f(x) = $ ' **- an expression in** x **-** '

<u>**Method-1:**</u>

Step-1 Let $x_1, x_2 \in A$ such that $f(x_1) = f(x_2)$

Step-2 Now $f(x_1) = f(x_2)$

$\Rightarrow$ Given expression in terms of x_1 = Given expression in terms of x_2

$\Rightarrow$ we will be able to find that $x_1 = x_2$

This will be true for every $x_1, x_2 \in A$

Step-3 We write $f(x_1) = f(x_2) \Rightarrow x_1 = x_2$ for every $x_1, x_2 \in A$

Hence the given function $f : A \rightarrow B$ is one-one.

<u>Method-2:</u>

Step-1 Let $x_1, x_2 \in A$ such that $x_1 \neq x_2$

Step-2 Now find $f(x_1)$ and $f(x_2)$ from the given expression.

$\Rightarrow$ we will be able to find that $f(x_1) \neq f(x_2)$

This will be true for every $x_1, x_2 \in A$

Step-3 We write $x_1 \neq x_2 \Rightarrow f(x_1) \neq f(x_2)$ for every $x_1, x_2 \in A$

Hence the given function $f : A \rightarrow B$ is one-one.

<u>Example</u>

Consider a function $f : \mathbf{R} \rightarrow \mathbf{R}$ given by $f(x) = 2x$ where $\mathbf{R}$ is set of real numbers.

<u>Method-1</u>:

Step-1: Let $x_1, x_2 \in \mathbf{R}$ such that $f(x_1) = f(x_2)$

Step-2: Now $f(x_1) = f(x_2) \Rightarrow 2x_1 = 2x_2 \qquad (\because f(x) = 2x)$

$\Rightarrow x_1 = x_2$

This will be true for every $x_1, x_2 \in \mathbf{R}$

Step-3: $\therefore f(x_1) = f(x_2) \Rightarrow x_1 = x_2$ for every $x_1, x_2 \in \mathbf{R}$

Hence the given function $f : \mathbf{R} \rightarrow \mathbf{R}$ is one-one.

<u>Method-2</u>:

Step-1: Let $x_1, x_2 \in \mathbf{R}$ such that $x_1 \neq x_2$

Step-2: $f(x_1) = 2x_1$ and $f(x_2) = 2x_2 \qquad (\because f(x) = 2x)$

Now $x_1 \neq x_2 \Rightarrow 2x_1 \neq 2x_2$

$\Rightarrow f(x_1) \neq f(x_2)$

This will be true for every $x_1, x_2 \in \mathbf{R}$

Step-3: $\therefore x_1 \neq x_2 \Rightarrow f(x_1) \neq f(x_2)$ for every $x_1, x_2 \in \mathbf{R}$

Hence the given function $f : \mathbf{R} \rightarrow \mathbf{R}$ is one-one.

8.2 Onto (or surjective) function

The function $f: A{\rightarrow}B$ *is said to be onto or surjective function* **if every element of set B is an image** *of some element in set* A *under the function f.*

Otherwise, it is *into function.*

- **Range of f will be equal to the complete set B for the function $f: A{\rightarrow}B$ to be an onto function.**

Example

A function $f: A \rightarrow B$ is defined as f = {(1,4), (2,5), (3,6), (4,6)} where A = {1,2,3,4} and B = {4,5,6}.

This function $f: A \rightarrow B$ can also be written as

$f(1) = 4, \quad f(2) = 5, \quad f(3) = 6, \quad f(4) = 6$.

Here, we observe that every element of set B i.e., '4', '5', and '6' is an image of at least one element of set A.

It means for element $y \in B$ there exists an element $x \in A$ such that $f(x) = y$

Or we can say that **Range of f = B**

$\therefore$ This is an onto function.

Example

A function $f: A \rightarrow B$ is defined as f = {(1,4), (2,5), (3,6)} where A = {1,2,3} and B = {4,5,6,7}.

This function $f: A \rightarrow B$ can also be written as

$f(1) = 4, \quad f(2) = 5, \quad f(3) = 6$

Here, we observe that an element '7' of set B is not an image of any element.

It means for element $7 \in B$ there doesn't exist any element $x \in A$ such that $f(x) = 7$

Or we can say that **Range of $f \neq$ B**

$\therefore$ This is *not* an onto function. It is an **into** function.

- Surjective (or onto) function in arrow diagram:

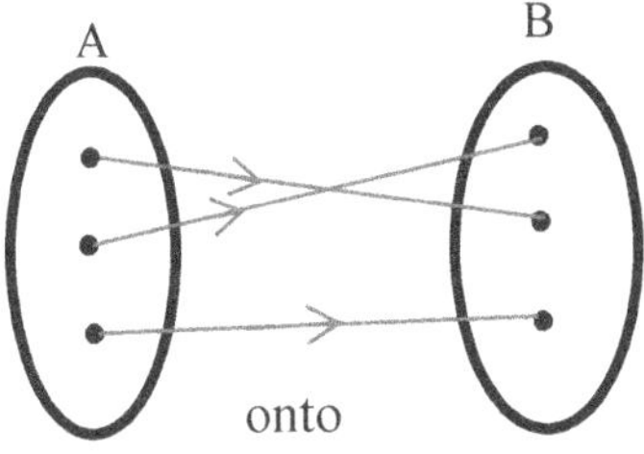

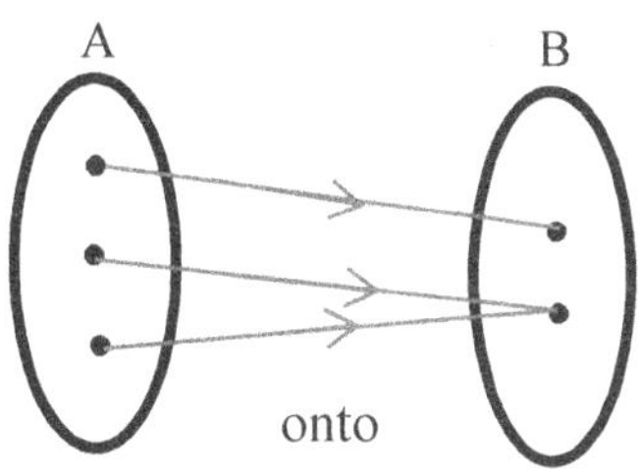

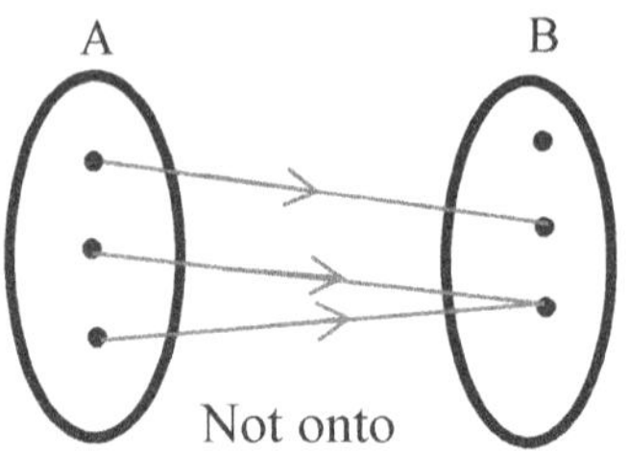

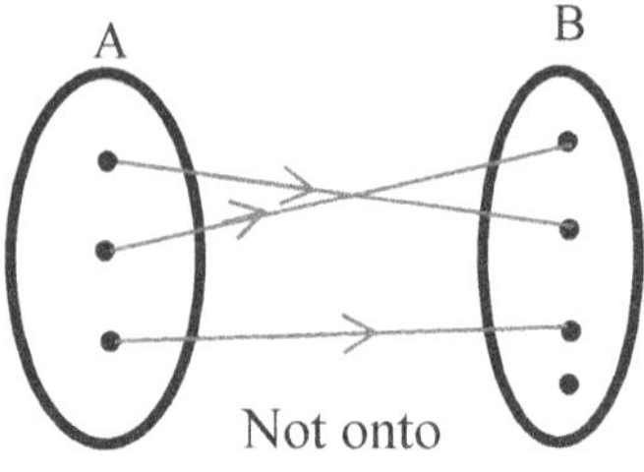

- We can prove that a function is onto by any of the following two methods:

  Method-1: If for every $y \in B$ there exists an element $x \in A$ such that $f(x) = y$, then $f: A \rightarrow B$ is onto function.

  Method-2: If Range of $f = B$, then $f: A \rightarrow B$ is onto function.

- If $f: A \rightarrow B$ is onto function, then Range of $f = B$.
- If a function is not onto, then it will be into.

8.2.1 Procedure to prove onto function

Given: Function $f: A \rightarrow B$ and $f(x) = $ ' - **an expression in x -** '

Method-1:

Step-1 Let $y \in B$ such that $y = f(x) = $ '- **an expression in x -**'

Step-2 Now we have $y = (- - \text{in terms of } x - -)$ from step-1

$\Rightarrow$ find $x = (- - \text{in terms of } y - -) \in A$

(we will be able to find that it will belong to set A)

Step-3 We write for every element $y \in B$ there exists an element $x \in A$ such that

$$f(x) = f(- - \text{in terms of } y \text{ from step-2- -}) = y$$

(on simplifying we will get y)

Hence the given function $f: A \rightarrow B$ is onto.

- **Method-2:**

Step-1 Find the range of given function.

We will see that Range of $f = B$

Step-2 We write Range of $f = B$

Hence the given function $f: A \rightarrow B$ is onto.

<u>Example</u>

Consider a function $f: \mathbf{R} \rightarrow \mathbf{R}$ given by $f(x) = 2x$ where $\mathbf{R}$ is set of real numbers.

Method-1:

Step-1: Let $y \in \mathbf{R}$ such that $y = f(x) = 2x$

(**Note:** We have to consider $y \in B$ for $f: A \rightarrow B$ but in this example, set B is **set R**)

Step-2: $y = 2x$

$$\Rightarrow x = \frac{y}{2} \in \mathbf{R} \text{ (as } y \text{ is real number, so } y/2 \text{ is also real)}$$

(Note: We should get $x \in$ A for $f : $ A→B but in this example, set A is **set R.)**

Step-3: ∴ for every element $y \in \mathbf{R}$ there exists an element

$$x \in \mathbf{R} \text{ such that } f(x) = f\left(\frac{y}{2}\right) = 2 \times \frac{y}{2} = y$$

Hence the given function $f : \mathbf{R} \to \mathbf{R}$ is onto.

Method-2:

Step-1: Let $x \in \mathbf{R}$ (because domain is set of real numbers)

$$\Rightarrow -\infty < x < \infty$$

$$\Rightarrow -\infty < 2x < \infty$$

$$\therefore \text{ Range of } f = \mathbf{R}$$

Step-2: ∵ Range of $f = \mathbf{R}$

Hence the given function $f : \mathbf{R} \to \mathbf{R}$ is onto.

8.3 Bijective function

The function $f :$ A→B is said to be bijective function if it is both one-one and onto.

- If a function $f :$ A → A is one-one, **then it will be onto** also and **vice-versa** where **A is a finite set**.

   (*Note: Here function is **from A to A** and not from A to B.*)

- Bijective (or one-one & onto both) function in arrow diagram:

-

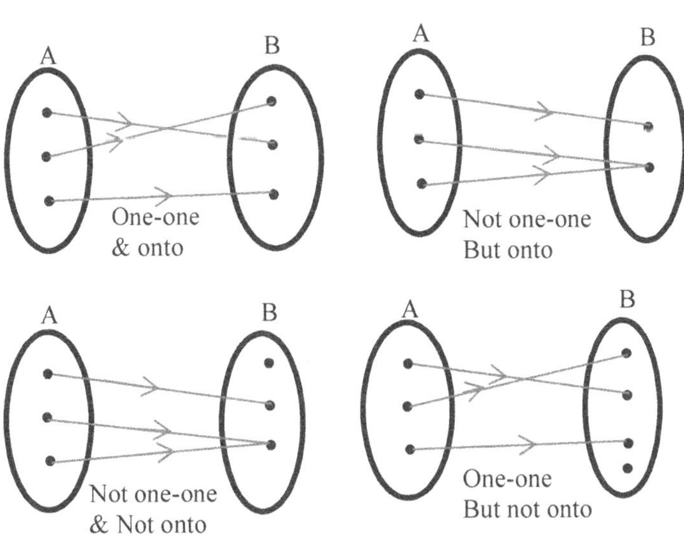

9   *Composite Function

If two functions are $f : A \to B$ and $g : B \to C$, then the composite function gof is defined as gof : A $\to$ C such that gof (x) = g(f (x)).

- $gof : A \to C$ function maps every element of set A to an element of set C.

   i.e., *gof* maps every element of rthe first set of function f to the second set of function g.

(i)   *gof* function is defined if **Range of f** is subset of **Domain of g**.

    fog function is defined if **Range of g** is subset of **Domain of f**.

<u>**Example**</u>

Functions $f : \{1,2,3,4\} \to \{3,4,5,6\}$ *and* $g : \{3,4,5,7\} \to \{1,2,3,8\}$ *are defined as* $f = \{(1,3), (2,4), (3,4), (4,5)\}$ *and*

$$g = \{(3,2), (4,1), (5,3), (7,8)\}$$

Here, **Range of f** = $\{3,4,5\}$ $\subset$ **Domain of g** = $\{3,4,5,7\}$

$\therefore gof : \{1,2,3,4\} \to \{1,2,3,8\}$ is defined.

But **Range of g** = $\{1,2,3,8\}$ $\not\subset$ **Domain of f** = $\{1,2,3,4\}$

$\therefore fog : \{1,2,3,8\} \to \{1,2,3,4\}$ is not defined.

<u>To find *gof*</u> :

We can write the function f and g respectively as:

$f(1) = 3, \qquad f(2) = 4, \qquad f(3) = 4, \qquad f(4) = 5$

$g(3) = 2, \qquad g(4) = 1, \qquad g(5) = 3, \qquad g(7) = 8$

Now $gof : \{1,2,3,4\} \to \{1,2,3,8\}$ is found by obtaining images of all elements of set $\{1,2,3,4\}$ as follows:

$gof(1) = g(f(1)) = g(3) = 2,$

$gof(2) = g(f(2)) = g(4) = 1,$

$gof(3) = g(f(3)) = g(4) = 1,$

$gof(4) = g(f(4)) = g(5) = 3,$

$\therefore gof(x) = \{(1,2), (2,1), (3,1), (4,3)\}$

<u>**Example**</u>

Functions $f : R \to R$ *and* $g : N \to N$ *are defined as* $f(x) = sin\ x$ *and* $g(x) = 2\ x$ *where* **N** *is set of natural numbers and* **R** *is set of real numbers.*

Here, **Range of f** = $[-1,1]$ is an interval in set of real numbers.

(It is because whatever be the value of angle θ, $\sin\theta \in [-1,1]$)

& **Domain of g** is set of natural numbers.

It means **Range of f** $\not\subset$ **Domain of g**

    $\therefore gof : R \to N$ is not defined.

But **Range of g** is set of even natural numbers.

(Since, if x is natural number, then $2x$ is even natural number.)
& **Domain of f = R** is a set of real numbers

It means **Range of g $\subset$ Domain of f**

$$\therefore fog \ : N \to R \ \text{is defined.}$$

Further, $fog \ : N \to R$ is defined as

$$fog(x) = f(g(x)) = f(2x) = sin \ 2 \ x$$

- **If gof is one-one, then f is necessarily one-one**, but g may or may not be one-one.

  i.e., gof is one-one $\Rightarrow$ f is one-one

- **If gof is onto, then g is necessarily onto**, but f may or may not be onto.

  i.e., gof is onto $\Rightarrow$ g is onto

10   *Invertible Function

*A function $f : A \to B$ is invertible if there exists another function,
$g : B \to A$ such that $gof = I_A$ and $fog = I_B$, where I_A and I_B
are identity functions in sets A and B respectively.*

The function g is inverse of f. i.e, $f^{-1} = g$.

- We can also conclude from this definition that $g^{-1} = f$.

  $$\Rightarrow (f^{-1})^{-1} = f.$$

- An identity function is the function in which an element is image of itself.

  i.e., $I(x) = x$ is an identity function.

- **A function $f : A \to B$ is invertible if and only if it is bijective (one-one and onto both).**

- Inverse of a function is **unique**, if it exists.

10.1   *Procedure to find inverse of a function

We can understand it with the help of following examples:

<u>Example</u>

A function $f : A \to B$ is defined as $f = \{(a,4), (b,5), (c,6)\}$
where A = $\{a,b,c\}$ and B = $\{4,5,6\}$.

This function $f : A \to B$ can also be written as

$$f(a) = 4, \ \ f(b) = 5, \ \ f(c) = 6 \ .$$

Here we observe that distinct elements of set A i.e., 'a', 'b' and 'c' have distinct images '4', '5', and '6' respectively.

     Also Range of $f = \{4,5,6\} = B$

$\therefore$ It is both one-one and onto function. i.e., it is a bijective function.

Hence, its inverse exists.

<u>To find inverse f^{-1}</u>

We define another function $g : B \to A$ containing ordered pairs which are reverse of pairs in f.

Here it will be $g = \{(4,a), (5,b), (6,c)\}$

(all pairs of f are reversed)

It can also be written as $g(4) = a$, $g(5) = b$, $g(6) = c$

Now under the function $gof : A \to A$, we find the image of every element of set A as follows :

$$gof(a) = g(f(a)) = g(4) = a,$$
$$gof(b) = g(f(b)) = g(5) = b,$$
$$gof(c) = g(f(c)) = g(6) = c,$$

we see that every element is the image of itself.

$\therefore$ gof is an identity function in set A. i.e., $gof = I_A$

Similarly, under the function $fog : B \to B$, we find the image of every element of set B as follows :

$$fog(4) = f(g(4)) = f(a) = 4,$$
$$fog(5) = f(g(5)) = f(b) = 5,$$
$$fog(6) = f(g(6)) = f(c) = 6,$$

we see that every element is the image of itself.

$\therefore$ gof is an identity function in set B. i.e., $gof = I_B$

$\because gof = I_A$ and $gof = I_B$

So, $f^{-1} = g$ where $g : B \to A$ defined as $g = \{(4,a), (5,b), (6,c)\}$

Example

Consider a function $f : N \to Y$ given by $f(x) = 2x + 3$ where R is set of real numbers and $Y = \{y \in N : y = 2x + 3 \text{ for } x \in N\}$.

Step-1: Let $y \in Y$

$\therefore$ $y = f(x) = 2x + 3$ where $x \in N$

Step-2: $y = 2x + 3$

$$\Rightarrow x = \frac{y-3}{2} \in N$$

Here, $y \in Y$ **and** $x \in N$

Step-3:

$\therefore$ We can define another function $g : Y \to N$ with $g(y) = \dfrac{y-3}{2}$

Step-4: find $gof : N \to N$ as follows:

$$gof(x) = g(f(x)) = g(2x + 3) = \frac{2x+3-3}{2} = x = I_N$$

It means gof is identity function in N

Step-5: find $fog : Y \to Y$ as follows:

$$fog\ (y) = f(g\ (y)) = f\left(\frac{y-3}{2}\right) = 2 \times \frac{y-3}{2} = y = \mathbf{I}_Y$$

It means fog is identity function in **Y**

Step-6: $\because gof = \mathbf{I}_N$ and $gof = \mathbf{I}_Y$

$\therefore f$ is invertible , and $f^{-1} = g$

It means $f^{-1} : \mathbf{Y} \rightarrow \mathbf{N}$ is a function defined as

$$f^{-1}\ (x) = g\ (x) = \frac{x-3}{2}$$

11 *Binary Operation

When we add two numbers, we get another number. Here, the operation is addition, and we perform this operation on two numbers. Now 'binary' means two. So, addition is a binary operation.

In general, the operation on two elements of a given set, which results in an element belonging to the same given set, is a binary operation on that set.

- A binary operation is denoted by $*$.

11.1 *Definition

A binary operation $*$ on a set A is a function $* : \mathbf{A} \times \mathbf{A} \rightarrow \mathbf{A}$.

- It means when operation $*$ is performed on any two elements of set A, the result is also an element of set A.
- '$a * b$' is read as 'a operated on b'.

11.2 *Addition, Subtraction, Multiplication, and Division

- **Addition on set of natural numbers N is a binary operation** because if we add two natural numbers, then the result is also a natural number.

  We write it as $+ : \mathbf{N} \times \mathbf{N} \rightarrow \mathbf{N}$ is a binary operation.

- **Multiplication on set of natural numbers N is a binary operation** because if we multiply two natural numbers, then the result is also a natural number.

  We write it as $\times : \mathbf{N} \times \mathbf{N} \rightarrow \mathbf{N}$ is a binary operation.

- **Subtraction on set of natural numbers N is <u>not</u> a binary operation** because if we subtract two natural numbers, then the result is not always a natural number.

  We write it as $- : \mathbf{N} \times \mathbf{N} \rightarrow \mathbf{N}$ is **not** a binary operation.

- **Division on set of natural numbers N is *not* a binary operation** because if we divide one natural number by another natural number, then the result is not always a natural number.

We write it as $\div : \text{N}\times\text{N} \rightarrow \text{N}$ is **not** a binary operation.

- **Addition, subtraction, and multiplication on set of real numbers R are all binary operation** because if we add, subtract or multiply two real numbers, then the result is also a real number. But **Division on real numbers is not a binary operation** because if we divide a real number by 0 (a real number), then the result is *Not Defined* .
  It means

  $+ : \text{R}\times\text{R} \rightarrow \text{R}$ is a binary operation.

  $- : \text{R}\times\text{R} \rightarrow \text{R}$ is a binary operation.

  $\times : \text{R}\times\text{R} \rightarrow \text{R}$ is a binary operation.

  $\div : \text{R}\times\text{R} \rightarrow \text{R}$ is *not* a binary operation.

- However, **Division on non-zero real numbers is a binary operation** because if we divide two non-zero real numbers, then the result is a non-zero real number.

  $\div : \text{R}_*\times\text{R}_* \rightarrow \text{R}_*$ is a binary operation. Here, R_* is a set of non-zero real numbers.

- Binary operations are not just addition, subtraction, multiplication or division. We can define other binary operations also.
  For example,
  (i)   HCF of two numbers on set of natural numbers is a binary operation.
  (ii) LCM of two numbers on set of natural numbers is a binary operation.
  (iii) The operation of two elements a and b from the set $\{1,2,3,4,5\}$ defined as $a * b =$ Greater of a and b , is a binary operation.

11.3 *Operation Table

- We can make an operation table of a binary operation on a finite set.

<u>**Example**</u>

Consider the binary operation defined as
$a * b =$ *Minimum of a and b on set $\{1,2,3\}$.*
We make a table having one extra number of rows and columns each than the number of elements in given set.
So, in this example, we draw a table having 4 rows and 4 columns because there are 3 elements in the given set.
In the first cell at top left corner we write the operation to be carried out (here it is 'Min').

Now to fill the remaining cells of first row, we enter an element each from the given set without repeating.
Remaining cells of first column are also filled in similar manner (as shown below).

Min	1	2	3
1			
2			
3			

Now we can fill the remaining cells by the result of operation of two elements present in first row and first column corresponding to the cell to be filled.

Here the operation is minimum of a and b , so we get the complete table as :

Min	1	2	3
1	1	1	1
2	1	2	2
3	1	2	3

11.4 *Commutative Binary Operation

A binary operation $*$ on set **A** *i.e.* $* : A \times A \to A$ *is said to be commutative if* $a * b = b * a$ *for every* $a , b \in A$.

- Commutative operation means it gives the same results by operating the two elements in any order. For example, in addition: $2+3 = 5$ and $3+2 = 5$. So addition is commutative.
- Addition and multiplication operations on set of real numbers, natural numbers, integers etc. are commutative.
  i.e., $+ : R \times R \to R$, $\times : R \times R \to R$, $+ : Z \times Z \to Z$, and $\times : Z \times Z \to Z$ are commutative binary operations.

11.5 *Associative Binary Operation

A binary operation $*$ on set **A** *i.e.* $* : A \times A \to A$ *is said to be associative if* $(a * b) * c = a * (b * c)$ *for every* $a, b, c \in A$.

- Addition and multiplication operations on set of real numbers, natural numbers, integers etc. are associative.
  i.e., $+ : R \times R \to R$, $\times : R \times R \to R$, $+ : Z \times Z \to Z$, and $\times : Z \times Z \to Z$ are associative binary operations.

11.6 *Identity Element of Binary *Operation*

An element $e \in \mathbf{A}$, if it exists, for a binary operation
$* : \mathbf{A} \times \mathbf{A} \rightarrow \mathbf{A}$ is called its identity element if
$a * e = e * a = a$ for every $a \in \mathbf{A}$.

- 0 is identity element of addition on set of real numbers $\mathbf{R}$.

    i.e., for $+ : \mathbf{R} \times \mathbf{R} \rightarrow \mathbf{R}$, 0 is identity element.

    It is because $a + 0 = 0 + a = a$ for every $a \in \mathbf{R}$.

- 0 is identity element of addition on set of integers $\mathbf{Z}$.

    i.e., for $+ : \mathbf{Z} \times \mathbf{Z} \rightarrow \mathbf{Z}$, 0 is identity element.

    It is because $a + 0 = 0 + a = a$ for every $a \in \mathbf{Z}$.

- 1 is identity element of multiplication on set of real numbers $\mathbf{R}$

    i.e., for $\times : \mathbf{R} \times \mathbf{R} \rightarrow \mathbf{R}$, 1 is identity element.

    It is because $a \times 1 = 1 \times a = a$ for every $a \in \mathbf{R}$.

- 1 is identity element of multiplication on set of integers $\mathbf{Z}$.

    i.e., for $\times : \mathbf{Z} \times \mathbf{Z} \rightarrow \mathbf{Z}$, 1 is identity element.

    It is because $a \times 1 = 1 \times a = a$ for every $a \in \mathbf{Z}$.

- **Identity element doesn't exist for subtraction and division operations on set of real numbers . It doesn't exist on set of integers also.**

11.7 *Invertible Element of Binary Operation

An element $a \in \mathbf{A}$ for a binary operation $* : \mathbf{A} \times \mathbf{A} \rightarrow \mathbf{A}$ is called an invertible element if there exists another element $b \in \mathbf{A}$ such that $a * b = b * a = e$ where e is the identity element of the operation.

In that case, b is called the inverse of a.

- Inverse of a is denoted by a^{-1}.

- If $a * b = b * a = e$ for a binary operation $* : \mathbf{A} \times \mathbf{A} \rightarrow \mathbf{A}$ where $a, b, e \in \mathbf{A}$ and e is the identity element of the operation

    then $a^{-1} = b$

    Also $b^{-1} = a$

    and $(a^{-1})^{-1} = a$

- For the addition binary operations $+ : \mathbf{R} \times \mathbf{R} \rightarrow \mathbf{R}$

    or $+ : \mathbf{Z} \times \mathbf{Z} \rightarrow \mathbf{Z}$, every element a is invertible with its inverse as $-a$.

    i.e., $a^{-1} = -a$.

- For the multiplication binary operation $\times : \mathbf{R} \times \mathbf{R} \to \mathbf{R}$, every **non-zero** element a is invertible with its inverse as $\dfrac{1}{a}$ i.e., $a^{-1} = \dfrac{1}{a}$.

Chapter-2   Inverse Trigonometry

1   Inverse of *sin* function (sin^{-1})

Inverse of *sine* function in the *principal value branch* is defined as $sin^{-1} : [-1,1] \rightarrow \left[-\frac{\pi}{2}, \frac{\pi}{2} \right]$, which is $y = sin^{-1}x$ such that $sin\, y = x$.

here, $x \in [-1,1]$ and $y \in \left[-\frac{\pi}{2}, \frac{\pi}{2} \right]$

- Domain $= [-1,1]$
- Principal Range $= \left[-\frac{\pi}{2}, \frac{\pi}{2} \right]$

- One of the other branches of range is $\left[\frac{\pi}{2}, \frac{3\pi}{2} \right]$

<u>Example</u>

Find the value of $sin^{-1}\left(-\frac{1}{2} \right)$ in the principal value branch.

Solution: Let $y = sin^{-1}\left(-\frac{1}{2} \right)$

According to definition of sin^{-1}, we write it as

$$sin\, y = -\frac{1}{2} \quad \text{where } y \in \left[-\frac{\pi}{2}, \frac{\pi}{2} \right] \text{ for principal}$$

branch

$$\Rightarrow \quad sin\, y = -sin\, \frac{\pi}{6}$$

$$\Rightarrow \quad sin\, y = sin\left(-\frac{\pi}{6} \right)$$

($\because$ In principal branch negative values of *sine* lie in 4th quadrant)

$$\Rightarrow \quad y = -\frac{\pi}{6}$$

$$\Rightarrow \quad sin^{-1}\left(-\frac{1}{2} \right) = -\frac{\pi}{6}$$

<u>Example</u>

Find the value of $sin^{-1}\left(\frac{1}{2} \right)$ in the principal value branch.

Solution: Let $y = sin^{-1}\left(\frac{1}{2} \right)$

According to definition of sin^{-1}, we write it as

$$sin\, y = \frac{1}{2} \quad \text{where } y \in \left[-\frac{\pi}{2}, \frac{\pi}{2} \right] \text{ for principal branch}$$

$$\Rightarrow \quad sin\, y = sin\, \frac{\pi}{6}$$

($\because$ In principal branch positive values of *sine* lie in 1st quadrant)

$$\Rightarrow \quad y = \frac{\pi}{6} \qquad \Rightarrow \quad \sin^{-1}\left(\frac{1}{2}\right) = \frac{\pi}{6}$$

2 Inverse of *cos* function (cos^{-1})

Inverse of *cosine* function in the *principal value branch* is defined as $cos^{-1} : [-1,1] \rightarrow [0, \pi]$, which is $y = cos^{-1}x$ such that $cos\, y = x$.

here, $\qquad x \in [-1,1] \qquad$ and $\quad y \in [0, \pi]$

- Domain $= [-1,1]$
- Principal Range $= [0, \pi]$
- One of the other branches of range is $[\pi, 2\pi]$

<u>**Example**</u>

Find the value of $cos^{-1}\left(-\frac{1}{2}\right)$ in the principal value branch.

Solution: $\qquad$ Let $y = cos^{-1}\left(-\frac{1}{2}\right)$

According to definition of cos^{-1}, we write it as

$$cos\, y = -\frac{1}{2} \quad \text{where } y \in [0, \pi] \text{ for principal branch}$$

$$\Rightarrow \quad cos\, y = -cos\frac{\pi}{3}$$

$$\Rightarrow \quad cos\, y = cos\left(\pi - \frac{\pi}{3}\right)$$

($\because$ In principal branch negative values of *cosine* lie in 2ⁿᵈ quadrant)

$$\Rightarrow \quad y = \frac{2\pi}{3}$$

$$\Rightarrow \quad cos^{-1}\left(-\frac{1}{2}\right) = \frac{2\pi}{3}$$

<u>**Example**</u>

Find the value of $cos^{-1}\left(\frac{1}{2}\right)$ in the principal value branch.

Solution: $\qquad$ Let $y = cos^{-1}\left(\frac{1}{2}\right)$

According to definition of cos^{-1}, we write it as

$$cos\, y = \frac{1}{2} \qquad \text{where } y \in [0, \pi] \text{ for principal branch}$$

$$\Rightarrow \quad cos\, y = cos\frac{\pi}{3}$$

($\because$ In principal branch positive values of *cosine* lie in 1ˢᵗ quadrant)

$$\Rightarrow \quad y = \frac{\pi}{3}$$

$$\Rightarrow \quad cos^{-1}\left(\frac{1}{2}\right) = \frac{\pi}{3}$$

3 Inverse of *tan* function (*tan⁻¹*)

Inverse of *tangent* function in the *principal value branch* is defined as $tan^{-1} : \mathbf{R} \to \left(-\frac{\pi}{2}, \frac{\pi}{2}\right)$, which is $y = tan^{-1}x$ such that $tan\, y = x$.

Where $\mathbf{R} = (-\infty, \infty)$ is set of real numbers.

Here, $\quad x \in (-\infty, \infty) \quad$ and $\quad y \in \left(-\frac{\pi}{2}, \frac{\pi}{2}\right)$

- Domain $= (-\infty, \infty) = \mathbf{R}$
- Principal Range $= \left(-\frac{\pi}{2}, \frac{\pi}{2}\right)$
- One of the other branches of range is $\left(\frac{\pi}{2}, \frac{3\pi}{2}\right)$

Example

Find the value of $tan^{-1}(-1)$ in the principal value branch.

Solution: Let $y = tan^{-1}(-1)$

According to definition of tan^{-1}, we write it as

$$tan\, y = -1 \quad \text{where } y \in \left(-\frac{\pi}{2}, \frac{\pi}{2}\right) \text{ for principal}$$

branch

$$\Rightarrow \quad tan\, y = -tan\, \frac{\pi}{4}$$

$$\Rightarrow \quad tan\, y = tan\left(-\frac{\pi}{4}\right)$$

($\because$ In principal branch negative values of *tangent* lie in 4th quadrant)

$$\Rightarrow \quad y = -\frac{\pi}{4}$$

$$\Rightarrow \quad tan^{-1}(-1) = -\frac{\pi}{4}$$

Example

Find the value of $tan^{-1}(1)$ in the principal value branch.

Solution: Let $y = tan^{-1}(1)$

According to definition of tan^{-1}, we write it as

$$tan\, y = 1 \quad \text{where } y \in \left(-\frac{\pi}{2}, \frac{\pi}{2}\right) \text{ for principal branch}$$

$$\Rightarrow \quad tan\, y = tan\, \frac{\pi}{4}$$

($\because$ In principal branch positive values of *tangent* lie in 1st quadrant)

$$\Rightarrow \quad y = \frac{\pi}{4}$$

$$\Rightarrow \quad tan^{-1}(1) = \frac{\pi}{4}$$

4   Inverse of *cosec* function (*cosec⁻¹*)

Inverse of *cosecant* function in the *principal value branch* is defined as

$$\operatorname{cosec}^{-1} : \mathbf{R} - (-1,1) \to \left[-\frac{\pi}{2}, \frac{\pi}{2}\right] - \{0\}, \text{ which is } y = \operatorname{cosec}^{-1} x$$

such that $\operatorname{cosec} y = x$.

Here, $\qquad x \in \mathbf{R} - (-1,1)$ and $y \in \left[-\frac{\pi}{2}, \frac{\pi}{2}\right] - \{0\}$

- Domain $= \mathbf{R} - (-1,1)$
- Principal Range $= \left[-\frac{\pi}{2}, \frac{\pi}{2}\right] - \{0\}$
- One of the other branches of range is $\left[\frac{\pi}{2}, \frac{3\pi}{2}\right] - \{\pi\}$

<u>Example</u>

Find the value of $\operatorname{cosec}^{-1}\left(-\sqrt{2}\right)$ in the principal value branch.

Solution: $\qquad$ Let $y = \operatorname{cosec}^{-1}\left(-\sqrt{2}\right)$

According to definition of $\operatorname{cosec}^{-1}$, we write it as

$\operatorname{cosec} y = -\sqrt{2}$ $\quad$ where $y \in \left[-\frac{\pi}{2}, \frac{\pi}{2}\right] - \{0\}$ for principal branch

$\Rightarrow \qquad \operatorname{cosec} y = -\operatorname{cosec} \dfrac{\pi}{4}$

$\Rightarrow \qquad \operatorname{cosec} y = \operatorname{cosec} \left(-\dfrac{\pi}{4}\right)$

($\because$ In principal branch negative values of *cosecant* lie in 4th quadrant)

$\Rightarrow \qquad y = -\dfrac{\pi}{4}$

$\Rightarrow \qquad \operatorname{cosec}^{-1}\left(-\sqrt{2}\right) = -\dfrac{\pi}{4}$

<u>Example</u>

Find the value of $\operatorname{cosec}^{-1}\left(\sqrt{2}\right)$ in the principal value branch.

Solution: $\qquad$ Let $y = \operatorname{cosec}^{-1}\left(\sqrt{2}\right)$

According to definition of $\operatorname{cosec}^{-1}$, we write it as

$\operatorname{cosec} y = \sqrt{2}$ $\quad$ where $y \in \left[-\frac{\pi}{2}, \frac{\pi}{2}\right] - \{0\}$ for principal branch

$\Rightarrow \qquad \operatorname{cosec} y = \operatorname{cosec} \dfrac{\pi}{4}$

($\because$ In principal branch positive values of *cosecant* lie in 1st quadrant)

$\Rightarrow \qquad y = \dfrac{\pi}{4}$

$\Rightarrow \qquad \operatorname{cosec}^{-1}\left(\sqrt{2}\right) = \dfrac{\pi}{4}$

---

5   Inverse of *sec* function (sec^{-1})

Inverse of *secant* function in the *principal value branch* is defined as $sec^{-1} : \mathbf{R} - (-1,1) \rightarrow [0, \pi] - \{\frac{\pi}{2}\}$, which is $y = sec^{-1}x$ such that $sec\, y = x$.

Here, $x \in \mathbf{R} - (-1,1)$ and $y \in [0, \pi] - \{\frac{\pi}{2}\}$

- Domain $= \mathbf{R} - (-1,1)$
- Principal Range $= [0, \pi] - \{\frac{\pi}{2}\}$

- One of the other branches of range is $[\pi, 2\pi] - \{\frac{3\pi}{2}\}$

<u>Example</u>

Find the value of $sec^{-1}(-2)$ in the principal value branch.

Solution: Let $y = sec^{-1}(-2)$

According to definition of sec^{-1}, we write it as

$sec\, y = -2$ where $y \in [0, \pi] - \{\frac{\pi}{2}\}$ for principal branch

$\Rightarrow$ $sec\, y = -sec\, \frac{\pi}{3}$

$\Rightarrow$ $sec\, y = sec\left(\pi - \frac{\pi}{3}\right)$

($\because$ In principal branch negative values of *secant* lie in 2nd quadrant)

$\Rightarrow$ $y = \frac{2\pi}{3}$

$\Rightarrow$ $sec^{-1}(-2) = \frac{2\pi}{3}$

<u>Example</u>

Find the value of $sec^{-1}(2)$ in the principal value branch.

Solution: Let $y = sec^{-1}(2)$

According to definition of sec^{-1}, we write it as

$sec\, y = 2$ where $y \in [0, \pi] - \{\frac{\pi}{2}\}$ for principal branch

$\Rightarrow$ $sec\, y = sec\, \frac{\pi}{3}$

($\because$ In principal branch positive values of *secant* lie in 1st quadrant)

$\Rightarrow$ $y = \frac{\pi}{3}$

$\Rightarrow$ $sec^{-1}(2) = \frac{\pi}{3}$

6   Inverse of *cot* function (cot^{-1})

Inverse of *cotangent* function in the *principal value branch* is defined as $cot^{-1} : \mathbf{R} \rightarrow (0, \pi)$, which is $y = cot^{-1}x$ such that

---

$cot\ y = x.$

Where $\mathbf{R} = (-\infty, \infty)$ is set of real numbers.

Here, $\qquad x \in (-\infty, \infty) \qquad$ and $\quad y \in (0, \pi)$

- Domain $= (-\infty, \infty) = \mathbf{R}$
- Principal Range $= (0, \pi)$
- One of the other branches of range is $(\pi,\ 2\pi)$

<u>Example</u>

Find the value of $cot^{-1}(-\sqrt{3})$ in the principal value branch.

Solution: $\qquad$ Let $y = cot^{-1}(-\sqrt{3})$

According to definition of cot^{-1}, we write it as

$cot\ y = -\sqrt{3} \qquad$ where $y \in (0, \pi)$ for principal branch

$\Rightarrow \quad cot\ y = -cot\ \dfrac{\pi}{6}$

$\Rightarrow \quad cot\ y = cot\left(\pi - \dfrac{\pi}{6}\right)$

($\because$ In principal branch negative values of *cotangent* lie in 2nd quadrant)

$\Rightarrow \quad y = \dfrac{5\pi}{6}$

$\Rightarrow \quad cot^{-1}(-\sqrt{3}) = \dfrac{5\pi}{6}$

<u>Example</u>

Find the value of $cot^{-1}(\sqrt{3})$ in the principal value branch.

Solution: $\qquad$ Let $y = cot^{-1}(\sqrt{3})$

According to definition of cot^{-1}, we write it as

$cot\ y = \sqrt{3} \quad$ where $y \in (0, \pi)$ for principal branch

$\Rightarrow \quad cot\ y = cot\ \dfrac{\pi}{6}$

($\because$ In principal branch positive values of *cotangent* lie in 1st quadrant)

$\Rightarrow \quad y = \dfrac{\pi}{6}$

$\Rightarrow \quad cot^{-1}(\sqrt{3}) = \dfrac{\pi}{6}$

Domain and range in principal branch of all inverse trigonometric functions are listed in the table on next page.

7 Domain and Range :

From the definitions of all inverse trigonometric functions, we summarise their domains and range in the following table:

S.N.	Functions	Domain	Principal Range
1)	$y = \sin^{-1}x$	$[-1, 1]$ *i.e.,* $-1 \leq x \leq 1$	$\left[-\dfrac{\pi}{2}, \dfrac{\pi}{2}\right]$ *i.e.,* $-\dfrac{\pi}{2} \leq y \leq \dfrac{\pi}{2}$
2)	$y = \cos^{-1}x$	$[-1, 1]$ *i.e.,* $-1 \leq x \leq 1$	$[0, \pi]$ *i.e.,* $0 \leq y \leq \pi$
3)	$y = \tan^{-1}x$	R *i.e.,* $-\infty < x < \infty$	$\left(-\dfrac{\pi}{2}, \dfrac{\pi}{2}\right)$ *i.e.,* $-\dfrac{\pi}{2} < y < \dfrac{\pi}{2}$
4)	$y = \operatorname{cosec}^{-1}x$	$R - (-1, 1)$ *i.e.,* $x \leq -1$ *or* $x \geq 1$ *i.e.,* $|x| \geq 1$	$\left[-\dfrac{\pi}{2}, \dfrac{\pi}{2}\right] - \{0\}$ *i.e.,* $-\dfrac{\pi}{2} \leq y < 0$ *or* $0 < y \leq \dfrac{\pi}{2}$
5)	$y = \sec^{-1}x$	$R - (-1, 1)$ *i.e.,* $x \leq -1$ *or* $x \geq 1$ *i.e.,* $|x| \geq 1$	$[0, \pi] - \left\{\dfrac{\pi}{2}\right\}$ *i.e.,* $0 \leq y < \dfrac{\pi}{2}$ *or* $\dfrac{\pi}{2} < y \leq \pi$
6)	$y = \cot^{-1}x$	R *i.e.,* $-\infty < x < \infty$	$(0, \pi)$ *i.e.,* $0 < y < \pi$

8   Results from definitions

$$
\begin{array}{lll}
(i) & sin^{-1}(sin\,x) = x & ; \quad if\ x \in [-\frac{\pi}{2}, \frac{\pi}{2}] \\[2mm]
(ii) & cos^{-1}(cos\ x) = x & ; \quad if\ x \in [0, \pi] \\[2mm]
(iii) & tan^{-1}(tan\ x) = x & ; \quad if\ x \in (-\frac{\pi}{2}, \frac{\pi}{2}) \\[2mm]
(iv) & cosec^{-1}(cosec\,x) = x & ; \quad if\ x \in [-\frac{\pi}{2}, \frac{\pi}{2}] - \{0\} \\[2mm]
(v) & sec^{-1}(sec\,x) = x & ; \quad if\ x \in [0, \pi] - \{\frac{\pi}{2}\} \\[2mm]
(vi) & cot^{-1}(cot\ x) = x & ; \quad if\ x \in (0, \pi)
\end{array}
$$

<u>Example</u>

(i) $sin^{-1}\left(sin\frac{\pi}{3}\right) = \frac{\pi}{3}$ $\left(\because \frac{\pi}{3} \in [-\frac{\pi}{2}, \frac{\pi}{2}]\right)$

(ii) $sin^{-1}\left(sin\frac{2\pi}{3}\right) \neq \frac{2\pi}{3}$ $\left(\because \frac{2\pi}{3} \notin [-\frac{\pi}{2}, \frac{\pi}{2}]\right)$

(iii) $cos^{-1}\left(cos\frac{2\pi}{3}\right) = \frac{2\pi}{3}$ $\left(\because \frac{2\pi}{3} \in [0, \pi]\right)$

(iv) $cos^{-1}\left(cos\left(-\frac{\pi}{3}\right)\right) \neq -\frac{\pi}{3}$ $\left(\because -\frac{\pi}{3} \notin [0, \pi]\right)$

Similarly we can conclude for tan^{-1}, $cosec^{-1}$, sec^{-1}, and cot^{-1}.

$$
\begin{array}{lll}
(i) & sin\,(sin^{-1} x) = x & ; \quad if\ x \in [-1, 1] \\[2mm]
(ii) & cos\,(cos^{-1} x) = x & ; \quad if\ x \in [-1, 1] \\[2mm]
(iii) & tan\,(tan^{-1} x) = x & ; \quad if\ x \in R \\[2mm]
(iv) & cosec\,(cosec^{-1} x) = x & ; \quad if\ x \in R - (-1, 1) \\[2mm]
(v) & sec\,(sec^{-1} x) = x & ; \quad if\ x \in R - (-1, 1) \\[2mm]
(vi) & cot\,(cot^{-1} x) = x & ; \quad if\ x \in R
\end{array}
$$

<u>Example</u>

(i) $sin\left(sin^{-1}\left(\frac{1}{3}\right)\right) = \frac{1}{3}$ $\left(\because \frac{1}{3} \in [-1,1]\right)$

(ii) $cos\left(cos^{-1}\left(\frac{1}{3}\right)\right) = \frac{1}{3}$ $\left(\because \frac{1}{3} \in [-1,1]\right)$

(iii) $sec\,(sec^{-1}(3)) = 3$ $\left(\because 3 \in \mathbf{R} - (-1,1)\right)$

(iv) $tan\,(tan^{-1}(2)) = 2$ $\left(\because 2 \in \mathbf{R}\right)$

Similarly we can conclude for $cosec^{-1}$ and cot^{-1}.

9 *Other Formulae

9.1 *Negative arguments

$$\left.\begin{array}{ll}(i) & sin^{-1}(-x) = -sin^{-1}x \\ (ii) & cosec^{-1}(-x) = -cosec^{-1}x \\ (iii) & tan^{-1}(-x) = -tan^{-1}x\end{array}\right\} \begin{array}{c}\text{whose } principal\ branch \\ is\ in \\ 1st\ and\ 4th\ quadrants\end{array}$$

$$\left.\begin{array}{ll}(iv) & cos^{-1}(-x) = \pi - cos^{-1}x \\ (v) & sec^{-1}(-x) = \pi - sec^{-1}x \\ (vi) & cot^{-1}(-x) = \pi - cot^{-1}x\end{array}\right\} \begin{array}{c}\text{whose } principal\ branch \\ is\ in \\ 1st\ and\ 2nd\ quadrants\end{array}$$

Example

(i) $sin^{-1}\left(-\dfrac{1}{3}\right) = -sin^{-1}\left(\dfrac{1}{3}\right)$

(ii) $cos^{-1}\left(-\dfrac{1}{3}\right) = \pi - cos^{-1}\left(\dfrac{1}{3}\right)$

Similarly we can conclude for tan^{-1}, $cosec^{-1}$, sec^{-1} and cot^{-1}.

9.2 *Reciprocal arguments

$$(i)\ sin^{-1}\dfrac{1}{x} = cosec^{-1}x \quad ; \quad if\ |x| \geq 1$$

$$(ii)\ cos^{-1}\dfrac{1}{x} = sec^{-1}x \quad ; \quad if\ |x| \geq 1$$

$$(iii)\ tan^{-1}\dfrac{1}{x} = cot^{-1}x \quad ; \quad if\ x > 0$$

$$(iv)\ cosec^{-1}\dfrac{1}{x} = sin^{-1}x \quad ; \quad if\ x \in [-1, 1] - \{0\}$$

$$(v)\ sec^{-1}\dfrac{1}{x} = cos^{-1}x \quad ; \quad if\ x \in [-1, 1] - \{0\}$$

$$(vi)\ cot^{-1}\dfrac{1}{x} = tan^{-1}x \quad ; \quad if\ x > 0$$

- Relationship between tan^{-1} and cot^{-1} is applicable only for positive x.

Example

(i) $sin^{-1}\left(\dfrac{1}{3}\right) = cosec^{-1}(3) \quad (\because |3| \geq 1)$

(ii) $cos^{-1}\left(-\dfrac{1}{3}\right) = sec^{-1}(-3) \quad (\because |-3| \geq 1)$

Similarly we can conclude for tan^{-1}, $cosec^{-1}$, sec^{-1} and cot^{-1}.

9.3   *Complementary of inverse functions

$(i)\quad \sin^{-1}x \;+\; \cos^{-1}x \;=\; \dfrac{\pi}{2}; \;\; if\; x \in [-1,1]$

$(ii)\quad \sec^{-1}x \;+\; \csc^{-1}x \;=\; \dfrac{\pi}{2}; \;\; if\; |x| \ge 1$

$(iii)\; \tan^{-1}x \;+\; \cot^{-1}x \;=\; \dfrac{\pi}{2}; \;\; if\; x \in R$

Example

(i) $\sin^{-1}\left(-\dfrac{1}{3}\right) \;+\; \cos^{-1}\left(-\dfrac{1}{3}\right) = \dfrac{\pi}{2}$

(ii) $\sec^{-1}(2) \;+\; \csc^{-1}(2) = \dfrac{\pi}{2}$

(iii) $\tan^{-1}\left(\dfrac{3}{2}\right) \;+\; \cot^{-1}\left(\dfrac{3}{2}\right) = \dfrac{\pi}{2}$

9.4   *sum / difference of inverse functions

$(i)\quad \tan^{-1}x + \tan^{-1}y = \tan^{-1}\dfrac{x+y}{1-xy} \qquad ;\, if\, xy < 1$

$(ii)\quad \tan^{-1}x + \tan^{-1}y = \pi + \tan^{-1}\dfrac{x+y}{1-xy}; \, if\, xy > 1\, and\, x,y > 0$

$(iii)\; \tan^{-1}x - \tan^{-1}y = \tan^{-1}\dfrac{x-y}{1+xy} \qquad ;\, if\, xy > -1$

Example

$$\tan^{-1}\left(\dfrac{3}{2}\right) + \tan^{-1}\left(\dfrac{3}{5}\right) = \tan^{-1}\dfrac{\frac{3}{2}+\frac{3}{5}}{1-\frac{3}{2}\times\frac{3}{5}} \qquad \left(\because \dfrac{3}{2}\times\dfrac{3}{5} = \dfrac{9}{10} < 1\right)$$

$$= \tan^{-1}(21)$$

Example

$$\tan^{-1}\left(\dfrac{3}{2}\right) + \tan^{-1}\left(\dfrac{5}{6}\right) = \pi + \tan^{-1}\dfrac{\frac{3}{2}+\frac{5}{6}}{1-\frac{3}{2}\times\frac{5}{6}}$$

$$\left(\because \dfrac{3}{2}\times\dfrac{5}{6} = \dfrac{15}{12} > 1\right)$$

$$= \pi + \tan^{-1}\left(-\dfrac{28}{3}\right)$$

$$= \pi - \tan^{-1}\left(\dfrac{28}{3}\right) \qquad (\because \tan^{-1}(-x) = -\tan^{-1}x)$$

Example

$$\tan^{-1}\left(\dfrac{3}{2}\right) - \tan^{-1}\left(\dfrac{3}{5}\right) = \tan^{-1}\dfrac{\frac{3}{2}-\frac{3}{5}}{1+\frac{3}{2}\times\frac{3}{5}} \qquad \left(\because \dfrac{3}{2}\times\dfrac{3}{5} = \dfrac{9}{10} > -1\right)$$

$$= \tan^{-1}\left(\dfrac{9}{19}\right)$$

9.5 *Double of inverse functions

$$(i) \quad 2\tan^{-1}x = \sin^{-1}\dfrac{2x}{1+x^2} \quad ; \quad if \ |x| \leq 1$$

$$(ii) \ 2\tan^{-1}x = \cos^{-1}\dfrac{1-x^2}{1+x^2} \quad ; \quad if \ x \geq 0$$

$$(iii) \ 2\tan^{-1}x = \tan^{-1}\dfrac{2x}{1-x^2} \quad ; \quad if \ |x| < 1$$

<u>Example</u>

$$2\tan^{-1}\left(-\tfrac{2}{3}\right) = \sin^{-1}\left(\dfrac{2\times\left(-\frac{2}{3}\right)}{1+\left(-\frac{2}{3}\right)^2}\right)\left(\because \left|-\tfrac{2}{3}\right| \leq 1\right)$$

$$=\sin^{-1}\left(-\tfrac{12}{13}\right)$$

$$=-\sin^{-1}\left(\tfrac{12}{13}\right) \qquad (\because \ sin^{-1}(-x) = -sin^{-1}x)$$

<u>Example</u>

$$2\tan^{-1}\left(\tfrac{2}{3}\right) = \cos^{-1}\left(\dfrac{1-\left(\frac{2}{3}\right)^2}{1+\left(\frac{2}{3}\right)^2}\right) \qquad \left(\because \tfrac{2}{3} \geq 0\right)$$

$$=\cos^{-1}\left(\tfrac{5}{13}\right)$$

<u>Example</u>

$$2\tan^{-1}\left(\tfrac{2}{3}\right) = 2\tan^{-1}\left(\dfrac{2\times\frac{2}{3}}{1-\left(\frac{2}{3}\right)^2}\right) \qquad \left(\because \left|\tfrac{2}{3}\right| < 1\right)$$

$$= \tan^{-1}\left(\tfrac{12}{5}\right)$$

$$(i) \ 2\sin^{-1}x = \sin^{-1}\left(2x\sqrt{1-x^2}\right) \quad ; \ if \ x \in \left[-\tfrac{1}{\sqrt{2}},\tfrac{1}{\sqrt{2}}\right]$$
$$= \cos^{-1}(1-2x^2) \quad ; \ if \ x \in [0,1]$$
$$(ii) \ 2\cos^{-1}x = \sin^{-1}\left(2x\sqrt{1-x^2}\right) \quad ; \ if \ x \in \left[\tfrac{1}{\sqrt{2}},1\right]$$
$$= \cos^{-1}(2x^2-1) \quad ; if \ x \in [0,1]$$

<u>Example</u>

$$2\sin^{-1}\left(-\tfrac{2}{3}\right) = \sin^{-1}\left(2\times\left(-\tfrac{2}{3}\right)\sqrt{1-\left(-\tfrac{2}{3}\right)^2}\right)$$

$$\left(\because -\tfrac{1}{\sqrt{2}} \leq -\tfrac{2}{3} \leq \tfrac{1}{\sqrt{2}}\right)$$

$$= \sin^{-1}\left(-\tfrac{4\sqrt{5}}{9}\right)$$

$$=-\sin^{-1}\left(\tfrac{4\sqrt{5}}{9}\right) \qquad (\because \ sin^{-1}(-x) = -sin^{-1}x)$$

<u>Example</u>

$$2 \sin^{-1}\left(\tfrac{3}{4}\right) = \cos^{-1}\left(1 - 2\left(\tfrac{3}{4}\right)^2\right) \qquad\qquad \left(\because 0 \le \tfrac{3}{4} \le 1\right)$$

$$= \cos^{-1}\left(-\tfrac{1}{8}\right)$$

$$= \pi - \cos^{-1}\left(\tfrac{1}{8}\right) \qquad \left(\because \cos^{-1}(-x) = \pi - \cos^{-1} x\right)$$

Example

$$2 \cos^{-1}\left(\tfrac{3}{4}\right) = \sin^{-1}\left(2 \times \left(\tfrac{3}{4}\right)\sqrt{1 - \left(\tfrac{3}{4}\right)^2}\right)$$

$$\left(\because \tfrac{1}{\sqrt{2}} \le \tfrac{3}{4} \le 1\right)$$

$$= \sin^{-1}\left(\tfrac{3\sqrt{7}}{8}\right)$$

Example

$$2 \cos^{-1}\left(\tfrac{3}{4}\right) = \cos^{-1}\left(2\left(\tfrac{3}{4}\right)^2 - 1\right) \qquad\qquad \left(\because 0 \le \tfrac{3}{4} \le 1\right)$$

$$= \cos^{-1}\left(\tfrac{1}{8}\right)$$

Chapter-3   Matrices

1   Definition

A matrix is a rectangular arrangement of given numbers or functions, in rows and columns, in an ordered manner.

- The numbers or functions in the matrix are known as its element.
- A matrix is denoted by a capital letter like A ,B, C etc., and its elements are represented as a_{ij} , b_{ij} , c_{ij} etc. respectively.

  where, a_{ij} = element in i^{th} row and j^{th} column of matrix A.

  b_{ij} = element in i^{th} row and j^{th} column of matrix B.
- Complete arrangement of the elements is enclosed in a *square or round brackets*.

Example

$$A = \begin{pmatrix} 3 & 6 \\ -1 & -2 \end{pmatrix}$$

We represent: element in 1st row and 1st column by a_{11}

element in 1st row and 2nd column by a_{12}

element in 2nd row and 1st column by a_{21}

element in 2nd row and 2nd column by a_{22}

Here, elements of matrix A are written as:

$$a_{11} = 3, \qquad a_{12} = 6,$$
$$a_{21} = -1, \qquad a_{22} = -2$$

Example

$$B = \begin{bmatrix} 0 & 3 & 4 \\ 1 & 2 & 5 \end{bmatrix}$$

Here, elements of matrix B are written as:

$$b_{11} = 0, \qquad b_{12} = 3, \qquad b_{13} = 4,$$
$$b_{21} = 1, \qquad b_{22} = 2 \qquad b_{23} = 5$$

2   Order of Matrix

- Number of rows and number of columns give the order of a matrix.
- Matrix A, having m rows and n columns, is said to have an order of $\boldsymbol{m \times n}$, and the matrix A is denoted as $A_{m \times n}$

  or $A = [a_{ij}]_{m \times n}$ where $i = 1,2,3,\ldots,m$ and $j = 1,2,3,\ldots,n$.

<u>**Example**</u>

If matrix A has 2 rows and 3 columns, then its order is **2×3**, and the matrix A is denoted as $A_{2\times3}$ or $A = [a_{ij}]_{2\times3}$ where $i = 1,2$ and $j = 1,2,3$.

So, matrix A with all its elements can be represented as

$$A = \begin{pmatrix} a_{11} & a_{12} & a_{13} \\ a_{21} & a_{22} & a_{23} \end{pmatrix}_{2\times3}$$

<u>**Example**</u>

If matrix B has 3 rows and 2 columns, then its order is **3×2**, and the matrix B is denoted as $B_{3\times2}$ or $B = [b_{ij}]_{3\times2}$ where $i = 1,2,3$ and $j = 1,2$.

So, matrix B with all its elements can be represented as

$$B = \begin{bmatrix} b_{11} & b_{12} \\ b_{21} & b_{22} \\ b_{31} & b_{32} \end{bmatrix}_{3\times2}$$

- Total number of elements in a matrix
  = product of number of rows and number of columns
  = mn (where m = no. of rows and n = no. of columns)

e.g. if the order of matrix B is 3×4, then total number of elements in it are 12.

3 Types of Matrices

3.1 Row Matrix

A matrix which has only one row is known as row matrix.

e.g. $[-2 \quad 4]$, $[\sqrt{2} \quad 1 \quad -3]$, $\left[0 \quad \frac{-7}{5} \quad 3 \quad 12\right]$ etc.

3.2 Column Matrix

A matrix which has only one column is known as column matrix.

e.g. $\begin{bmatrix} 3 \\ \frac{1}{2} \end{bmatrix}$, , $\begin{bmatrix} \sqrt{3} \\ 5 \\ -1 \end{bmatrix}$, $\begin{bmatrix} -5 \\ \frac{3}{2} \\ 23 \\ -4 \end{bmatrix}$ etc.

3.3 Square Matrix

*A matrix which has **equal number of rows and columns** is known as square matrix.*

e.g. $\begin{bmatrix} 6 & -8 \\ -5 & 3/5 \end{bmatrix}$, $\begin{bmatrix} -3 & 7 & 5 \\ \sqrt{2} & 9 & -4 \\ \sqrt{3} & 1 & 0 \end{bmatrix}$ etc.

- A square matrix of order $m \times m$ is simply said to be of order m.

Thus, 2×2 square matrix is simply said to be of order 2, 3×3 square matrix is simply said to be of order 3 etc.

3.3.1 Diagonal of square matrix

*Elements of a square matrix lying diagonally from top of 1st column to the bottom of last column constitute **principal diagonal (or diagonal)** of matrix.*

- **Elements whose row number and column number are same constitute the diagonal of matrix.**

  i.e. in the matrix $A = [a_{ij}]_{m \times m}$,

  a_{ij} represents element of the diagonal if $i = j$.

  It means a_{11} , a_{22} , a_{33} , ..., a_{mm} are diagonal elements.

<u>Example</u>

In square matrix of order 3 the elements a_{11} , a_{22} , a_{33} are diagonal elements.

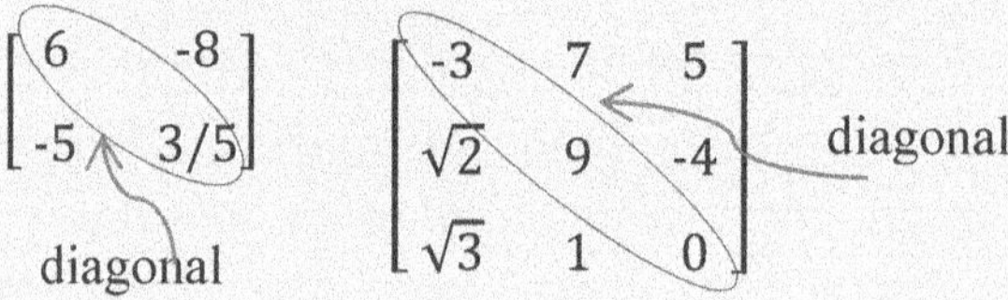

$$\begin{pmatrix} a_{11} & a_{12} & a_{13} \\ a_{21} & a_{22} & a_{23} \\ a_{31} & a_{32} & a_{33} \end{pmatrix} \quad \text{diagonal}$$

- Encircled elements in the following matrices are diagonal elements

$$\begin{bmatrix} 6 & -8 \\ -5 & 3/5 \end{bmatrix} \quad \text{diagonal} \qquad \begin{bmatrix} -3 & 7 & 5 \\ \sqrt{2} & 9 & -4 \\ \sqrt{3} & 1 & 0 \end{bmatrix} \quad \text{diagonal}$$

3.4 Diagonal Matrix

*A **square matrix**, whose all non-diagonal elements are **0** , is known as diagonal matrix.*

- $A = [a_{ij}]_{m \times m}$ is a diagonal matrix if and only if $a_{ij} = 0$ *for all $i \neq j$*

  e.g. $\begin{bmatrix} 6 & 0 \\ 0 & 3/5 \end{bmatrix}$, $\begin{bmatrix} -3 & 0 & 0 \\ 0 & 9 & 0 \\ 0 & 0 & 2 \end{bmatrix}$, $\begin{bmatrix} -3 & 0 & 0 \\ 0 & 0 & 0 \\ 0 & 0 & 2 \end{bmatrix}$ etc.

3.5 Scalar Matrix

A **square matrix**, *whose all non-diagonal elements are* **0** , *and all diagonal elements are* **equal**, *is known as scalar matrix.*

- $A = [a_{ij}]_{m \times m}$ is a scalar matrix if and only if

$$a_{ij} = \begin{cases} 0 & for \ i \neq j \\ k & for \ i = j \end{cases} \quad \text{where } k \text{ is a constant.}$$

e.g. $\begin{bmatrix} 6 & 0 \\ 0 & 6 \end{bmatrix}$, $\begin{bmatrix} -3 & 0 & 0 \\ 0 & -3 & 0 \\ 0 & 0 & -3 \end{bmatrix}$ etc.

- **Scalar matrix is a diagonal matrix also.**

3.6 Identity Matrix (or unit matrix)

A **square matrix**, *whose all non-diagonal elements are* **0** , *and all diagonal elements are* equal to **1** , *is known as identity or unit matrix.*

- $A = [a_{ij}]_{m \times m}$ is an identity matrix if and only if

$$a_{ij} = \begin{cases} 0 & for \ i \neq j \\ 1 & for \ i = j \end{cases}$$

- Identity matrix is generally denoted by $\mathbf{I}_n$, where n is order of the matrix.

e.g. $\mathbf{I}_2 = \begin{bmatrix} 1 & 0 \\ 0 & 1 \end{bmatrix}$, $\mathbf{I}_3 = \begin{bmatrix} 1 & 0 & 0 \\ 0 & 1 & 0 \\ 0 & 0 & 1 \end{bmatrix}$ etc.

- Unit matrix is a **diagonal matrix and** a **scalar matrix** also.

3.7 Zero Matrix (or null matrix)

A matrix, whose each element is **0** *, is known as zero or null matrix.*

- Zero matrix is generally denoted by **O**.

e.g.

$$\mathbf{O}_{2 \times 2} = \begin{pmatrix} 0 & 0 \\ 0 & 0 \end{pmatrix}, \ \mathbf{O}_{2 \times 3} = \begin{pmatrix} 0 & 0 & 0 \\ 0 & 0 & 0 \end{pmatrix}, \ \mathbf{O}_{3 \times 3} = \begin{bmatrix} 0 & 0 & 0 \\ 0 & 0 & 0 \\ 0 & 0 & 0 \end{bmatrix} \text{etc.}$$

4 Equal Matrices

Two matrices are equal if and only if their orders are same and their corresponding elements are equal.

- If we have matrices $A = [a_{ij}]_{m \times n}$ and $B = [b_{ij}]_{p \times q}$, then they are equal if

  (i) $m = p$ and $n = q$ (same order)

  (ii) $a_{ij} = b_{ij}$ for all i and j (equal corresponding elements)

Example

If matrix $A = \begin{pmatrix} a_{11} & a_{12} & a_{13} \\ a_{21} & a_{22} & a_{23} \end{pmatrix}_{2 \times 3}$ and $B = \begin{bmatrix} b_{11} & b_{12} \\ b_{21} & b_{22} \\ b_{31} & b_{32} \end{bmatrix}_{3 \times 2}$

then $A \neq B$ as they **do not have same order**. Matrix A has order 2×3 while B has 3×2.

Example

If matrix $A = \begin{pmatrix} a_{11} & a_{12} & a_{13} \\ a_{21} & a_{22} & a_{23} \end{pmatrix}_{2 \times 3}$

and $B = \begin{bmatrix} b_{11} & b_{12} & b_{13} \\ b_{21} & b_{22} & b_{23} \end{bmatrix}_{2 \times 3}$

such that $A = B$, then

$$a_{11} = b_{11}, \qquad a_{12} = b_{12}, \qquad a_{13} = b_{13}$$
$$a_{21} = b_{21}, \qquad a_{22} = b_{22}, \qquad a_{23} = b_{23}$$

Example

If matrix $A = \begin{pmatrix} x & y & z \\ u & v & w \end{pmatrix}$ and $B = \begin{pmatrix} a & b & c \\ d & e & f \end{pmatrix}$, then **A can be equal to B** as they have same order 2×3 provided,

$$x = a, \quad y = b, \quad z = c, \quad u = d, \quad v = e, \quad w = f.$$

Example

If matrix $A = \begin{pmatrix} 2 & 3 & 4 \\ 1 & -7 & -5 \end{pmatrix}$ and $B = \begin{pmatrix} 3 & 4 & 2 \\ -7 & -5 & 1 \end{pmatrix}$,

then $A \neq B$ because their corresponding elements are not equal though they have same order 3×2.

Example

If matrix $A = \begin{pmatrix} 2 & 3 & 4 \\ 1 & -7 & -5 \end{pmatrix}$ and $B = \begin{pmatrix} 2 & 3 & 4 \\ 1 & -7 & -5 \end{pmatrix}$

then $A = B$ because their corresponding elements are equal, and they have same order 3×2.

5   Multiplication of a matrix by a scalar

A matrix of any order can be multiplied by a scalar (a number or a function), and their product is obtained by **multiplying each element of the matrix by that scalar**.

- The order of resulting matrix is same as that of the given matrix.
- If we have matrix $A = [a_{ij}]_{m \times n}$ and a scalar k, then

$$k A = [k\, a_{ij}]_{m \times n} \text{ for all } i \text{ and } j \text{ (}multiplying\ every\ element\ by\ k\text{)}$$

<u>**Example**</u>

If matrix $A = \begin{pmatrix} x & y & z \\ u & v & w \end{pmatrix}$ and a scalar is k, then

$$k\,A = k \begin{pmatrix} x & y & z \\ u & v & w \end{pmatrix}$$

$$\Rightarrow \quad k\,A = \begin{pmatrix} kx & ky & kz \\ ku & kv & kw \end{pmatrix} \quad \text{it has } \textbf{same order 2×3 as A.}$$

<u>**Example**</u>

If matrix $A = \begin{pmatrix} 2 & 3 & 4 \\ 1 & -7 & -5 \end{pmatrix}$ and we multiply it by a scalar, -3 ,

then $\quad -3\,A = -3 \begin{pmatrix} 2 & 3 & 4 \\ 1 & -7 & -5 \end{pmatrix}$

$$\Rightarrow \quad -3\,A = \begin{pmatrix} -3 \times 2 & -3 \times 3 & -3 \times 4 \\ -3 \times 1 & -3 \times -7 & -3 \times -5 \end{pmatrix}$$

$$= \begin{pmatrix} -6 & -9 & -12 \\ -3 & 21 & 15 \end{pmatrix}$$

5.1 Negative of matrix

Negative of a matrix is multiplication of the matrix by **–1**.
i.e. negative of matrix A is –A which is obtained by changing the sign of every element of matrix A.

- If we have matrix $A = [a_{ij}]_{m \times n}$, then

  $- A = [-a_{ij}]_{m \times n}$ for all i and j

  (multiplying every element by –1)

  e.g., If $A = \begin{pmatrix} 2 & 3 & 4 \\ 1 & -7 & -5 \end{pmatrix}$,

  then $-A = \begin{pmatrix} -2 & -3 & -4 \\ -1 & 7 & 5 \end{pmatrix}$

6 Addition of matrices

Two matrices can be added only if their **orders are same**, and *their sum is obtained by* **adding their corresponding elements**.

- The order of resulting matrix is same as that of the matrices added.
- If we have matrices $A = [a_{ij}]_{m \times n}$ and $B = [b_{ij}]_{p \times q}$, then

  (i) they can be added only if $m = p$ and $n = q$
     (i.e., if they have same order)

  (ii) The order of matrix A+ B will be $m \times n$ or $p \times q$

  (iii) $A + B = [c_{ij}]_{m \times n}$ or $[c_{ij}]_{p \times q}$ such that

  $$[c_{ij}] = [a_{ij} + b_{ij}]$$
  for all $i = 1,2,3,\ldots,m$ and $j = 1,2,3,\ldots,n$.

  (adding corresponding elements)

<u>**Example**</u>

If matrix $A = \begin{pmatrix} a_{11} & a_{12} & a_{13} \\ a_{21} & a_{22} & a_{23} \end{pmatrix}_{2 \times 3}$

and $B = \begin{bmatrix} b_{11} & b_{12} & b_{13} \\ b_{21} & b_{22} & b_{23} \end{bmatrix}_{2 \times 3}$

then **A and B can be added** as they have same order 2×3, and the resulting matrix is,

$$A + B = \begin{pmatrix} a_{11} + b_{11} & a_{12} + b_{12} & a_{13} + b_{13} \\ a_{21} + b_{21} & a_{22} + b_{22} & a_{23} + b_{23} \end{pmatrix}$$

which has the **order 2×3, same as A and B**.

<u>**Example**</u>

If matrix $A = \begin{pmatrix} x & y & z \\ u & v & w \end{pmatrix}$ and $B = \begin{bmatrix} a & d \\ b & e \\ c & f \end{bmatrix}$, then **A and B**

cannot be added because they do not have same order (Matrix A has order 2×3 while B has 3×2).

<u>**Example**</u>

If matrix $A = \begin{pmatrix} 2 & 3 & 4 \\ 1 & -7 & -5 \end{pmatrix}$ and $B = \begin{pmatrix} 3 & 4 & 2 \\ -7 & -5 & 1 \end{pmatrix}$

then $A + B = \begin{pmatrix} 2+3 & 3+4 & 4+2 \\ 1-7 & -7-5 & -5+1 \end{pmatrix} = \begin{pmatrix} 5 & 7 & 6 \\ -6 & -12 & -4 \end{pmatrix}$

7   Subtraction of matrices

Two matrices can be subtracted only if their **orders are same,** *and their difference is obtained by* **subtracting their corresponding elements**.

- Actually, difference $A - B$ is sum of A and (–B).
  i.e. $A - B = A + (-B)$
- The order of resulting matrix is same as that of the matrices subtracted.
- If we have matrices $A = [a_{ij}]_{m \times n}$ and $B = [b_{ij}]_{p \times q}$, then

  (i) they can be subtracted only if $m = p$ and $n = q$
       (i.e., if they have same order)

  (ii) The order of matrix $A - B$ will be $m \times n$ or $p \times q$

  (iii) $A - B = [c_{ij}]_{m \times n}$ or $[c_{ij}]_{p \times q}$ such that

  $$[c_{ij}] = [a_{ij} - b_{ij}]$$

  for all $i = 1,2,3,\dots,m$ and $j = 1,2,3,\dots,n$.

  (subtracting corresponding elements)

Example

If matrix $A = \begin{pmatrix} a_{11} & a_{12} & a_{13} \\ a_{21} & a_{22} & a_{23} \end{pmatrix}_{2 \times 3}$

and $B = \begin{bmatrix} b_{11} & b_{12} & b_{13} \\ b_{21} & b_{22} & b_{23} \end{bmatrix}_{2 \times 3}$

then **A and B can be subtracted** as they have same order 2×3 and the resulting matrix is,

$$A - B = \begin{pmatrix} a_{11} - b_{11} & a_{12} - b_{12} & a_{13} - b_{13} \\ a_{21} - b_{21} & a_{22} - b_{22} & a_{23} - b_{23} \end{pmatrix}$$

which has the **order 2×3, same as A and B**.

Example

If matrix $A = \begin{pmatrix} x & y & z \\ u & v & w \end{pmatrix}$ and $B = \begin{bmatrix} a & d \\ b & e \\ c & f \end{bmatrix}$

then **A and B cannot be subtracted** as they do not have same order. (Matrix A has order 2×3 while B has 3×2).

Example

If matrix $A = \begin{pmatrix} 2 & 3 & 4 \\ 1 & -7 & -5 \end{pmatrix}$ and $B = \begin{pmatrix} 3 & 4 & 2 \\ -7 & -5 & 1 \end{pmatrix}$

then $A - B = \begin{pmatrix} 2-3 & 3-4 & 4-2 \\ 1+7 & -7+5 & -5-1 \end{pmatrix} = \begin{pmatrix} -1 & -1 & 2 \\ 8 & -2 & -6 \end{pmatrix}$

8 Properties of scalar multiplication

If A & B are 2 matrices of same order , and k & l are any scalars, then

(i) $k(A + B) = kA + kB$

(ii) $(k + l)A = kA + lA$

9 Properties of matrix addition

Matrices A, B & C of same order hold the following properties on addition

(i) **Commutative**: $A + B = B + A$

(ii) **Associative**: $(A + B) + C = A + (B + C)$

(iii) **Additive identity**: Additive identity of matrix $A_{m \times n}$ is **Zero matrix $O_{m \times n}$**.

   i.e. $A + O = A$ and $O + A = A$

e.g. if $A = \begin{bmatrix} 3 & 5 \\ -2 & 1 \\ 4 & 0 \end{bmatrix}$, then its additive identity is $O_{3 \times 2} = \begin{bmatrix} 0 & 0 \\ 0 & 0 \\ 0 & 0 \end{bmatrix}$

(iv) **Additive inverse**: $-A$ is additive inverse of matrix A.

$$\text{i.e.,} \quad A + (-A) = O \quad \text{and} \quad (-A) + A = O$$

e.g.   if $A = \begin{bmatrix} 3 & 5 \\ -2 & 1 \\ 4 & 0 \end{bmatrix}$

then its additive inverse is $-A = \begin{bmatrix} -3 & -5 \\ 2 & -1 \\ -4 & 0 \end{bmatrix}$

10 Multiplication of matrices

Two matrices can be multiplied only if the **number of columns in first matrix is equal to the number of rows in the second matrix**.

- The order of resulting matrix is given by the number of rows in first matrix and the number of columns of second matrix.
- If we have matrices $A = [a_{ij}]_{m \times n}$ and $B = [b_{ij}]_{p \times q}$, then

  (i) the product AB is defined only if $n = p$

    (No. of columns of A = No. of rows of B)

  (ii) The order of matrix AB will be $m \times q$

  (iii) $AB = [c_{ij}]_{m \times q}$ such that

  $$[c_{ij}] = [a_{i1} b_{1j} + a_{i2} b_{2j} + \ldots + a_{in} b_{nj}]$$

  for all $i = 1,2,3,\ldots,m$ and $j = 1,2,3,\ldots,p$.

- If product AB is defined, then the product BA is not necessarily defined.

Example

If matrix $A = \begin{pmatrix} x & y & z \\ u & v & w \end{pmatrix}_{2 \times 3}$ and $B = \begin{pmatrix} a & b & c \\ d & e & f \end{pmatrix}_{2 \times 3}$

then the product **AB is not defined** because the number of columns in matrix A is 3, and number of rows in B is 2, which are not equal.

BA is also not defined because the number of columns in matrix B is 3, and number of rows in A is 2, which are not equal.

Example

If matrix $A = \begin{pmatrix} a_{11} & a_{12} \\ a_{21} & a_{22} \end{pmatrix}_{2 \times 2}$ and $B = \begin{bmatrix} b_{11} & b_{12} & b_{13} \\ b_{21} & b_{22} & b_{23} \end{bmatrix}_{2 \times 3}$

then the product **AB is defined** because the number of columns in matrix A and number of rows in B are both equal (equal to 2)

The order of matrix AB will be 2×3.

But the product **BA is not defined** because the number of columns in matrix B is 3, and number of rows in A is 2, which are not equal.

<u>**Example**</u>

If matrix $A = \begin{pmatrix} a_{11} & a_{12} & a_{13} \\ a_{21} & a_{22} & a_{23} \end{pmatrix}_{2 \times 3}$ and $B = \begin{bmatrix} b_{11} & b_{12} \\ b_{21} & b_{22} \\ b_{31} & b_{32} \end{bmatrix}_{3 \times 2}$

then the product **AB is defined** because the number of columns in matrix A and number of rows in B are both equal (equal to 3) **The order of matrix AB will be 2×2.**
Also the product **BA is defined** because the number of columns in matrix B and number of rows in A are both equal (equal to 2) **The order of matrix BA will be 3×3.**

10.1 Procedure to multiply two matrices

Given: Two matrices $A = \begin{bmatrix} a_{11} & a_{12} \\ a_{21} & a_{22} \\ a_{31} & a_{32} \end{bmatrix}$

and $B = \begin{bmatrix} b_{11} & b_{12} & b_{13} \\ b_{21} & b_{22} & b_{23} \end{bmatrix}$

To find: Product, AB

Step-1 To obtain the product, we mark row numbers in the first matrix, A and column numbers in the second matrix, B as shown below:

$$A B = \begin{matrix} R_1 \to \\ R_2 \to \\ R_3 \to \end{matrix} \begin{bmatrix} a_{11} & a_{12} \\ a_{21} & a_{22} \\ a_{31} & a_{32} \end{bmatrix} \begin{matrix} C_1 & C_2 & C_3 \\ \downarrow & \downarrow & \downarrow \\ \end{matrix} \begin{pmatrix} b_{11} & b_{12} & b_{13} \\ b_{21} & b_{22} & b_{23} \end{pmatrix}$$

Step-2 Now we multiply elements of R_1 with the corresponding elements of C_1, and add them to obtain the **first element in the first row** of the product. We are showing it by $R_1 C_1$ in the matrix below.

$$\begin{pmatrix} R_1 C_1 & -- & -- \\ -- & -- & -- \\ -- & -- & -- \end{pmatrix}$$

Here , $R_1 C_1 = a_{11} \times b_{11} + a_{12} \times b_{21}$

Similarly, to obtain the **second element in first row of the product** we multiply elements of R_1 with the corresponding elements of C_2, and add them. We show it by $R_1 C_2$.

And so on for other elements. Finally, we write the matrix as follows:

$$\begin{pmatrix} R_1C_1 & R_1C_2 & R_1C_3 \\ R_2C_1 & R_2C_2 & R_2C_3 \\ R_3C_1 & R_3C_2 & R_3C_3 \end{pmatrix}$$

$$\begin{aligned}
\text{Where} \quad R_1C_1 &= a_{11} \times b_{11} + a_{12} \times b_{21} \\
R_1C_2 &= a_{11} \times b_{12} + a_{12} \times b_{22} \\
R_1C_3 &= a_{11} \times b_{13} + a_{12} \times b_{23} \\
R_2C_1 &= a_{21} \times b_{11} + a_{22} \times b_{21} \\
R_2C_2 &= a_{21} \times b_{12} + a_{22} \times b_{22} \\
R_2C_3 &= a_{21} \times b_{13} + a_{22} \times b_{23} \\
R_3C_1 &= a_{31} \times b_{11} + a_{32} \times b_{21} \\
R_3C_2 &= a_{31} \times b_{12} + a_{32} \times b_{22} \\
R_3C_3 &= a_{31} \times b_{13} + a_{32} \times b_{23}
\end{aligned}$$

Step-3 So, we write as follows:

$$AB = \begin{bmatrix} a_{11} & a_{12} \\ a_{21} & a_{22} \\ a_{31} & a_{32} \end{bmatrix} \begin{pmatrix} b_{11} & b_{12} & b_{13} \\ b_{21} & b_{22} & b_{23} \end{pmatrix}$$

$$= \begin{bmatrix} a_{11} \times b_{11} + a_{12} \times b_{21} & a_{11} \times b_{12} + a_{12} \times b_{22} & a_{11} \times b_{13} + a_{12} \times b_{23} \\ a_{21} \times b_{11} + a_{22} \times b_{21} & a_{21} \times b_{12} + a_{22} \times b_{22} & a_{21} \times b_{13} + a_{22} \times b_{23} \\ a_{31} \times b_{11} + a_{32} \times b_{21} & a_{31} \times b_{12} + a_{32} \times b_{22} & a_{31} \times b_{13} + a_{32} \times b_{23} \end{bmatrix}$$

<u>Example</u>

If matrix $A = \begin{pmatrix} 2 & 3 & 4 \\ 1 & -7 & -5 \end{pmatrix}$ and $B = \begin{bmatrix} -8 & -12 \\ 9 & -10 \\ -6 & 0 \end{bmatrix}$, then AB and BA are both defined.

$$AB = \begin{matrix} R_1 \to \\ R_2 \to \end{matrix} \begin{pmatrix} 2 & 3 & 4 \\ 1 & -7 & -5 \end{pmatrix} \begin{matrix} C_1 & C_2 \\ \downarrow & \downarrow \end{matrix} \begin{bmatrix} -8 & -12 \\ 9 & -10 \\ -6 & 0 \end{bmatrix}$$

$$= \begin{pmatrix} R_1C_1 & R_1C_2 \\ R_2C_1 & R_2C_2 \end{pmatrix} =$$

$$\begin{bmatrix} (2)(-8) + (3)(9) + (4)(-6) & (2)(-12) + (3)(-10) + (4)(0) \\ (1)(-8) + (-7)(9) + (-5)(-6) & (1)(-12) + (-7)(-10) + (-5)(0) \end{bmatrix}$$

$$= \begin{pmatrix} -13 & -54 \\ -41 & 58 \end{pmatrix}$$

Similarly, we can find BA as follows:

$$BA = \begin{bmatrix} -8 & -12 \\ 9 & -10 \\ -6 & 0 \end{bmatrix} \begin{pmatrix} 2 & 3 & 4 \\ 1 & -7 & -5 \end{pmatrix}$$

$$= \begin{bmatrix} (-8)(2)+(-12)(1) & (-8)(3)+(-12)(-7) & (-8)(4)+(-12)(-5) \\ (9)(2)+(-10)(1) & (9)(3)+(-10)(-7) & (9)(4)+(-10)(-5) \\ (-6)(2)+(0)(1) & (-6)(3)+(0)(-7) & (-6)(4)+(0)(-5) \end{bmatrix}$$

$$= \begin{bmatrix} -28 & 60 & 28 \\ 8 & 97 & 86 \\ -12 & -18 & -24 \end{bmatrix}$$

Important:

- *Product of two non-zero matrices can be a zero matrix.*

e.g. If $A = \begin{bmatrix} 4 & 2 \\ -6 & -3 \end{bmatrix}$ and $B = \begin{bmatrix} -1 & 1 \\ 2 & -2 \end{bmatrix}$, then $AB = \begin{bmatrix} 0 & 0 \\ 0 & 0 \end{bmatrix}$

11 Properties of matrix multiplication

Matrices A, B & C hold the following properties on multiplication (if the products involved are defined):

(i) **Non-Commutative**: AB is not necessarily equal to BA.

(ii) **Associative**: $(A\,B)\,C = A\,(B\,C)$

(iii) **Multiplicative identity**: Multiplicative identity of square matrix $A_{n \times n}$ is **Identity matrix I_n**, of same order.

i.e. $A\,\mathbf{I} = A$ and $\mathbf{I}\,A = A$

e.g., if $A = \begin{bmatrix} 3 & 5 & 6 \\ -2 & 1 & 7 \\ 4 & 0 & 8 \end{bmatrix}$,

then its multiplicative identity is $I_3 = \begin{bmatrix} 1 & 0 & 0 \\ 0 & 1 & 0 \\ 0 & 0 & 1 \end{bmatrix}$

(iv) **Distributive Property**: $A\,(B + C) = AB + AC$

and $(A + B)\,C = AC + BC$

Also, $A\,(B - C) = AB - AC$

And $(A - B)\,C = AC - BC$

(This property holds, only if the products, additions, and subtractions involved are defined).

12 Transpose of matrix

The matrix obtained by **interchanging rows with columns** *of a given matrix or vice-versa is known as transpose matrix of given matrix.*

- Transpose of matrix A is denoted as $\mathbf{A}^{\mathrm{T}}$ or $\mathbf{A'}$.
- **Order of $\mathbf{A}^{\mathrm{T}}$ is reverse** of the order of matrix A.
  i.e. If order of A is $m \times n$, then order of A^{T} is $n \times m$
- If $A = [a_{ij}]_{m \times n}$, then $\mathbf{A}^{\mathrm{T}} = [\mathbf{a}_{ji}]_{n \times m}$
  where $i = 1,2,3,\dots,m$ and $j = 1,2,3,\dots,n$.

e.g., if $\quad A = \begin{pmatrix} x & y & z \\ u & v & w \end{pmatrix}_{2 \times 3}$ $\quad$ then $\quad \mathbf{A}^{\mathrm{T}} = \begin{pmatrix} x & u \\ y & v \\ z & w \end{pmatrix}_{3 \times 2}$

13 Properties of Transpose

(i) $\quad (A^{\mathrm{T}})^{\mathrm{T}} = A$

(ii) $\quad (kA)^{\mathrm{T}} = kA^{\mathrm{T}}$ where k is any scalar

(iii) $\quad (A \pm B)^{\mathrm{T}} = A^{\mathrm{T}} \pm B^{\mathrm{T}}$

(iv) $\quad \mathbf{(AB)^{\mathrm{T}} = B^{\mathrm{T}} A^{\mathrm{T}}}$

14 Symmetric Matrix

If $\mathbf{A}^{\mathrm{T}} = \mathbf{A}$, then *A is called a symmetric matrix.*
- It is defined only for a square matrix.
- $A = [a_{ij}]_{n \times n}$ is symmetric matrix if and only if
  $a_{ij} = a_{ji} \quad$ for all $i = 1,2,3,\dots,n$ and $j = 1,2,3,\dots,n$.

<u>Example</u>

If $\quad A = \begin{bmatrix} 3 & 5 & 6 \\ 5 & 1 & 7 \\ 6 & 7 & 8 \end{bmatrix}$ then $\quad A^{\mathrm{T}} = \begin{bmatrix} 3 & 5 & 6 \\ 5 & 1 & 7 \\ 6 & 7 & 8 \end{bmatrix}$

$\therefore \quad A^{\mathrm{T}} = A$

$\Rightarrow \quad$ A is symmetric matrix.

15 Skew Symmetric Matrix

If $\mathbf{A}^{\mathrm{T}} = -\mathbf{A}$, then *A is called a skew symmetric matrix.*
- It is defined only for a square matrix.
- $A = [a_{ij}]_{n \times n}$ is skew symmetric matrix if and only if
  $a_{ij} = -a_{ji}$ for all $i = 1,2,3,\dots,n$ and $j = 1,2,3,\dots,n$.
- **All diagonal elements of a skew symmetric matrix are 0.**
  i.e., $\quad a_{ii} = 0 \quad$ for all $i = 1,2,3,\dots,n$

<u>Example</u>

If $\quad A = \begin{bmatrix} 0 & 5 & -6 \\ -5 & 0 & -7 \\ 6 & 7 & 0 \end{bmatrix}$

then $\quad A^{T} = \begin{bmatrix} 0 & -5 & 6 \\ 5 & 0 & 7 \\ -6 & -7 & 0 \end{bmatrix}$

$$= -\begin{bmatrix} 0 & 5 & -6 \\ -5 & 0 & -7 \\ 6 & 7 & 0 \end{bmatrix}$$

$\Rightarrow \quad A^{T} = -A$

$\therefore \quad$ A is skew symmetric matrix.

Important

- **Zero** square matrix is **symmetric as well skew symmetric** matrix
- $A + A^{T}$ *is always a symmetric matrix for a square matrix* **A**.
- $A - A^{T}$ *is always a skew symmetric matrix for a square matrix* **A**.

16 Expressing Square Matrix as Sum of a Symmetric and a Skew Symmetric Matrix

Any Square matrix **A** *can be expressed as sum of a symmetric and a skew symmetric matrix as follows:*

$$A = \underbrace{\frac{1}{2}(A + A^{T})}_{Symmetric} + \underbrace{\frac{1}{2}(A - A^{T})}_{Skew\ Symmetric}$$

<u>**Example**</u>

Express matrix, $A = \begin{bmatrix} 3 & 5 & 6 \\ -2 & 1 & 7 \\ 4 & 0 & 8 \end{bmatrix}$ *as sum of a symmetric and a skew symmetric matrix.*

Solution:

Here, $\quad A = \begin{bmatrix} 3 & 5 & 6 \\ -2 & 1 & 7 \\ 4 & 0 & 8 \end{bmatrix} \quad \Rightarrow \quad A^{T} = \begin{bmatrix} 3 & -2 & 4 \\ 5 & 1 & 0 \\ 6 & 7 & 8 \end{bmatrix}$

Let $P = \frac{1}{2}(A + A^{T})$ and $Q = \frac{1}{2}(A - A^{T})$

$\therefore \quad P = \frac{1}{2}\left\{ \begin{bmatrix} 3 & 5 & 6 \\ -2 & 1 & 7 \\ 4 & 0 & 8 \end{bmatrix} + \begin{bmatrix} 3 & -2 & 4 \\ 5 & 1 & 0 \\ 6 & 7 & 8 \end{bmatrix} \right\}$

$$= \frac{1}{2}\begin{bmatrix} 6 & 3 & 10 \\ 3 & 2 & 7 \\ 10 & 7 & 16 \end{bmatrix}$$

$$\Rightarrow \quad P = \begin{bmatrix} 3 & \frac{3}{2} & 5 \\ \frac{3}{2} & 1 & \frac{7}{2} \\ 5 & \frac{7}{2} & 8 \end{bmatrix}$$

$$\Rightarrow \quad P^T = \begin{bmatrix} 3 & \frac{3}{2} & 5 \\ \frac{3}{2} & 1 & \frac{7}{2} \\ 5 & \frac{7}{2} & 8 \end{bmatrix}$$

(By interchanging rows with columns or vice-versa
of matrix P, we can obtain transpose of P)

$$\Rightarrow \quad P^T = P$$

$$\therefore \quad P = \begin{bmatrix} 3 & \frac{3}{2} & 5 \\ \frac{3}{2} & 1 & \frac{7}{2} \\ 5 & \frac{7}{2} & 8 \end{bmatrix} \quad \text{is a symmetric matrix}$$

Now $Q = \dfrac{1}{2}(A - A^T)$

$$\Rightarrow \quad Q = \frac{1}{2}\left\{ \begin{bmatrix} 3 & 5 & 6 \\ -2 & 1 & 7 \\ 4 & 0 & 8 \end{bmatrix} - \begin{bmatrix} 3 & -2 & 4 \\ 5 & 1 & 0 \\ 6 & 7 & 8 \end{bmatrix} \right\}$$

$$= \frac{1}{2}\begin{bmatrix} 0 & 7 & 2 \\ -7 & 0 & 7 \\ -2 & -7 & 0 \end{bmatrix}$$

$$\Rightarrow \quad Q = \begin{bmatrix} 0 & \frac{7}{2} & 1 \\ -\frac{7}{2} & 0 & \frac{7}{2} \\ -1 & -\frac{7}{2} & 0 \end{bmatrix}$$

$$\Rightarrow \quad Q^T = \begin{bmatrix} 0 & -\frac{7}{2} & -1 \\ \frac{7}{2} & 0 & -\frac{7}{2} \\ 1 & \frac{7}{2} & 0 \end{bmatrix}$$

(By interchanging rows with columns or vice-versa
of matrix Q, we can obtain transpose of Q)

$$\Rightarrow \quad Q^T = -\begin{bmatrix} 0 & \frac{7}{2} & 1 \\ -\frac{7}{2} & 0 & \frac{7}{2} \\ -1 & -\frac{7}{2} & 0 \end{bmatrix}$$

$$\text{(Taking minus sign common out of the matrix,}$$
$$\text{sign of all elements gets reversed)}$$

$$\Rightarrow \quad Q^{T} = -Q$$

$$\therefore \quad Q = \begin{bmatrix} 0 & \dfrac{7}{2} & 1 \\[2mm] -\dfrac{7}{2} & 0 & \dfrac{7}{2} \\[2mm] -1 & -\dfrac{7}{2} & 0 \end{bmatrix} \quad \text{is a skew symmetric matrix.}$$

$$\text{Now} \quad P + Q = \begin{bmatrix} 3 & \dfrac{3}{2} & 5 \\[2mm] \dfrac{3}{2} & 1 & \dfrac{7}{2} \\[2mm] 5 & \dfrac{7}{2} & 8 \end{bmatrix} + \begin{bmatrix} 0 & \dfrac{7}{2} & 1 \\[2mm] -\dfrac{7}{2} & 0 & \dfrac{7}{2} \\[2mm] -1 & -\dfrac{7}{2} & 0 \end{bmatrix}$$

$$= \begin{bmatrix} 3 & 5 & 6 \\ -2 & 1 & 7 \\ 4 & 0 & 8 \end{bmatrix}$$

$$= A$$

$$\therefore \quad \text{We can write} \quad A = P + Q$$

$$\Rightarrow \quad A = \underbrace{\begin{bmatrix} 3 & \dfrac{3}{2} & 5 \\[2mm] \dfrac{3}{2} & 1 & \dfrac{7}{2} \\[2mm] 5 & \dfrac{7}{2} & 8 \end{bmatrix}}_{symmetric\ matrix} + \underbrace{\begin{bmatrix} 0 & \dfrac{7}{2} & 1 \\[2mm] -\dfrac{7}{2} & 0 & \dfrac{7}{2} \\[2mm] -1 & -\dfrac{7}{2} & 0 \end{bmatrix}}_{skew\ symmetric\ matrix}$$

17 *Elementary Operations (or Transformations)

17.1 *Types of elementary operations

Two types of elementary operations are:
(i) elementary row operations (ii) elementary column operations
For each of these types there are 3 operations. So, we have 6
elementary operations in total.

17.1.1 *Elementary Row Operations

(i) $R_i \leftrightarrow R_j$ **(Interchanging any two rows)**: In this
operation, we interchange any two rows of the given
matrix.

Example

In matrix $\begin{bmatrix} a & b & c \\ d & e & f \\ g & h & i \end{bmatrix}$

Applying $\mathbf{R}_1 \leftrightarrow \mathbf{R}_3$, we get $\begin{bmatrix} g & h & i \\ d & e & f \\ a & b & c \end{bmatrix}$

(ii) $\mathbf{R}_i \to \mathbf{kR}_i$ **(Multiplying a row with a number)**: In this operation, we multiply each element of a row of the given matrix by a non-zero number k.

Example

In matrix $\begin{bmatrix} a & b & c \\ d & e & f \\ g & h & i \end{bmatrix}$

Applying $\mathbf{R}_2 \to (-2)\mathbf{R}_2$, we get $\begin{bmatrix} a & b & c \\ -2d & -2e & -2f \\ g & h & i \end{bmatrix}$

(iii) $\mathbf{R}_i \to \mathbf{R}_i + \mathbf{k}\,\mathbf{R}_j$ **(Addition of a row after multiplying it by a non-zero number k to another row)**: In this operation we add each element of a row $\mathbf{R}_j$ of the given matrix, after multiplying them by a non-zero number $\boldsymbol{k}$, to the corresponding elements of another row $\mathbf{R}_i$ of the matrix.

Example

In matrix $\begin{bmatrix} a & b & c \\ d & e & f \\ g & h & i \end{bmatrix}$

Applying $\mathbf{R}_1 \to \mathbf{R}_1 + 3\mathbf{R}_3$, we get $\begin{bmatrix} a+3g & b+3h & c+3i \\ d & e & f \\ g & h & i \end{bmatrix}$

17.1.2 *Elementary Column Operations

(i) $\mathbf{C}_i \leftrightarrow \mathbf{C}_j$ **(Interchanging any two columns)**: In this operation, we interchange any two columns of the given matrix.

Example

In matrix $\begin{bmatrix} a & b & c \\ d & e & f \\ g & h & i \end{bmatrix}$

Applying $\mathbf{C}_1 \leftrightarrow \mathbf{C}_2$, we get $\begin{bmatrix} b & a & c \\ e & d & f \\ h & g & i \end{bmatrix}$

(ii) $C_i \rightarrow kC_i$ **(Multiplying a column with a number)**: In this operation, we multiply each element of a column of the given matrix by a non-zero number k.

<u>Example</u>

In matrix $\begin{bmatrix} a & b & c \\ d & e & f \\ g & h & i \end{bmatrix}$

Applying $C_3 \rightarrow 2C_3$, we get $\begin{bmatrix} a & b & 2c \\ d & e & 2f \\ g & h & 2i \end{bmatrix}$

(iii) $C_i \rightarrow C_i + k\,C_j$ **(Addition of a column after multiplying it by a non-zero number k to another column)**: In this operation we add each element of a column C_j of the given matrix, after multiplying them by a non-zero number k, to the corresponding elements of another column C_i of the matrix.

<u>Example</u>

In matrix $\begin{bmatrix} a & b & c \\ d & e & f \\ g & h & i \end{bmatrix}$

Applying $C_3 \rightarrow C_3 + (-2)C_1$, we get $\begin{bmatrix} a & b & c-2a \\ d & e & f-2d \\ g & h & i-2g \end{bmatrix}$

17.2 *Elementary Operation on Matrix Equation

In a matrix equation, $P = AB$:

(i) If we apply a row operation on P, then we have to apply same row operation on **matrix A only, keeping B unchanged** to maintain the equality.

<u>Example</u>

Consider the matrix equation:

$$\begin{pmatrix} -3 & -6 \\ -1 & 9 \end{pmatrix} = \begin{pmatrix} -2 & 1 \\ 3 & 4 \end{pmatrix} \begin{pmatrix} 1 & 3 \\ -1 & 0 \end{pmatrix}$$

On applying $R_1 \rightarrow R_1 - 3R_2$, the equation changes to

$$\begin{pmatrix} -3-3(-1) & -6-3(9) \\ -1 & 9 \end{pmatrix} = \begin{pmatrix} -2-3(3) & 1-3(4) \\ 3 & 4 \end{pmatrix} \underbrace{\begin{pmatrix} 1 & 3 \\ -1 & 0 \end{pmatrix}}_{unchanged}$$

$$\Rightarrow \begin{pmatrix} 0 & -33 \\ -1 & 9 \end{pmatrix} = \begin{pmatrix} -11 & -11 \\ 3 & 4 \end{pmatrix} \underbrace{\begin{pmatrix} 1 & 3 \\ -1 & 0 \end{pmatrix}}_{unchanged}$$

Here, we have applied the operation on LHS and on First matrix on RHS.

(ii) If we apply a column operation on P, then we have to apply same column operation on matrix **B only, keeping A unchanged** to maintain the equality.

Example

Consider the matrix equation:

$$\begin{pmatrix} -3 & -6 \\ -1 & 9 \end{pmatrix} = \begin{pmatrix} -2 & 1 \\ 3 & 4 \end{pmatrix} \begin{pmatrix} 1 & 3 \\ -1 & 0 \end{pmatrix}$$

On applying $\mathbf{C_2 \to C_2 - 2C_1}$, the equation changes to

$$\begin{pmatrix} -3 & -6-2(-3) \\ -1 & 9-2(-1) \end{pmatrix} = \underbrace{\begin{pmatrix} -2 & 1 \\ 3 & 4 \end{pmatrix}}_{unchanged} \begin{pmatrix} 1 & 3-2(1) \\ -1 & 0-2(-1) \end{pmatrix}$$

$$\Rightarrow \begin{pmatrix} -3 & 0 \\ -1 & 11 \end{pmatrix} = \underbrace{\begin{pmatrix} -2 & 1 \\ 3 & 4 \end{pmatrix}}_{unchanged} \begin{pmatrix} 1 & 1 \\ -1 & 2 \end{pmatrix}$$

Here, we have applied the operation on LHS and on Second matrix on RHS.

18 Invertible matrix

Square Matrix **A** *of order m is said to be invertible if there exists a square matrix* **B** *of the same order m such that* $\mathbf{AB = BA = I}$ *, where* **I** *is identity matrix of the order m.*

And we say that multiplicative inverse of matrix **A** *= matrix* **B**.

- Multiplicative Inverse of **A** is denoted by $\mathbf{A^{-1}}$.
- $\mathbf{A^{-1} = B}$
- Also, $\mathbf{B^{-1} = A}$ and $\mathbf{(A^{-1})^{-1} = A}$
- **Multiplicative inverse of a matrix doesn't exist if it is not a square matrix.**

Example

If $\quad A = \begin{bmatrix} 1 & -1 & 2 \\ 0 & 2 & -3 \\ 3 & -2 & 4 \end{bmatrix}$ and $B = \begin{bmatrix} -2 & 0 & 1 \\ 9 & 2 & -3 \\ 6 & 1 & -2 \end{bmatrix}$

then $\quad AB = \begin{bmatrix} 1 & -1 & 2 \\ 0 & 2 & -3 \\ 3 & -2 & 4 \end{bmatrix} \begin{bmatrix} -2 & 0 & 1 \\ 9 & 2 & -3 \\ 6 & 1 & -2 \end{bmatrix} = \begin{bmatrix} 1 & 0 & 0 \\ 0 & 1 & 0 \\ 0 & 0 & 1 \end{bmatrix}$

$$= \mathbf{I} \text{ (Identity matrix)}$$

Also, $\quad BA = \begin{bmatrix} -2 & 0 & 1 \\ 9 & 2 & -3 \\ 6 & 1 & -2 \end{bmatrix} \begin{bmatrix} 1 & -1 & 2 \\ 0 & 2 & -3 \\ 3 & -2 & 4 \end{bmatrix} = \begin{bmatrix} 1 & 0 & 0 \\ 0 & 1 & 0 \\ 0 & 0 & 1 \end{bmatrix}$

$$= \mathbf{I} \text{ (Identity matrix)}$$

$\because \quad AB = BA = \mathbf{I}$

$\therefore \quad A^{-1} = B$

$$\Rightarrow \quad \begin{bmatrix} 1 & -1 & 2 \\ 0 & 2 & -3 \\ 3 & -2 & 4 \end{bmatrix}^{-1} = \begin{bmatrix} -2 & 0 & 1 \\ 9 & 2 & -3 \\ 6 & 1 & -2 \end{bmatrix}$$

Also, $B^{-1} = A$

$$\Rightarrow \quad \begin{bmatrix} -2 & 0 & 1 \\ 9 & 2 & -3 \\ 6 & 1 & -2 \end{bmatrix}^{-1} = \begin{bmatrix} 1 & -1 & 2 \\ 0 & 2 & -3 \\ 3 & -2 & 4 \end{bmatrix}$$

18.1 Properties of inverse

- If matrix A is invertible, then its inverse (A^{-1}) **is unique**.
- $A\,A^{-1} = \mathbf{I}$ and $A^{-1}\,A = \mathbf{I}$
- $(A^{-1})^{-1} = A$
- $(AB)^{-1} = B^{-1}\,A^{-1}$

19 *To find inverse using elementary operations

Inverse of a square matrix **A** can be found
(i) by Elementary Row Operations or
(ii) by Elementary Column Operations

19.1 *Inverse using Elementary Row Operations

Step-1 Write A = I A   (where I is identity matrix)

Now write the complete matrix on LHS in place of A.
Also write complete identity matrix in place of I on RHS.
The equation will look like as follows:

$$\Rightarrow \quad \begin{bmatrix} \end{bmatrix} = \begin{bmatrix} 1 & 0 & 0 \\ 0 & 1 & 0 \\ 0 & 0 & 1 \end{bmatrix} A \qquad (\text{ if A is a } 3\times3 \text{ matrix })$$

$$\text{or} \quad \begin{bmatrix} \end{bmatrix} = \begin{bmatrix} 1 & 0 \\ 0 & 1 \end{bmatrix} A \qquad (\text{ if A is a } 2\times2 \text{ matrix })$$

Step-2 Now apply some row operations, one by one, in matrix on
LHS such that it becomes an identity matrix. Also apply the
same row operations in identity matrix on RHS. Finally, the
equation looks like,

$$\begin{bmatrix} 1 & 0 & 0 \\ 0 & 1 & 0 \\ 0 & 0 & 1 \end{bmatrix} = \begin{bmatrix} \end{bmatrix} A \qquad (\text{ if A is a } 3\times3 \text{ matrix })$$

$$\text{or} \quad \begin{bmatrix} 1 & 0 \\ 0 & 1 \end{bmatrix} = \begin{bmatrix} \end{bmatrix} A \qquad (\text{ if A is a } 2\times2 \text{ matrix })$$

Step-3 The first matrix on RHS will be A^{-1}.

So, $\qquad A^{-1} = \begin{bmatrix} & & \\ & & \\ & & \end{bmatrix}$ or $A^{-1} = \begin{bmatrix} & \end{bmatrix}$

***Important**
- If all the elements of any one row or any one column becomes 0 in the matrix on LHS at any step, then A^{-1} **does not exist**.

Example

Find A^{-1} by elementary row operations if $A = \begin{bmatrix} 1 & -1 & 2 \\ 0 & 2 & -3 \\ 3 & -2 & 4 \end{bmatrix}$

Solution:

Step-1: We write $A = I\,A$

$$\Rightarrow \quad \begin{bmatrix} 1 & -1 & 2 \\ 0 & 2 & -3 \\ 3 & -2 & 4 \end{bmatrix} = \begin{bmatrix} 1 & 0 & 0 \\ 0 & 1 & 0 \\ 0 & 0 & 1 \end{bmatrix} A \quad ----- (i)$$

Step-2: We have to make LHS an identity matrix using row operations.

First of all, we convert the elements in 1st column C_1 into the required elements for the matrix on LHS to look like $\begin{bmatrix} 1 \\ 0 \\ 0 \end{bmatrix}$.

For this, observe that we have to convert only the element in 3rd row and 1st column from 3 to 0 by using any row operation.

So, we apply $\mathbf{R_3 \rightarrow R_3 - 3R_1}$ to get

$$\begin{bmatrix} 1 & -1 & 2 \\ 0 & 2 & -3 \\ 0 & 1 & -2 \end{bmatrix} = \begin{bmatrix} 1 & 0 & 0 \\ 0 & 1 & 0 \\ -3 & 0 & 1 \end{bmatrix} A \quad ----- (ii)$$

(Remember, while applying a row operation in matrix equation like the above, it is applied only to first matrix in the product of two matrices. So, we keep the matrix A on RHS as unchanged, and apply the operation on identity matrix. *See* 'Elementary Operation on Matrix Equation')

Step-3: Now we will convert elements in 2nd column C_2 on LHS of eqn. (ii) to the required elements to get the matrix which looks like $\begin{bmatrix} 1 & 0 \\ 0 & 1 \\ 0 & 0 \end{bmatrix}$.

[*Caution*: we must apply only those row operations which do not change the elements in C_1 on LHS because now C_1 already contains the required elements.]

We first convert the middle element of this column to 1 by applying any row operation, keeping in mind that elements in C_1 do not get changed.

Apply $\mathbf{R_2 \leftrightarrow R_3}$ in eqn. (ii) to get

$$\begin{bmatrix} 1 & -1 & 2 \\ 0 & 1 & -2 \\ 0 & 2 & -3 \end{bmatrix} = \begin{bmatrix} 1 & 0 & 0 \\ -3 & 0 & 1 \\ 0 & 1 & 0 \end{bmatrix} A \quad ----- \text{(iii)}$$

Now we will convert other two elements in C_2 to 0, keeping in mind that elements in C_1 and middle element of C_2 do not change.

Apply $\mathbf{R_1 \rightarrow R_1 + R_2}$ and $\mathbf{R_3 \rightarrow R_3 - 2R_2}$ in eqn. (iii) to get

$$\begin{bmatrix} 1 & 0 & 0 \\ 0 & 1 & -2 \\ 0 & 0 & 1 \end{bmatrix} = \begin{bmatrix} -2 & 0 & 1 \\ -3 & 0 & 1 \\ 6 & 1 & -2 \end{bmatrix} A \qquad ----- \text{(iv)}$$

Step-4: Now we will convert elements in 3rd column C_3 on LHS of eqn. (iv) to the required elements to get the identity matrix $\begin{bmatrix} 1 & 0 & 0 \\ 0 & 1 & 0 \\ 0 & 0 & 1 \end{bmatrix}$.

[*Caution*: we must apply only those row operations which do not change the elements in C_1 and C_2 on LHS.]

First, we should convert the last element of C_3 to 1, but we observe that it is already 1.

After that we have to convert other two elements of C_3 to 0. Out of which 1st element is already 0. So, we have to convert only the 2nd element of C_3 to 0 by applying row operation, keeping in mind that all other elements on LHS do not get changed.

Apply $\mathbf{R_2 \rightarrow R_2 + 2R_3}$ in eqn. (iv) to get

$$\begin{bmatrix} 1 & 0 & 0 \\ 0 & 1 & 0 \\ 0 & 0 & 1 \end{bmatrix} = \begin{bmatrix} -2 & 0 & 1 \\ 9 & 2 & -3 \\ 6 & 1 & -2 \end{bmatrix} A \quad ----- \text{(v)}$$

Step-5: The matrix before A on RHS is A^{-1}

$$\therefore \quad A^{-1} = \begin{bmatrix} -2 & 0 & 1 \\ 9 & 2 & -3 \\ 6 & 1 & -2 \end{bmatrix}$$

19.2 *Inverse using Elementary Column Operations

Step-1 Write A = A I $\qquad$ (where I is identity matrix)

Now write the complete matrix on LHS in place of A. Also write complete identity matrix in place of I on RHS. The equation will look like as follows:

$$\Rightarrow \quad \begin{bmatrix} \end{bmatrix} = A \begin{bmatrix} 1 & 0 & 0 \\ 0 & 1 & 0 \\ 0 & 0 & 1 \end{bmatrix} \qquad (\text{ if A is a } 3\times3 \text{ matrix })$$

Or $\quad \begin{bmatrix} \end{bmatrix} = A \begin{bmatrix} 1 & 0 \\ 0 & 1 \end{bmatrix} \qquad (\text{ if A is a } 2\times2 \text{ matrix })$

Step-2 Now apply some column operations, one by one, in matrix on LHS such that it becomes an identity matrix. Also apply the same column operations in identity matrix on RHS. Finally, the equation looks like

$$\begin{bmatrix} 1 & 0 & 0 \\ 0 & 1 & 0 \\ 0 & 0 & 1 \end{bmatrix} = A \begin{bmatrix} \end{bmatrix} \qquad (\text{ if A is a } 3\times3 \text{ matrix })$$

or $\quad \begin{bmatrix} 1 & 0 \\ 0 & 1 \end{bmatrix} = A \begin{bmatrix} \end{bmatrix} \qquad (\text{ if A is a } 2\times2 \text{ matrix })$

Step-3 The second matrix on RHS will be A^{-1}.

So, $\quad A^{-1} = \begin{bmatrix} \end{bmatrix} \qquad$ or $\qquad A^{-1} = \begin{bmatrix} \end{bmatrix}$

***Important**

- If all the elements of any one row or any one column becomes 0 in the matrix on LHS at any step, then **A^{-1} does not exist**.

Example

Find A^{-1} by elementary row operations if $A = \begin{bmatrix} -2 & 0 & 1 \\ 9 & 2 & -3 \\ 6 & 1 & -2 \end{bmatrix}$

Solution:

Step-1: We write A = A I

$$\Rightarrow \quad \begin{bmatrix} -2 & 0 & 1 \\ 9 & 2 & -3 \\ 6 & 1 & -2 \end{bmatrix} = A \begin{bmatrix} 1 & 0 & 0 \\ 0 & 1 & 0 \\ 0 & 0 & 1 \end{bmatrix} \quad \text{-----(i)}$$

Step-2: We have to make LHS an identity matrix using column operations.

First of all, we convert the elements in 1st row R_1 into the required elements for the matrix on LHS to look like $\begin{bmatrix} 1 & 0 & 0 \\ & & \\ & & \end{bmatrix}$.

We should convert first element of R_1 to 1 before making other elements 0.

So, we apply $\mathbf{C_1 \leftrightarrow C_3}$ to get

$$\begin{bmatrix} 1 & 0 & -2 \\ -3 & 2 & 9 \\ -2 & 1 & 6 \end{bmatrix} = A \begin{bmatrix} 0 & 0 & 1 \\ 0 & 1 & 0 \\ 1 & 0 & 0 \end{bmatrix} \quad \text{- - - - - (ii)}$$

(Remember, while applying a column operation in matrix equation like the above, it is applied only to second matrix in the product of two matrices. So, we keep the matrix A on RHS as unchanged, and apply the operation on identity matrix. *See* 'Elementary Operation on Matrix Equation')

Now the second element of R_1 on LHS is already 0.

We have to just convert 3rd element of R_1 to 0.

So, we apply $\mathbf{C_3 \rightarrow C_3 + 2C_1}$ in eqn. (ii) to get

$$\begin{bmatrix} 1 & 0 & 0 \\ -3 & 2 & 3 \\ -2 & 1 & 2 \end{bmatrix} = A \begin{bmatrix} 0 & 0 & 1 \\ 0 & 1 & 0 \\ 1 & 0 & 2 \end{bmatrix} \quad \text{- - - - - (iii)}$$

Step-3: Now we will convert elements in 2nd row R_2 on LHS of eqn. (iii) to the required elements to get the matrix which look like $\begin{bmatrix} 1 & 0 & 0 \\ 0 & 1 & 0 \\ & & \end{bmatrix}$.

[*Caution*: we must apply only those column operations which do not change the elements in R_1 on LHS because R_1 already contains the required elements.]

We first convert the middle element of this row to 1 by applying any column operation keeping in mind that elements in R_1 do not get changed.

Apply $\mathbf{C_2 \rightarrow \dfrac{1}{2} C_2}$ in eqn. (iii) to get

$$\begin{bmatrix} 1 & 0 & 0 \\ -3 & 1 & 3 \\ -2 & \frac{1}{2} & 2 \end{bmatrix} = A \begin{bmatrix} 0 & 0 & 1 \\ 0 & \frac{1}{2} & 0 \\ 1 & 0 & 2 \end{bmatrix} \quad \text{- - - - - (iv)}$$

Now on we will convert other two elements in R_2 to 0 keeping in mind that elements in R_1 and middle element of R_2 do not change.

Apply $C_1 \to C_1 + 3C_2$ and $C_3 \to C_3 - 3C_2$ in eqn. (iv) to get

$$\begin{bmatrix} 1 & 0 & 0 \\ 0 & 1 & 0 \\ -\frac{1}{2} & \frac{1}{2} & \frac{1}{2} \end{bmatrix} = A \begin{bmatrix} 0 & 0 & 1 \\ \frac{3}{2} & \frac{1}{2} & -\frac{3}{2} \\ 1 & 0 & 2 \end{bmatrix} \qquad ----- (v)$$

Step-4: Now we will convert elements in 3rd row R_3 on LHS of eqn. (v) to the required elements to get the identity

matrix $\begin{bmatrix} 1 & 0 & 0 \\ 0 & 1 & 0 \\ 0 & 0 & 1 \end{bmatrix}$.

[*Caution*: we must apply only those column operations which do not change the elements in R_1 and R_2 on LHS.]

First, we should convert the last element of R_3 to 1.

So, we apply $C_3 \to 2C_3$ in eqn. (v) to get

$$\begin{bmatrix} 1 & 0 & 0 \\ 0 & 1 & 0 \\ -\frac{1}{2} & \frac{1}{2} & 1 \end{bmatrix} = A \begin{bmatrix} 0 & 0 & 2 \\ \frac{3}{2} & \frac{1}{2} & -3 \\ 1 & 0 & 4 \end{bmatrix} \qquad ----- (v)$$

After this we have to convert other two elements of R_3 to 0 keeping in mind that all other elements on LHS do not get changed.

Apply $C_1 \to C_1 + \frac{1}{2} C_3$ and $C_2 \to C_2 - \frac{1}{2} C_3$ in eqn.(iv) to get

$$\begin{bmatrix} 1 & 0 & 0 \\ 0 & 1 & 0 \\ 0 & 0 & 1 \end{bmatrix} = A \begin{bmatrix} 1 & -1 & 2 \\ 0 & 2 & -3 \\ 3 & -2 & 4 \end{bmatrix} \qquad ----- (vi)$$

Step-5: The matrix after A on RHS is A^{-1}

$$\therefore \qquad A^{-1} = \begin{bmatrix} 1 & -1 & 2 \\ 0 & 2 & -3 \\ 3 & -2 & 4 \end{bmatrix}$$

Chapter-4   Determinants

1 Definition

A **unique number (exactly one number)** *can be assigned to a* **square matrix** , *which is known as its determinant.*

- A determinant is usually denoted by Δ.
- However, the determinant of matrix 'A' is written as $|A|$ (or sometimes as $\text{Det}(A)$).
  Similarly, determinants of square matrices B, C etc. are written as $|B|$, $|C|$ etc. respectively.
- $|A|$ is read as determinant of A, and **not** as **modulus** of A.
- To represent a determinant, complete arrangement of the elements is enclosed in ***straight bars*** while to represent a matrix, round or square brackets are used.

  <u>Example</u>

  If matrix, $A = \begin{pmatrix} 3 & 6 \\ -1 & -2 \end{pmatrix}$

  then determinant of A is written as $|A| = \Delta = \begin{vmatrix} 3 & 6 \\ -1 & -2 \end{vmatrix}$

  <u>Example</u>

  If matrix, $B = \begin{bmatrix} 0 & 3 & 4 \\ 1 & 2 & 5 \\ -3 & 1 & 4 \end{bmatrix}$

  then determinant of B is written as $|B| = \Delta = \begin{vmatrix} 0 & 3 & 4 \\ 1 & 2 & 5 \\ -3 & 1 & 4 \end{vmatrix}$

  Important

- Remember, **only a square matrix can have determinant**.
- Observe that, to represent a matrix, we enclose the elements in round or square brackets while to represent a determinant, we enclose the elements in straight bars.

2 Determinant of matrix of order One

- There is only one element in a matrix of order one, and its determinant is that element itself.

  <u>Example</u>

  If matrix $A = [a]$ then $|A| = \Delta = a$

  <u>Example</u>

  If matrix $B = [-1.5]$ then $|B| = \Delta = -1.5$

3 Determinant of matrix of order Two

- Determinant of square matrix $A = [a_{ij}]_{2\times2} = \begin{pmatrix} a_{11} & a_{12} \\ a_{21} & a_{22} \end{pmatrix}$ is obtained by cross multiplying the elements as follows:

$$|A| = \begin{vmatrix} a_{11} & a_{12} \\ a_{21} & a_{22} \end{vmatrix} = a_{11}\,a_{22} - a_{21}\,a_{12}$$

Example

If matrix, $A = \begin{pmatrix} 3 & -6 \\ -1 & -2 \end{pmatrix}$,

then $|A| = \Delta = \begin{vmatrix} 3 & -6 \\ -1 & -2 \end{vmatrix} = 3(-2) - (-1)(-6) = -6 - 6 = -12$

4 Determinant of matrix of order Three

There are 6 ways to obtain determinant of a matrix of order 3.

(i) Expand along R_1 (along 1st row)

(ii) Expand along R_2 (along 2nd row)

(iii) Expand along R_3 (along 3rd row)

(iv) Expand along C_1 (along 1st column)

(v) Expand along C_2 (along 2nd column)

(vi) Expand along C_3 (along 3rd column)

Procedure to find determinant

We follow the following steps to get the determinant by any of the above 6 ways:

Step-1 Choose a row or a column for expanding.

Step-2 Pick first element of that row or column.

Step-3 If the sum of the row number and the column number of that element is odd change the sign of the picked element otherwise keep the same sign.

Step-4 Obtain the determinant of order 2 by removing the row and column in which the picked element is present, and expand it as explained for **determinant of order 2**. (*See* art3 of this chapter)

Step-5 Multiply the numbers obtained in step 3 and 4.

Step-6 Repeat the steps 2, 3, 4 & 5 for other two elements also, of the chosen row or column.

In this way, we get 3 products one each corresponding to the elements of chosen row or column.

After that, we add all the three products to get the required determinant.

We can obtain the determinant of square matrix,

$$A = \begin{bmatrix} a_{ij} \end{bmatrix}_{3\times3} = \begin{pmatrix} a_{11} & a_{12} & a_{13} \\ a_{21} & a_{22} & a_{23} \\ a_{31} & a_{32} & a_{33} \end{pmatrix}$$

i.e., $|A| = \begin{vmatrix} a_{11} & a_{12} & a_{13} \\ a_{21} & a_{22} & a_{23} \\ a_{31} & a_{32} & a_{33} \end{vmatrix}$ in the following ways:

4.1 Expanding along R_1

Let square matrix $A = \left[a_{ij}\right]_{3\times3} = \begin{pmatrix} a_{11} & a_{12} & a_{13} \\ a_{21} & a_{22} & a_{23} \\ a_{31} & a_{32} & a_{33} \end{pmatrix}$

$$\therefore |A| = \begin{vmatrix} a_{11} & a_{12} & a_{13} \\ a_{21} & a_{22} & a_{23} \\ a_{31} & a_{32} & a_{33} \end{vmatrix}$$

$$= (a_{11})\begin{vmatrix} a_{22} & a_{23} \\ a_{32} & a_{33} \end{vmatrix} + (-a_{12})\begin{vmatrix} a_{21} & a_{23} \\ a_{31} & a_{33} \end{vmatrix} + (a_{13})\begin{vmatrix} a_{21} & a_{22} \\ a_{31} & a_{32} \end{vmatrix}$$

$$= a_{11}(a_{22}a_{33} - a_{32}a_{23}) + (-a_{12})(a_{21}a_{33} - a_{31}a_{23})$$
$$+ (a_{13})(a_{21}a_{32} - a_{31}a_{22})$$

<u>**Explanation:**</u>

Step-1: Choose 1st row (R_1) for expanding.

Step-2: Pick the 1st element (a_{11}) of R_1.

Step-3: The sum of the row number and the column number of a_{11} is 1+1 =2, which is even. So, we keep the same sign of a_{11}.

Step-4: As a_{11} is present in 1st row and 1st column, so we remove 1st row and 1st column as shown

$$\begin{vmatrix} a_{11} & a_{12} & a_{13} \\ a_{21} & a_{22} & a_{23} \\ a_{31} & a_{32} & a_{33} \end{vmatrix}$$

and obtain the determinant of order 2, which is
$$\begin{vmatrix} a_{22} & a_{23} \\ a_{32} & a_{33} \end{vmatrix} = a_{22}a_{33} - a_{32}a_{23}$$

Step-5: Multiply the numbers obtained in step 3 and 4 as
$$a_{11}\begin{vmatrix} a_{22} & a_{23} \\ a_{32} & a_{33} \end{vmatrix} = a_{11}(a_{22}a_{33} - a_{32}a_{23})$$

Step-6: Repeat steps 2, 3, 4 & 5 for other elements a_{12} & a_{13} of R_1.

For a_{12}, remove 1st row and 2nd column from the given determinant to obtain 2nd order determinant and multiply it by $(-a_{12})$.

Removing 1st row and 2nd column: $\begin{vmatrix} a_{11} & a_{12} & a_{13} \\ a_{21} & a_{22} & a_{23} \\ a_{31} & a_{32} & a_{33} \end{vmatrix}$, *we get* $\begin{vmatrix} a_{21} & a_{23} \\ a_{31} & a_{33} \end{vmatrix}$

So, we write:

$$(-a_{12})\begin{vmatrix} a_{21} & a_{23} \\ a_{31} & a_{33} \end{vmatrix} = (-a_{12})(a_{21}a_{33} - a_{31}a_{23})$$

Similarly, for a_{13}, remove 1ˢᵗ row and 3ʳᵈ column from the given determinant to obtain 2ⁿᵈ order determinant and multiply it by (a_{13}).

Removing 1ˢᵗ row and 3ʳᵈ column: $\begin{vmatrix} a_{11} & a_{12} & a_{13} \\ a_{21} & a_{22} & a_{23} \\ a_{31} & a_{32} & a_{33} \end{vmatrix}$, *we get* $\begin{vmatrix} a_{21} & a_{22} \\ a_{31} & a_{32} \end{vmatrix}$

So, we write as:

$$(a_{13})\begin{vmatrix} a_{21} & a_{22} \\ a_{31} & a_{32} \end{vmatrix} = (a_{13})\,(a_{21}\,a_{32} - a_{31}\,a_{22})$$

Now we add all the three products corresponding to each element of R_1 to get the required determinant.

→ We needn't write each and every step as explained above. All the above steps in short, can be written as follows:

$$|A| = \begin{vmatrix} a_{11} & a_{12} & a_{13} \\ a_{21} & a_{22} & a_{23} \\ a_{31} & a_{32} & a_{33} \end{vmatrix}$$

$$= (a_{11})\begin{vmatrix} a_{22} & a_{23} \\ a_{32} & a_{33} \end{vmatrix} + (-a_{12})\begin{vmatrix} a_{21} & a_{23} \\ a_{31} & a_{33} \end{vmatrix} + (a_{13})\begin{vmatrix} a_{21} & a_{22} \\ a_{31} & a_{32} \end{vmatrix}$$

$$= a_{11}(a_{22}a_{33} - a_{32}a_{23}) + (-a_{12})(a_{21}a_{33} - a_{31}a_{23})$$
$$+ (a_{13})(a_{21}a_{32} - a_{31}a_{22})$$

Example

If matrix, $A = \begin{pmatrix} 2 & 3 & -4 \\ 1 & 2 & 5 \\ -3 & 1 & 4 \end{pmatrix}$

then $|A| = \Delta = \begin{vmatrix} 2 & 3 & -4 \\ 1 & 2 & 5 \\ -3 & 1 & 4 \end{vmatrix}$

Expanding along R_1, we get

$$|A| = 2 \times \begin{vmatrix} 2 & 3 & -4 \\ 1 & 2 & 5 \\ -3 & 1 & 4 \end{vmatrix} + (-3) \times \begin{vmatrix} 2 & 3 & -4 \\ 1 & 2 & 5 \\ -3 & 1 & 4 \end{vmatrix} + (-4) \times \begin{vmatrix} 2 & 3 & -4 \\ 1 & 2 & 5 \\ -3 & 1 & 4 \end{vmatrix}$$

$$= 2\begin{vmatrix} 2 & 5 \\ 1 & 4 \end{vmatrix} + (-3)\begin{vmatrix} 1 & 5 \\ -3 & 4 \end{vmatrix} + (-4)\begin{vmatrix} 1 & 2 \\ -3 & 1 \end{vmatrix}$$

$$= 2(2\times4 - 1\times5) + (-3)\,[1\times4 - (-3)\times5] + (-4)\,[1\times1 - (-3)\times2]$$

$$= 2(8-5) - 3(4+15) - 4(1+6)$$

$$= 2\times3 - 3\times19 - 4\times7 = 6 - 57 - 28 = -79$$

4.2   Expanding along R_2

Let square matrix $A = \left[a_{ij}\right]_{3\times3} = \begin{pmatrix} a_{11} & a_{12} & a_{13} \\ a_{21} & a_{22} & a_{23} \\ a_{31} & a_{32} & a_{33} \end{pmatrix}$

$$\therefore |A| = \begin{vmatrix} a_{11} & a_{12} & a_{13} \\ a_{21} & a_{22} & a_{23} \\ a_{31} & a_{32} & a_{33} \end{vmatrix}$$

$$= (-a_{21}) \times \begin{vmatrix} a_{11} & a_{12} & a_{13} \\ a_{21} & a_{22} & a_{23} \\ a_{31} & a_{32} & a_{33} \end{vmatrix} + (a_{22}) \times \begin{vmatrix} a_{11} & a_{12} & a_{13} \\ a_{21} & a_{22} & a_{23} \\ a_{31} & a_{32} & a_{33} \end{vmatrix} + (-a_{23}) \times \begin{vmatrix} a_{11} & a_{12} & a_{13} \\ a_{21} & a_{22} & a_{23} \\ a_{31} & a_{32} & a_{33} \end{vmatrix}$$

$$= (-a_{21}) \begin{vmatrix} a_{12} & a_{13} \\ a_{32} & a_{33} \end{vmatrix} + (a_{22}) \begin{vmatrix} a_{11} & a_{13} \\ a_{31} & a_{33} \end{vmatrix} + (-a_{23}) \begin{vmatrix} a_{11} & a_{12} \\ a_{31} & a_{32} \end{vmatrix}$$

$$= (-a_{21})(a_{12}\,a_{33} - a_{32}\,a_{13}) + (a_{22})(a_{11}\,a_{33} - a_{31}\,a_{13})$$
$$+ (-a_{23})(a_{11}\,a_{32} - a_{31}\,a_{12})$$

Example

If matrix, $A = \begin{pmatrix} 2 & 3 & -4 \\ 1 & 2 & 5 \\ -3 & 1 & 4 \end{pmatrix}$

then $|A| = \Delta = \begin{vmatrix} 2 & 3 & -4 \\ 1 & 2 & 5 \\ -3 & 1 & 4 \end{vmatrix}$

Expanding along R_2, we get

$$|A| = (-1) \times \begin{vmatrix} 2 & 3 & -4 \\ 1 & 2 & 5 \\ -3 & 1 & 4 \end{vmatrix} + 2 \times \begin{vmatrix} 2 & 3 & -4 \\ 1 & 2 & 5 \\ -3 & 1 & 4 \end{vmatrix} + (-5) \times \begin{vmatrix} 2 & 3 & -4 \\ 1 & 2 & 5 \\ -3 & 1 & 4 \end{vmatrix}$$

$$= (-1) \begin{vmatrix} 3 & -4 \\ 1 & 4 \end{vmatrix} + (2) \begin{vmatrix} 2 & -4 \\ -3 & 4 \end{vmatrix} + (-5) \begin{vmatrix} 2 & 3 \\ -3 & 1 \end{vmatrix}$$

$$= (-1)[3 \times 4 - 1 \times (-4)] + (2)[2 \times 4 - (-3) \times (-4)]$$
$$+ (-5)[2 \times 1 - (-3) \times 3]$$

$$= (-1)(12+4) + 2(8-12) - 5(2+9)$$
$$= (-1) \times 16 + 2 \times (-4) - 5 \times 11$$
$$= -16 - 8 - 55$$
$$= -79$$

4.3 Expanding along R_3

Let square matrix $A = \begin{bmatrix} a_{ij} \end{bmatrix}_{3 \times 3} = \begin{pmatrix} a_{11} & a_{12} & a_{13} \\ a_{21} & a_{22} & a_{23} \\ a_{31} & a_{32} & a_{33} \end{pmatrix}$

$$\therefore |A| = \begin{vmatrix} a_{11} & a_{12} & a_{13} \\ a_{21} & a_{22} & a_{23} \\ a_{31} & a_{32} & a_{33} \end{vmatrix}$$

$$= (a_{31}) \times \begin{vmatrix} a_{11} & a_{12} & a_{13} \\ a_{21} & a_{22} & a_{23} \\ a_{31} & a_{32} & a_{33} \end{vmatrix} + (-a_{32}) \times \begin{vmatrix} a_{11} & a_{12} & a_{13} \\ a_{21} & a_{22} & a_{23} \\ a_{31} & a_{32} & a_{33} \end{vmatrix} + (a_{33}) \times \begin{vmatrix} a_{11} & a_{12} & a_{13} \\ a_{21} & a_{22} & a_{23} \\ a_{31} & a_{32} & a_{33} \end{vmatrix}$$

$$= (a_{31}) \begin{vmatrix} a_{12} & a_{13} \\ a_{22} & a_{23} \end{vmatrix} + (-a_{32}) \begin{vmatrix} a_{11} & a_{13} \\ a_{21} & a_{23} \end{vmatrix} + (a_{33}) \begin{vmatrix} a_{11} & a_{12} \\ a_{21} & a_{22} \end{vmatrix}$$

$$= (a_{31})(a_{12}a_{23} - a_{22}a_{13}) + (-a_{32})(a_{11}a_{23} - a_{21}a_{13}) + (a_{23})(a_{11}a_{22} - a_{21}a_{12})$$

<u>Example</u>

If matrix, $A = \begin{pmatrix} 2 & 3 & -4 \\ 1 & 2 & 5 \\ -3 & 1 & 4 \end{pmatrix}$

then $|A| = \Delta = \begin{vmatrix} 2 & 3 & -4 \\ 1 & 2 & 5 \\ -3 & 1 & 4 \end{vmatrix}$

Expanding along R_3, we get

$$|A| = (-3) \times \begin{vmatrix} 2 & 3 & -4 \\ 1 & 2 & 5 \\ -3 & 1 & 4 \end{vmatrix} + (-1) \times \begin{vmatrix} 2 & 3 & -4 \\ 1 & 2 & 5 \\ -3 & 1 & 4 \end{vmatrix} + 4 \times \begin{vmatrix} 2 & 3 & -4 \\ 1 & 2 & 5 \\ -3 & 1 & 4 \end{vmatrix}$$

$$= (-3) \begin{vmatrix} 3 & -4 \\ 2 & 5 \end{vmatrix} + (-1) \begin{vmatrix} 2 & -4 \\ 1 & 5 \end{vmatrix} + (4) \begin{vmatrix} 2 & 3 \\ 1 & 2 \end{vmatrix}$$

$$= (-3)[3 \times 5 - 2 \times (-4)] + (-1)[2 \times 5 - 1 \times (-4)] + (4)[2 \times 2 - 1 \times 3]$$

$$= (-3)(15 + 8) + (-1)(10 + 4) + 4(4 - 3)$$

$$= (-3) \times 23 + (-1) \times (14) + 4 \times 1$$

$$= -69 - 14 + 4$$

$$= -79$$

4.4   Expanding along C_1

Let square matrix $A = \left[a_{ij} \right]_{3 \times 3} = \begin{pmatrix} a_{11} & a_{12} & a_{13} \\ a_{21} & a_{22} & a_{23} \\ a_{31} & a_{32} & a_{33} \end{pmatrix}$

$$\therefore |A| = \begin{vmatrix} a_{11} & a_{12} & a_{13} \\ a_{21} & a_{22} & a_{23} \\ a_{31} & a_{32} & a_{33} \end{vmatrix}$$

$$= (a_{11}) \times \begin{vmatrix} a_{11} & a_{12} & a_{13} \\ a_{21} & a_{22} & a_{23} \\ a_{31} & a_{32} & a_{33} \end{vmatrix} + (-a_{21}) \times \begin{vmatrix} a_{11} & a_{12} & a_{13} \\ a_{21} & a_{22} & a_{23} \\ a_{31} & a_{32} & a_{33} \end{vmatrix} + (a_{31}) \times \begin{vmatrix} a_{11} & a_{12} & a_{13} \\ a_{21} & a_{22} & a_{23} \\ a_{31} & a_{32} & a_{33} \end{vmatrix}$$

$$= (a_{11}) \begin{vmatrix} a_{22} & a_{23} \\ a_{32} & a_{33} \end{vmatrix} + (-a_{21}) \begin{vmatrix} a_{12} & a_{13} \\ a_{32} & a_{33} \end{vmatrix} + (a_{31}) \begin{vmatrix} a_{12} & a_{13} \\ a_{22} & a_{23} \end{vmatrix}$$

$$= (a_{11})(a_{22}a_{33} - a_{32}a_{23}) + (-a_{21})(a_{12}a_{33} - a_{32}a_{13}) + (a_{31})(a_{12}a_{23} - a_{22}a_{13})$$

<u>Example</u>

If matrix, $A = \begin{pmatrix} 2 & 3 & -4 \\ 1 & 2 & 5 \\ -3 & 1 & 4 \end{pmatrix}$

then $|A| = \Delta = \begin{vmatrix} 2 & 3 & -4 \\ 1 & 2 & 5 \\ -3 & 1 & 4 \end{vmatrix}$

Expanding along C_1, we get

$$|A| = 2 \times \begin{vmatrix} 2 & 3 & -4 \\ 1 & 2 & 5 \\ -3 & 1 & 4 \end{vmatrix} + (-1) \times \begin{vmatrix} 2 & 3 & -4 \\ 1 & 2 & 5 \\ -3 & 1 & 4 \end{vmatrix} + (-3) \times \begin{vmatrix} 2 & 3 & -4 \\ 1 & 2 & 5 \\ -3 & 1 & 4 \end{vmatrix}$$

$$= (2) \begin{vmatrix} 2 & 5 \\ 1 & 4 \end{vmatrix} + (-1) \begin{vmatrix} 3 & -4 \\ 1 & 4 \end{vmatrix} + (-3) \begin{vmatrix} 3 & -4 \\ 2 & 5 \end{vmatrix}$$

$$= (2)[2\times4 - 1\times5] + (-1)[3\times4 - 1\times(-4)] + (-3)[3\times5 - 2\times(-4)]$$

$$= (2)(8-5) + (-1)(12+4) - 3(15+8)$$

$$= 2\times3 + (-1)\times16 - 3\times23$$

$$= 6 - 16 - 69$$

$$= -79$$

4.5   Expanding along C_2

Let square matrix $A = \left[a_{ij} \right]_{3\times3} = \begin{pmatrix} a_{11} & a_{12} & a_{13} \\ a_{21} & a_{22} & a_{23} \\ a_{31} & a_{32} & a_{33} \end{pmatrix}$

$$\therefore |A| = \begin{vmatrix} a_{11} & a_{12} & a_{13} \\ a_{21} & a_{22} & a_{23} \\ a_{31} & a_{32} & a_{33} \end{vmatrix}$$

$$= (-a_{12}) \times \begin{vmatrix} a_{11} & a_{12} & a_{13} \\ a_{21} & a_{22} & a_{23} \\ a_{31} & a_{32} & a_{33} \end{vmatrix} + (a_{22}) \times \begin{vmatrix} a_{11} & a_{12} & a_{13} \\ a_{21} & a_{22} & a_{23} \\ a_{31} & a_{32} & a_{33} \end{vmatrix} + (-a_{32}) \times \begin{vmatrix} a_{11} & a_{12} & a_{13} \\ a_{21} & a_{22} & a_{23} \\ a_{31} & a_{32} & a_{33} \end{vmatrix}$$

$$= (-a_{12}) \begin{vmatrix} a_{21} & a_{23} \\ a_{31} & a_{33} \end{vmatrix} + (a_{22}) \begin{vmatrix} a_{11} & a_{13} \\ a_{31} & a_{33} \end{vmatrix} + (-a_{32}) \begin{vmatrix} a_{11} & a_{13} \\ a_{21} & a_{23} \end{vmatrix}$$

$$= (-a_{12})(a_{21}a_{33} - a_{31}a_{23}) + (a_{22})(a_{11}a_{33} - a_{31}a_{13}) + (-a_{32})(a_{11}a_{23} - a_{21}a_{13})$$

Example

If matrix, $A = \begin{pmatrix} 2 & 3 & -4 \\ 1 & 2 & 5 \\ -3 & 1 & 4 \end{pmatrix}$

then $|A| = \Delta = \begin{vmatrix} 2 & 3 & -4 \\ 1 & 2 & 5 \\ -3 & 1 & 4 \end{vmatrix}$

Expanding along C_2, we get

$$|A| = (-3) \times \begin{vmatrix} 2 & 3 & -4 \\ 1 & 2 & 5 \\ -3 & 1 & 4 \end{vmatrix} + (2) \times \begin{vmatrix} 2 & 3 & -4 \\ 1 & 2 & 5 \\ -3 & 1 & 4 \end{vmatrix} + (-1) \times \begin{vmatrix} 2 & 3 & -4 \\ 1 & 2 & 5 \\ -3 & 1 & 4 \end{vmatrix}$$

$$= (-3) \begin{vmatrix} 1 & 5 \\ -3 & 4 \end{vmatrix} + (2) \begin{vmatrix} 2 & -4 \\ -3 & 4 \end{vmatrix} + (-1) \begin{vmatrix} 2 & -4 \\ 1 & 5 \end{vmatrix}$$

$$= (-3)[1\times4 - (-3)\times5] + (2)[2\times4 - (-3)\times(-4)] + (-1)[2\times5 - 1\times(-4)]$$

$$= (-3)(4+15) + (2)(8-12) + (-1)(10+4)$$

$$= -3 \times 19 + 2 \times (-4) - 1 \times 14$$
$$= -57 - 8 - 14$$
$$= -79$$

4.6 Expanding along C_3

Let square matrix $A = \left[a_{ij}\right]_{3\times3} = \begin{pmatrix} a_{11} & a_{12} & a_{13} \\ a_{21} & a_{22} & a_{23} \\ a_{31} & a_{32} & a_{33} \end{pmatrix}$

$$\therefore |A| = \begin{vmatrix} a_{11} & a_{12} & a_{13} \\ a_{21} & a_{22} & a_{23} \\ a_{31} & a_{32} & a_{33} \end{vmatrix}$$

$$= (a_{13}) \times \begin{vmatrix} a_{11} & a_{12} & a_{13} \\ a_{21} & a_{22} & a_{23} \\ a_{31} & a_{32} & a_{33} \end{vmatrix} + (-a_{23}) \times \begin{vmatrix} a_{11} & a_{12} & a_{13} \\ a_{21} & a_{22} & a_{23} \\ a_{31} & a_{32} & a_{33} \end{vmatrix} + (a_{33}) \times \begin{vmatrix} a_{11} & a_{12} & a_{13} \\ a_{21} & a_{22} & a_{23} \\ a_{31} & a_{32} & a_{33} \end{vmatrix}$$

$$= (a_{13}) \begin{vmatrix} a_{21} & a_{22} \\ a_{31} & a_{32} \end{vmatrix} + (-a_{23}) \begin{vmatrix} a_{11} & a_{12} \\ a_{31} & a_{32} \end{vmatrix} + (a_{33}) \begin{vmatrix} a_{11} & a_{12} \\ a_{21} & a_{22} \end{vmatrix}$$

$$= (a_{13})(a_{21}a_{32} - a_{31}a_{22}) + (-a_{23})(a_{11}a_{32} - a_{31}a_{12}) + (a_{33})(a_{11}a_{22} - a_{21}a_{12})$$

Example

If matrix, $A = \begin{pmatrix} 2 & 3 & -4 \\ 1 & 2 & 5 \\ -3 & 1 & 4 \end{pmatrix}$

then $|A| = \Delta = \begin{vmatrix} 2 & 3 & -4 \\ 1 & 2 & 5 \\ -3 & 1 & 4 \end{vmatrix}$

$$|A| = (-4) \times \begin{vmatrix} 2 & 3 & -4 \\ 1 & 2 & 5 \\ -3 & 1 & 4 \end{vmatrix} + (-5) \times \begin{vmatrix} 2 & 3 & -4 \\ 1 & 2 & 5 \\ -3 & 1 & 4 \end{vmatrix} + (4) \times \begin{vmatrix} 2 & 3 & -4 \\ 1 & 2 & 5 \\ -3 & 1 & 4 \end{vmatrix}$$

Expanding along C_3, we get

$$= (-4) \begin{vmatrix} 1 & 2 \\ -3 & 1 \end{vmatrix} + (-5) \begin{vmatrix} 2 & 3 \\ -3 & 1 \end{vmatrix} + (4) \begin{vmatrix} 2 & 3 \\ 1 & 2 \end{vmatrix}$$

$$= (-4)[1 \times 1 - (-3) \times 2] + (-5)[2 \times 1 - (-3) \times 3] + (4)[2 \times 2 - 1 \times 3]$$

$$= (-4)(1+6) + (-5)(2+9) + 4(4-3)$$

$$= -4 \times 7 + (-5) \times 11 + 4 \times 1$$

$$= -28 - 55 + 4$$

$$= -79$$

5 Area of triangle in a plane (using determinant)

If three vertices of a triangle are $A(x_1, y_1)$, $B(x_2, y_2)$ and $C(x_3, y_3)$, then

$$\text{Area of } \Delta ABC = \frac{1}{2} \begin{vmatrix} x_1 & y_1 & 1 \\ x_2 & y_2 & 1 \\ x_3 & y_3 & 1 \end{vmatrix}$$

- As **area cannot be negative**, we take absolute value after calculating determinant from the above expression.
- If area is given, then we take both positive and negative sign with the value of area while putting it in this expression.

<u>**Example**</u>

Find area of a triangle whose vertices are (5,3), (2,2) and (4,4)

Solution:

$$\text{Area of } \Delta = \frac{1}{2} \begin{vmatrix} 5 & 3 & 1 \\ 2 & 2 & 1 \\ 4 & 4 & 1 \end{vmatrix}$$

$$= \frac{1}{2} [5(2-4) - 3(2-4) + (8-8)]$$

(Expanding along 1st row)

$$= \frac{1}{2} \times [-10 + 6 + 0] = -2$$

$\because$ Area can't be negative

$\therefore$ Required area of $\Delta = 2$ sq. units

<u>**Example**</u>

Find the value of k if area of a triangle formed by the point (5,k), (2,2) and (4,4) is 2 sq units.

Solution:

$$\text{Area of } \Delta = \frac{1}{2} \begin{vmatrix} 5 & k & 1 \\ 2 & 2 & 1 \\ 4 & 4 & 1 \end{vmatrix}$$

$$= \frac{1}{2} [5(2-4) - k(2-4) + (8-8)]$$

(Expanding along 1st row)

$$= \frac{1}{2} \times [-10 + 2k + 0] = -5 + k$$

$\because$ Area can't be negative, we take its absolute value

$\therefore$ Area of $\Delta = |-5 + k|$

According to question it should be 2 sq units

$\therefore \ |-5 + k| = 2$

$\Rightarrow \ -5 + k = \pm 2$

$\Rightarrow \ -5 + k = 2 \qquad$ or $\qquad -5 + k = -2$

$\Rightarrow \ k = 7 \qquad\quad$ or $\qquad k = 3$

6   Collinearity of 3 points

For three points A(x_1, y_1), B(x_2, y_2) and C(x_3, y_3) to be collinear

Area of $\Delta ABC = 0$

$$\therefore \quad \begin{vmatrix} x_1 & y_1 & 1 \\ x_2 & y_2 & 1 \\ x_3 & y_3 & 1 \end{vmatrix} = 0$$

(This is the **condition of collinearity** of 3 points)

<u>**Example**</u>
Check collinearity of three points whose coordinates are
(2,–1), (–1,–10) and (3,2).
Solution:
Condition for collinearity of points (x_1, y_1), (x_2, y_2) and (x_3, y_3) is

$$\begin{vmatrix} x_1 & y_1 & 1 \\ x_2 & y_2 & 1 \\ x_3 & y_3 & 1 \end{vmatrix} = 0$$

$\therefore$ we must find $\begin{vmatrix} 2 & -1 & 1 \\ -1 & -10 & 1 \\ 3 & 2 & 1 \end{vmatrix}$

Expanding it along 1st row, we get its determinant as follows:
$\Delta = 2\,(-10 - 2) + 1\,(-1 - 3) + 1\,(-2 + 30)]$
$ = -24 - 4 + 28$
$ = 0$

$\therefore$ Points *(2,–1), (–1,–10) and (3,2)* are collinear.

7   Equation of straight line (using determinant)

Given: Coordinates of two points A(x_1, y_1) and B(x_2, y_2) in a cartesian plane.

Required equation: Equation of line passing through A and B is found by

$$\begin{vmatrix} x & y & 1 \\ x_1 & y_1 & 1 \\ x_2 & y_2 & 1 \end{vmatrix} = 0$$

<u>**Explanation**</u>
We consider a general point P(x, y) on the line passing through A(x_1, y_1) & B(x_2, y_2).

$\because$ Points P, A and B lie on the same line, we can apply condition of collinearity for them, which will be $\begin{vmatrix} x & y & 1 \\ x_1 & y_1 & 1 \\ x_2 & y_2 & 1 \end{vmatrix} = 0$

By expanding the determinant along first row, we get the required equation of straight line.

<u>**Example**</u>
Find the equation of straight line passing through the points (5,3), (2,4).
Solution:
   Let the given points are A(5,3) and B(2,4).
   Let P(x, y) be a point on the line passing through A and B.
By applying condition of collinearity to P, A & B , we get

$$\begin{vmatrix} x & y & 1 \\ 5 & 3 & 1 \\ 2 & 4 & 1 \end{vmatrix} = 0$$

$\Rightarrow \quad x\,(3-4) - y\,(5-2) + 1(20-6) = 0$

(Expanding along 1st row)

$\Rightarrow \quad -x + 3y + 14 = 0$

$\Rightarrow \quad x - 3y - 14 = 0$

This is the required equation of straight line.

8 Minors

The minor of an element of given determinant is the determinant obtained by removing the row and the column in which the element is present.

- i.e., The minor of element a_{ij} of given determinant is the determinant obtained by removing i^{th} row and the jth column.

- The minor of element a_{ij} is denoted by M_{ij}.

<u>Explanation</u>

Given: $\Delta = \begin{vmatrix} a_{11} & a_{12} & a_{13} \\ a_{21} & a_{22} & a_{23} \\ a_{31} & a_{32} & a_{33} \end{vmatrix}$

We write minor of a_{11} as M_{11},

Minor of a_{12} as M_{12},

Minor of a_{13} as M_{13}, and so on.

To find them we proceed as follows:

(i) a_{11} is present in 1st row and 1st column, so we remove 1st row and 1st column as shown

$$\begin{vmatrix} a_{11} & a_{12} & a_{13} \\ a_{21} & a_{22} & a_{23} \\ a_{31} & a_{32} & a_{33} \end{vmatrix}$$

and obtain the determinant of order 2, which is $\begin{vmatrix} a_{22} & a_{23} \\ a_{32} & a_{33} \end{vmatrix}$

$\therefore \qquad M_{11} = \begin{vmatrix} a_{22} & a_{23} \\ a_{32} & a_{33} \end{vmatrix} = a_{22}\,a_{33} - a_{32}\,a_{23}$

(ii) a_{12} is present in 1st row and 2nd column, so we remove 1st row and 2nd column as shown

$$\begin{vmatrix} a_{11} & a_{12} & a_{13} \\ a_{21} & a_{22} & a_{23} \\ a_{31} & a_{32} & a_{33} \end{vmatrix}$$

and obtain the determinant of order 2, which is $\begin{vmatrix} a_{21} & a_{23} \\ a_{31} & a_{33} \end{vmatrix}$

$\therefore \qquad M_{12} = \begin{vmatrix} a_{21} & a_{23} \\ a_{31} & a_{33} \end{vmatrix} = a_{21}\,a_{33} - a_{31}\,a_{23}$

Similarly, we can find minors of other elements also.

Example

Given: $\Delta = \begin{vmatrix} 2 & 3 & -4 \\ 1 & 2 & 5 \\ -3 & 1 & 4 \end{vmatrix}$

Minor of $a_{11} = M_{11} = \begin{vmatrix} 2 & 3 & -4 \\ 1 & 2 & 5 \\ -3 & 1 & 4 \end{vmatrix} = \begin{vmatrix} 2 & 5 \\ 1 & 4 \end{vmatrix} = 2 \times 4 - 1 \times 5 = 3$

Minor of $a_{12} = M_{12} = \begin{vmatrix} 2 & 3 & -4 \\ 1 & 2 & 5 \\ -3 & 1 & 4 \end{vmatrix} = \begin{vmatrix} 1 & 5 \\ -3 & 4 \end{vmatrix} = 1 \times 4 - (-3) \times 5 = 19$

Minor of $a_{13} = M_{13} = \begin{vmatrix} 2 & 3 & -4 \\ 1 & 2 & 5 \\ -3 & 1 & 4 \end{vmatrix} = \begin{vmatrix} 1 & 2 \\ -3 & 1 \end{vmatrix} = 1 \times 1 - (-3) \times 2 = 7$

Similarly, other minors can be obtained.

Example

Given: $\Delta = \begin{vmatrix} 2 & -5 \\ 1 & 4 \end{vmatrix}$

Minor of $a_{11} = M_{11} = \begin{vmatrix} 2 & -5 \\ 1 & 4 \end{vmatrix} = 4$

Minor of $a_{12} = M_{12} = \begin{vmatrix} 2 & -5 \\ 1 & 4 \end{vmatrix} = 1$

Minor of $a_{21} = M_{21} = \begin{vmatrix} 2 & -5 \\ 1 & 4 \end{vmatrix} = -5$

Minor of $a_{22} = M_{22} = \begin{vmatrix} 2 & -5 \\ 1 & 4 \end{vmatrix} = 2$

- Minor of any element of determinant of order n is the determinant of order $n - 1$.
  i.e., minor of any element of determinant of order 3 has order 2.
  and minor of any element of determinant of order 2 has order 1.
- Minor of determinant of order 1 does not exist.

9 Cofactors

The cofactor of an element a_{ij} is obtained when the minor M_{ij} of that element is multiplied by $(-1)^{i+j}$.

- The cofactor of element a_{ij} is usually denoted by A_{ij}.
- Thus, cofactor of a_{ij} is

  $A_{ij} = (-1)^{i+j} M_{ij}$ where M_{ij} = minor of a_{ij}

Explanation

Given: $\Delta = \begin{vmatrix} a_{11} & a_{12} & a_{13} \\ a_{21} & a_{22} & a_{23} \\ a_{31} & a_{32} & a_{33} \end{vmatrix}$

We can write cofactor of a_{11} as A_{11},

cofactor of a_{12} as A_{12},

cofactor of a_{13} as A_{13}, and so on.

To find them we use, $A_{ij} = (-1)^{i+j} M_{ij}$

where M_{ij} = minor of a_{ij} and proceed as follows:

(i) $A_{11} = (-1)^{1+1} M_{11} = M_{11}$

It means cofactor of a_{11} = minor of $a_{11} = M_{11}$

We can calculate M_{11} as explained earlier in 'Minors', and find A_{11} as follows:

$$A_{11} = M_{11} = \begin{vmatrix} a_{22} & a_{23} \\ a_{32} & a_{33} \end{vmatrix} = a_{22}\,a_{33} - a_{32}\,a_{23}$$

(ii) $A_{12} = (-1)^{1+2} M_{12} = -M_{12}$

It means cofactor of a_{12} = negative of minor of $a_{12} = -M_{12}$

We can calculate M_{12} as explained earlier in 'Minors', and find A_{12} as follows:

$$A_{12} = -M_{12} = -\begin{vmatrix} a_{21} & a_{23} \\ a_{31} & a_{33} \end{vmatrix} = -(a_{21}\,a_{33} - a_{31}\,a_{23})$$

Similarly, we can find cofactors of other elements also.

Example

Given: $\Delta = \begin{vmatrix} 2 & 3 & -4 \\ 1 & 2 & 5 \\ -3 & 1 & 4 \end{vmatrix}$

Let's denote cofactor of element a_{ij} as A_{ij}

(i) Cofactor of $a_{11} = (-1)^{1+1} M_{11} = M_{11}$

$$\Rightarrow A_{11} = \begin{vmatrix} 2 & 3 & -4 \\ 1 & 2 & 5 \\ -3 & 1 & 4 \end{vmatrix} \qquad \text{(delete 1}^{\text{st}}\text{ row and 1}^{\text{st}}\text{ column)}$$

$$= \begin{vmatrix} 2 & 5 \\ 1 & 4 \end{vmatrix} = 2\times 4 - 1\times 5 = 3$$

(ii) Cofactor of $a_{12} = (-1)^{1+2} M_{12}$

$$\Rightarrow A_{12} = -\begin{vmatrix} 2 & 3 & -4 \\ 1 & 2 & 5 \\ -3 & 1 & 4 \end{vmatrix} \qquad \text{(delete 1}^{\text{st}}\text{ row and 2}^{\text{nd}}\text{ column)}$$

$$= -\begin{vmatrix} 1 & 5 \\ -3 & 4 \end{vmatrix} = -[1\times 4 - (-3)\times 5] = -19$$

(iii) Cofactor of $a_{13} = (-1)^{1+3} M_{13} = M_{13}$

$$\Rightarrow A_{13} = \begin{vmatrix} 2 & 3 & -4 \\ 1 & 2 & 5 \\ -3 & 1 & 4 \end{vmatrix} \qquad \text{(delete 1}^{\text{st}}\text{ row and 3}^{\text{rd}}\text{ column)}$$

---

*Asterisk (*) marked article (if any) is **not** in CBSE 2025-26 syllabus.*

$$= \begin{vmatrix} 1 & 2 \\ -3 & 1 \end{vmatrix} = 1 \times 1 - (-3) \times 2 = 7$$

Similarly, other cofactors can be obtained.

<u>Example</u>

Given: $\Delta = \begin{vmatrix} 2 & -5 \\ 1 & 4 \end{vmatrix}$

Let's denote cofactor of element a_{ij} as A_{ij}

Cofactor of $a_{11} = (-1)^{1+1} M_{11} = M_{11}$

$\Rightarrow A_{11} = \begin{vmatrix} 2 & -5 \\ 1 & 4 \end{vmatrix} = 4$

Cofactor of $a_{12} = (-1)^{1+2} M_{12} = - M_{12}$

$\Rightarrow A_{12} = - \begin{vmatrix} 2 & -5 \\ 1 & 4 \end{vmatrix} = -1$

Cofactor of $a_{21} = (-1)^{2+1} M_{21} = - M_{21}$

$\Rightarrow A_{21} = \begin{vmatrix} 2 & -5 \\ 1 & 4 \end{vmatrix} = -(-5) = 5$

Cofactor of $a_{22} = (-1)^{2+2} M_{22} = M_{22}$

$\Rightarrow A_{22} = \begin{vmatrix} 2 & -5 \\ 1 & 4 \end{vmatrix} = 2$

Important

- **If the elements of any row or column are multiplied by their corresponding cofactors, and then these products are added, the result is the determinant.**

i.e., if $\Delta = \begin{vmatrix} a_{11} & a_{12} & a_{13} \\ a_{21} & a_{22} & a_{23} \\ a_{31} & a_{32} & a_{33} \end{vmatrix}$, then

(i) $\Delta = a_{11} A_{11} + a_{12} A_{12} + a_{13} A_{13}$

   (Elements of 1st row multiplied by cofactors of 1st row)

  - This is same as the expansion along R_1 .

(ii) $\Delta = a_{21} A_{21} + a_{22} A_{22} + a_{23} A_{23}$

   (Elements of 2nd row multiplied by cofactors of 2nd row)

  - This is same as expansion along R_2 .

(iii) $\Delta = a_{31} A_{31} + a_{32} A_{32} + a_{33} A_{33}$

   (Elements of 3rd row multiplied by cofactors of 3rd row)

  - This is same as expansion along R_3 .

(iv) $\Delta = a_{11} A_{11} + a_{21} A_{21} + a_{31} A_{31}$

   (Elements of 1st column multiplied by cofactors of 1st column)

  - This is same as expansion along C_1

(v) $\Delta = a_{12} A_{12} + a_{22} A_{22} + a_{32} A_{32}$

   (Elements of 2nd column multiplied by cofactors of 2nd column)

  - This is same as expansion along C_2

(vi) $\Delta = a_{13}\,A_{13}\, + \,a_{23}\,A_{23}\, + \,a_{33}\,A_{33}$

(Elements of 3rd column multiplied by cofactors of 3rd column)

- This is same as expansion along C$_3$

<u>Example</u>

Given: $\Delta = \begin{vmatrix} 2 & 3 & -4 \\ 1 & 2 & 5 \\ -3 & 1 & 4 \end{vmatrix}$

We can evaluate by expanding along any row or column as explained in 'Determinant of matrix of order 3'.

We find that $\Delta = 79$ $\quad$ - - - - - - (i)

To verify the result $a_{11}\,A_{11}\, + \,a_{12}\,A_{12}\, + \,a_{13}\,A_{13}\, = \,\Delta$, we proceed as follows:

A_{11} = Cofactor of a_{11} = $(-1)^{1+1}\,M_{11}$ = M_{11}

$\Rightarrow A_{11} = \begin{vmatrix} 2 & 3 & -4 \\ 1 & 2 & 5 \\ -3 & 1 & 4 \end{vmatrix}$ $\qquad$ (delete 1st row and 1st column)

$= \begin{vmatrix} 2 & 5 \\ 1 & 4 \end{vmatrix} = 2{\times}4 - 1{\times}5 = 3$

A_{12} = Cofactor of a_{12} = $(-1)^{1+2}\,M_{12}$

$\Rightarrow A_{12} = -\begin{vmatrix} 2 & 3 & -4 \\ 1 & 2 & 5 \\ -3 & 1 & 4 \end{vmatrix}$ $\qquad$ (delete 1st row and 2nd column)

$= -\begin{vmatrix} 1 & 5 \\ -3 & 4 \end{vmatrix} = -[1{\times}4 - (-3){\times}5] = -19$

A_{13} = Cofactor of a_{13} = $(-1)^{1+3}\,M_{13}$ = M_{13}

$\Rightarrow A_{13} = \begin{vmatrix} 2 & 3 & -4 \\ 1 & 2 & 5 \\ -3 & 1 & 4 \end{vmatrix}$ $\qquad$ (delete 1st row and 3rd column)

$= \begin{vmatrix} 1 & 2 \\ -3 & 1 \end{vmatrix} = 1{\times}1 - (-3){\times}2 = 7$

Now we multiply elements of 1st row with their corresponding cofactors, and add the products, i.e.,

$a_{11}\,A_{11} + a_{12}\,A_{12} + a_{13}\,A_{13} = (2)(3) + (3)(-19) + (-4)(7) = 79$

Also, from eqn.(i) , $\Delta = 79$

$\therefore\ a_{11}\,A_{11}\, + \,a_{12}\,A_{12}\, + \,a_{13}\,A_{13}\, = \,\Delta$ $\quad$ is verified.

Similarly, we can verify other results.

- **Also, if the elements of any row (or column) are multiplied by the corresponding cofactors of other row (or column), and then these products are added, the result is 0.**

---

i.e., if $\Delta = \begin{vmatrix} a_{11} & a_{12} & a_{13} \\ a_{21} & a_{22} & a_{23} \\ a_{31} & a_{32} & a_{33} \end{vmatrix}$, then

(i) $a_{11} A_{21} + a_{12} A_{22} + a_{13} A_{23} = 0$

(Elements of 1st row multiplied by cofactors of 2nd row)

(ii) $a_{11} A_{31} + a_{12} A_{32} + a_{13} A_{33} = 0$

(Elements of 1st row multiplied by cofactors of 3rd row)

(iii) $a_{21} A_{11} + a_{22} A_{12} + a_{23} A_{13} = 0$

(Elements of 2nd row multiplied by cofactors of 1st row)

(iv) $a_{21} A_{31} + a_{22} A_{32} + a_{23} A_{33} = 0$

(Elements of 2nd row multiplied by cofactors of 3rd row)

(v) $a_{31} A_{11} + a_{32} A_{12} + a_{33} A_{13} = 0$

(Elements of 3rd row multiplied by cofactors of 1st row)

(vi) $a_{31} A_{21} + a_{32} A_{22} + a_{33} A_{23} = 0$

(Elements of 3rd row multiplied by cofactors of 2nd row)

(vii) $a_{11} A_{12} + a_{21} A_{22} + a_{31} A_{32} = 0$

(Elements of 1st column multiplied by cofactors of 2nd column)

(viii) $a_{11} A_{13} + a_{21} A_{23} + a_{31} A_{33} = 0$

(Elements of 1st column multiplied by cofactors of 3rd column)

(ix) $a_{12} A_{11} + a_{22} A_{21} + a_{32} A_{31} = 0$

(Elements of 2nd column multiplied by cofactors of 1st column)

(x) $a_{12} A_{13} + a_{22} A_{23} + a_{32} A_{33} = 0$

(Elements of 2nd column multiplied by cofactors of 3rd column)

(xi) $a_{13} A_{11} + a_{23} A_{21} + a_{33} A_{31} = 0$

(Elements of 3rd column multiplied by cofactors of 1st column)

(xii) $a_{13} A_{12} + a_{23} A_{22} + a_{33} A_{32} = 0$

(Elements of 3rd column multiplied by cofactors of 2nd column)

<u>**Example**</u>

Given: $\Delta = \begin{vmatrix} 2 & 3 & -4 \\ 1 & 2 & 5 \\ -3 & 1 & 4 \end{vmatrix}$

To verify the result $a_{31}\,A_{11} + a_{32}\,A_{12} + a_{33}\,A_{13} = 0$, we proceed as follows:

A_{11} = Cofactor of a_{11} = $(-1)^{1+1}\,M_{11}$ = M_{11}

$\Rightarrow A_{11} = \begin{vmatrix} 2 & 3 & -4 \\ 1 & 2 & 5 \\ -3 & 1 & 4 \end{vmatrix}$ (delete 1st row and 1st column)

$= \begin{vmatrix} 2 & 5 \\ 1 & 4 \end{vmatrix} = 2\times 4 - 1\times 5 = 3$

A_{12} = Cofactor of a_{12} = $(-1)^{1+2}\,M_{12}$

$\Rightarrow A_{12} = -\begin{vmatrix} 2 & 3 & -4 \\ 1 & 2 & 5 \\ -3 & 1 & 4 \end{vmatrix}$ (delete 1st row and 2nd column)

$= -\begin{vmatrix} 1 & 5 \\ -3 & 4 \end{vmatrix} = -[1\times 4 - (-3)\times 5] = -19$

A_{13} = Cofactor of a_{13} = $(-1)^{1+3}\,M_{13}$ = M_{13}

$\Rightarrow A_{13} = \begin{vmatrix} 2 & 3 & -4 \\ 1 & 2 & 5 \\ -3 & 1 & 4 \end{vmatrix}$ (delete 1st row and 3rd column)

$= \begin{vmatrix} 1 & 2 \\ -3 & 1 \end{vmatrix} = 1\times 1 - (-3)\times 2 = 7$

Now we multiply elements of 3rd row with the corresponding cofactors of 1st row, and add the products, i.e.,

$a_{31}\,A_{11} + a_{32}\,A_{12} + a_{33}\,A_{13} = (-3)(3) + (1)(-19) + (4)(7) = 0$

$\therefore\ a_{11}\,A_{11} + a_{12}\,A_{12} + a_{13}\,A_{13} = 0$ is verified.

Similarly, we can verify other results.

10 Adjoint of matrix

If $A = [\,a_{ij}\,]$ *is a square matrix and* A_{ij} *are the cofactors of its elements, then the* **transpose of the cofactor matrix** $[\,A_{ij}\,]$ *is called as* **adjoint** *of the matrix* A.

* Adjoint of matrix A is denoted by *adj* A.

<u>**Example**</u>

Given: $A = \begin{pmatrix} 2 & 3 & -4 \\ 1 & 2 & 5 \\ -3 & 1 & 4 \end{pmatrix}$

To find *adj* A , we have to find cofactors A_{ij} of all elements of the matrix (*see* 'Cofactors' in this chapter), and write them as follows:

$$A_{11} = 3 \qquad A_{12} = -19 \qquad A_{13} = 7$$
$$A_{21} = -16 \qquad A_{22} = -4 \qquad A_{23} = -11$$
$$A_{31} = 23 \qquad A_{32} = -14 \qquad A_{33} = 1$$

So, the cofactor matrix is $= \begin{pmatrix} 3 & -19 & 7 \\ -16 & -4 & -11 \\ 23 & -14 & 1 \end{pmatrix}$

Its transpose is adjoint of A.

$$\therefore \ adj\ A \ = \begin{pmatrix} 3 & -16 & 23 \\ -19 & -4 & -14 \\ 7 & -11 & 1 \end{pmatrix}$$

Example

Given: $A = \begin{pmatrix} 2 & -5 \\ 1 & 4 \end{pmatrix}$

To find *adj* A , we have to find cofactors A_{ij} of all elements of the matrix (*see* 'Cofactors' in this chapter), and write them as follows:

$$A_{11} = 4 \qquad A_{12} = -1$$
$$A_{21} = 5 \qquad A_{22} = 2$$

So, the cofactor matrix is $= \begin{pmatrix} 4 & -1 \\ 5 & 2 \end{pmatrix}$

Its transpose is adjoint.

$$\therefore \ adj\ A \ = \begin{pmatrix} 4 & 5 \\ -1 & 2 \end{pmatrix}$$

- We can obtain adjoint of 2×2 matrix directly, by interchanging the positions of elements in the principal diagonal, and changing the sign of the remaining elements.

i.e., if $A = [a_{ij}]_{2\times2} = \begin{pmatrix} a_{11} & a_{12} \\ a_{21} & a_{22} \end{pmatrix}$

then $adj\ A = \begin{pmatrix} a_{22} & -a_{12} \\ -a_{21} & a_{11} \end{pmatrix}$

Example

Given: $A = \begin{pmatrix} 2 & -5 \\ 1 & 4 \end{pmatrix}$

To find *adj* A , we just change the position of 2 & 4, and change the sign of -5 & 1.

$$\therefore \ adj\ A \ = \begin{pmatrix} 4 & 5 \\ -1 & 2 \end{pmatrix}$$

11 Singular matrix

If the determinant of a square matrix is **0** *, then the matrix is called as singular matrix.*

i.e., **If** $|A| = 0$ **, then A is a singular matrix.**

and **If** $|A| \neq 0$ **, then A is a non-singular matrix.**

<u>**Example**</u>

Given: $A = \begin{pmatrix} 2 & 3 & -4 \\ 1 & 2 & 5 \\ -3 & 1 & 4 \end{pmatrix}$

$\Rightarrow |A| = \begin{vmatrix} 2 & 3 & -4 \\ 1 & 2 & 5 \\ -3 & 1 & 4 \end{vmatrix} = 79$

(by expanding along any row or column)

$\Rightarrow |A| \neq 0$

$\therefore$ A is a non-singular matrix.

<u>**Example**</u>

Given: $A = \begin{pmatrix} 3 & -2 \\ 6 & -4 \end{pmatrix}$

$\Rightarrow |A| = \begin{vmatrix} 3 & -2 \\ 6 & -4 \end{vmatrix} = 0$

$\Rightarrow |A| = 0$

$\therefore$ A is a singular matrix.

12 Inverse of square matrix

If square matrix A is non-singular matrix then its inverse exists, and

$$A^{-1} = \frac{1}{|A|} \, (adj\ A).$$

<u>**Example**</u>

Given: $A = \begin{pmatrix} 2 & 1 & 3 \\ 4 & -1 & 0 \\ -7 & 2 & 1 \end{pmatrix}$

$\Rightarrow |A| = \begin{vmatrix} 2 & 1 & 3 \\ 4 & -1 & 0 \\ -7 & 2 & 1 \end{vmatrix} = -3$

(by expanding along any row or column)

$\Rightarrow |A| \neq 0$

$\therefore A^{-1}$ exists

To find A^{-1}, we have to find *adj* A (*see 'Adjoint of matrix' in this chapter*) as follows:

Cofactors:

$$A_{11} = -1 \qquad A_{12} = -4 \qquad A_{13} = 1$$
$$A_{21} = 5 \qquad A_{22} = 23 \qquad A_{23} = -11$$
$$A_{31} = 3 \qquad A_{32} = 12 \qquad A_{33} = -6$$

So, the cofactor matrix is $= \begin{pmatrix} -1 & -4 & 1 \\ 5 & 23 & -11 \\ 3 & 12 & -6 \end{pmatrix}$

Its transpose is adjoint.

$$\therefore \quad adj \; \mathrm{A} \;\; = \begin{pmatrix} -1 & 5 & 3 \\ -4 & 23 & 12 \\ 1 & -11 & -6 \end{pmatrix}$$

Now $\;\; \mathrm{A}^{-1} = \dfrac{1}{|\mathrm{A}|} \left(adj \; \mathrm{A} \right)$

$$\therefore \quad \mathrm{A}^{-1} = \dfrac{1}{-3} \begin{pmatrix} -1 & 5 & 3 \\ -4 & 23 & 12 \\ 1 & -11 & -6 \end{pmatrix} = \begin{pmatrix} \frac{1}{3} & \frac{5}{3} & -1 \\ \frac{4}{3} & \frac{23}{3} & -4 \\ \frac{-1}{3} & \frac{-11}{3} & 2 \end{pmatrix}$$

Example

Given: $\; \mathrm{P} = \begin{pmatrix} 2 & 1 & 6 \\ 4 & -1 & 0 \\ -7 & 2 & 1 \end{pmatrix}$

$$\Rightarrow |\mathrm{P}| \;\; = \begin{vmatrix} 2 & 1 & 6 \\ 4 & -1 & 0 \\ -7 & 2 & 1 \end{vmatrix} = 0$$

(by expanding along any row or column)

$\Rightarrow |\mathrm{P}| \; = 0$

$\therefore \; \mathrm{P}^{-1} \;$ **doesn't exists**

Example

Given: $\; \mathrm{A} = \begin{pmatrix} 2 & 2 \\ 4 & 3 \end{pmatrix}$

$\Rightarrow |\mathrm{A}| \;\; = \begin{vmatrix} 2 & 2 \\ 4 & 3 \end{vmatrix} = -2$

$\Rightarrow |\mathrm{A}| \;\neq 0$

$\therefore \; \mathrm{A}^{-1} \;$ exists

To find A^{-1} , we have to find *adj* A (*see* 'Adjoint of matrix' in this chapter) as follows:

Cofactors:

$$\mathrm{A}_{11} = 3 \qquad \mathrm{A}_{12} = -4$$
$$\mathrm{A}_{21} = -2 \qquad \mathrm{A}_{22} = 2$$

So, the cofactor matrix is $\; = \begin{pmatrix} 3 & -4 \\ -2 & 2 \end{pmatrix}$

Its transpose is adjoint.

$$\therefore \quad adj \; \mathrm{A} \;\; = \begin{pmatrix} 3 & -2 \\ -4 & 2 \end{pmatrix}$$

Now $\qquad \mathrm{A}^{-1} = \dfrac{1}{|\mathrm{A}|} \left(adj \; \mathrm{A} \right)$

$$\therefore \quad \mathrm{A}^{-1} = \dfrac{1}{-2} \begin{pmatrix} 3 & -2 \\ -4 & 2 \end{pmatrix} = \begin{pmatrix} \frac{-3}{2} & 1 \\ 2 & -1 \end{pmatrix}$$

13 Important formulae

- $|k\,A| = k^n\,|A|$
  where n is order of matrix A and k is any real number.
- Inverse of a square matrix exists only if it is non-singular.
  i.e. if $|A| \neq 0$, then A^{-1} exists.
  and if $|A| = 0$, then A^{-1} does not exist.
- **Inverse of a matrix is unique if it exists.**
- If A^{-1} exists, then $\quad |A^{-1}| = \dfrac{1}{|A|}$
- $A\,(adj\,A) = |A|\,\mathbf{I}\quad$ and $\quad(adj\,A)\,A = |A|\,\mathbf{I}$
- If A and B are two non-singular matrices of the same order,

  then $|AB| = |A|\,|B|$.
- $|adj\,A| = |A|^{n-1}$ where n is order of matrix A.
- $(\mathbf{AB})^{-1} = \mathbf{B}^{-1}\mathbf{A}^{-1}\ldots$ for two non-singular matrices A and B

14 Find A^{-1} using given equation

If we are given a square matrix A, and a matrix equation like
$aA^2 + bA + cI = O$, then we can find A^{-1} using this equation as
explained in the following example:

<u>Example</u>

If $A = \begin{pmatrix} 3 & 1 \\ -1 & 2 \end{pmatrix}$, *which satisfy the equation* $A^2 - 5A + 7\,I = O$
where I is identity matrix, and O is zero matrix of same order as that
of A, *then find* A^{-1}.

Solution:

Given : $A^2 - 5A + 7\,I = O$

Post multiplying both sides by A^{-1} to get

$A^2\,(A^{-1}) - 5A(A^{-1}) + 7\,I\,(A^{-1}) = O\,(A^{-1})$

$\Rightarrow AA\,(A^{-1}) - 5A(A^{-1}) + 7\,(A^{-1}) = O$

$$[\because I(A^{-1}) = A^{-1} \text{ and } OA^{-1} = O]$$

$\Rightarrow AI - 5\,I + 7\,A^{-1} = O \qquad\ldots\ldots\ldots\ldots[\because A\,A^{-1} = I\,]$

$\Rightarrow A - 5\,I + 7\,A^{-1} = O \qquad\ldots\ldots\ldots\ldots[\because AI = A\,]$

$\Rightarrow 7\,A^{-1} = -A + 5\,I$

$\Rightarrow 7\,A^{-1} = -\begin{pmatrix} 3 & 1 \\ -1 & 2 \end{pmatrix} + 5\begin{pmatrix} 1 & 0 \\ 0 & 1 \end{pmatrix}$

$\Rightarrow 7\,A^{-1} = \begin{pmatrix} 2 & -1 \\ 1 & 3 \end{pmatrix}$

$\Rightarrow A^{-1} = \dfrac{1}{7}\begin{pmatrix} 2 & -1 \\ 1 & 3 \end{pmatrix} \qquad \Rightarrow A^{-1} = \begin{pmatrix} \frac{2}{7} & \frac{-1}{7} \\ \frac{1}{7} & \frac{3}{7} \end{pmatrix}$

15 Solution of system of Linear Equations (Matrix method)

- If a system of equations has solutions (unique solution or many solutions), then this system is said to be **Consistent**.
- If a system of equations has no solution, then this system is said to be **Inconsistent**.

Step-1 First, we have to write matrix form of given system of equations as follows:

(i) For a system of linear equations in 3 variables

$$a_1 x + b_1 y + c_1 z = d_1$$
$$a_2 x + b_2 y + c_2 z = d_2$$
$$a_3 x + b_3 y + c_3 z = d_3$$

We write 3 matrices:

Coefficient matrix, $A = \begin{bmatrix} a_1 & b_1 & c_1 \\ a_2 & b_2 & c_2 \\ a_3 & b_3 & c_3 \end{bmatrix}$

[coefficients of x, y and z of 1st eqn are written in 1st row, that of 2nd eqn in 2nd row and that of 3rd eqn in 3rd row]

Constant matrix, $B = \begin{bmatrix} d_1 \\ d_2 \\ d_3 \end{bmatrix}$

[this is the matrix formed by constants on RHS of the eqns]

Variable matrix, $X = \begin{bmatrix} x \\ y \\ z \end{bmatrix}$

[this is the matrix formed by variables involved in the eqns]

If we find the product AX, and equate it with B, we will get complete given system of equations.

∴ Matrix form of given system of equations is
$$AX = B$$

(ii) For a system of linear equations in 2 variables

$$a_1 x + b_1 y = c_1$$
$$a_2 x + b_2 y = c_2$$

Here, we write 3 matrices for this system:

Coefficient matrix, $A = \begin{bmatrix} a_1 & b_1 \\ a_2 & b_2 \end{bmatrix}$

[coefficients of x and y of 1st eqn are written in 1st row and that of 2nd eqn in 2nd row]

Constant matrix, $B = \begin{bmatrix} c_1 \\ c_2 \end{bmatrix}$

[*this is the matrix formed by constants on* RHS *of the eqns*]

Variable matrix, $X = \begin{bmatrix} x \\ y \end{bmatrix}$

[*this is the matrix formed by variables involved in the eqns*]

$\therefore$ Matrix form of given system of equations is

$$AX = B$$

Step-2 Now, we find

$|A| = \text{----}$ and $adj\ A = \text{----}$

Also find $(adj\ A)B = \text{----}$

Step-3 From step 2, we can have one of the following cases:

$\longrightarrow$ **Case 1 :** If $|A| \neq 0$,

then there is **unique** solution and system is **consistent.**

Find $A^{-1} = \text{----}$

Find the unique solution by: $X = A^{-1}B$

$\longrightarrow$ **Case 2 :** If $|A| = 0$ and $(adj\ A)\ B \neq O$,

(O is zero matrix)

then there is **no** solution and system is **inconsistent** .

$\longrightarrow$ **Case 3 :** If $|A| = 0$ and $(adj\ A)\ B = O$,

then there is **no** solution or **many** solutions.

And the system may be **inconsistent** or **consistent.**

<u>Example</u>

Solve the following system of equations:

$$2x + 3y + 3z = 5$$
$$x - 2y + z = -1$$
$$3x - y - 2z = 3$$

Solution:

Step-1 : Here, we have

Coefficient matrix, $A = \begin{bmatrix} 2 & 3 & 3 \\ 1 & -2 & 1 \\ 3 & -1 & -2 \end{bmatrix}$

[*coefficients of x, y and z of 1st eqn are written in 1st row,*
that of 2nd eqn in 2nd row and that of 3rd eqn in 3rd row]

Constant matrix, $\text{B} = \begin{bmatrix} 5 \\ -4 \\ 3 \end{bmatrix}$

[*this is the matrix formed by constants on* RHS *of the eqns.*]

Variable matrix, $\text{X} = \begin{bmatrix} x \\ y \\ z \end{bmatrix}$

[*this is the matrix formed by variables involved in the eqns*]

$\therefore$ Matrix form of given system of equations is
$$\text{AX} = \text{B}$$

Step-2 : Now we can find $|A|$ by expanding the determinant along any row or any column.

So, by expanding along R_1 , we get

$$|A| = 2[(-2)(-2) - (-1)(1)] - 3[(1)(-2) - (3)(1)]$$
$$+ 3[(1)(-1) - (3)(-2)]$$
$$= 2 \times 5 - 3 \times (-5) + 3 \times 5$$
$$= 40$$

Step-3 :

$$\because \ |A| \neq 0$$

$\therefore$ **There is unique solution, which is found by** $\text{X} = \text{A}^{-1}\,\text{B}$

Now we have to find A^{-1} (*see* 'Inverse of square matrix' in this chapter).

For this find cofactor matrix of A as discussed in article 'Cofactors' of this chapter. By following that method, we get

$$\text{Cofactor matrix of A} = \begin{bmatrix} 5 & 5 & 5 \\ 3 & -13 & 11 \\ 9 & 1 & -7 \end{bmatrix}$$

$$\therefore \quad adj\ \text{A} = \begin{bmatrix} 5 & 3 & 9 \\ 5 & -13 & 1 \\ 5 & 11 & -7 \end{bmatrix}$$

$$\text{And} \quad \text{A}^{-1} = \frac{1}{40}\begin{bmatrix} 5 & 3 & 9 \\ 5 & -13 & 1 \\ 5 & 11 & -7 \end{bmatrix}$$

Now $\text{X} = \text{A}^{-1}\,\text{B}$

$$\Rightarrow \quad \begin{bmatrix} x \\ y \\ z \end{bmatrix} = \frac{1}{40}\begin{bmatrix} 5 & 3 & 9 \\ 5 & -13 & 1 \\ 5 & 11 & -7 \end{bmatrix}\begin{bmatrix} 5 \\ -4 \\ 3 \end{bmatrix}$$

$$= \frac{1}{40} \begin{bmatrix} 40 \\ 80 \\ -40 \end{bmatrix}$$

$$\Rightarrow \quad \begin{bmatrix} x \\ y \\ z \end{bmatrix} = \begin{bmatrix} 1 \\ 2 \\ -1 \end{bmatrix}$$

$$\Rightarrow \quad x = 1, \qquad y = 2 \qquad \text{and} \qquad z = -1$$

Example

Solve the following system of equations:

$$x + 3y = 5$$
$$2x + 6y = 4$$

Solution:

Step-1 : Here, we have

Coefficient matrix, $A = \begin{bmatrix} 1 & 3 \\ 2 & 6 \end{bmatrix}$

> *[coefficients of x and y of 1st eqn are written in 1st row and that of 2nd eqn in 2nd row]*

Constant matrix, $B = \begin{bmatrix} 5 \\ 4 \end{bmatrix}$

> *[this is the matrix formed by constants on RHS of the eqns.]*

Variable matrix, $X = \begin{bmatrix} x \\ y \end{bmatrix}$

> *[this is the matrix formed by variables involved in the eqns]*

$\therefore$ Matrix form of given system of equations is
$$AX = B$$

Step-2 : Now $|A| = (1)(6) - (2)(3) = 0$

Step-3 :

$\because$ $|A| = 0$

$\therefore$ We find adjoint A (*see 'Adjoint of matrix' in this chapter*).
By following that method, we get

$$adj\ A = \begin{bmatrix} 6 & -2 \\ -3 & 1 \end{bmatrix}$$

Now $(adj\ A)\ B = \begin{bmatrix} 6 & -2 \\ -3 & 1 \end{bmatrix} \begin{bmatrix} 5 \\ 4 \end{bmatrix}$

$$= \begin{bmatrix} 22 \\ -11 \end{bmatrix}$$

$\because$ $(adj\ A)\ B \neq O$ (i.e., $(adj\ A)\ B$ is not a zero matrix)
But $|A| = 0$

$\therefore$ **There is no solution and system of equations is inconsistent.**

---

16 *Properties of Determinants

(i) The value of the determinant remains unchanged if its rows and columns are interchanged.

Symbolically, this property is represented as $C_i \leftrightarrow R_i$

- $|A'| = |A|$ where A is a square matrix

For example, if $\Delta = \begin{vmatrix} a & b & c \\ d & e & f \\ g & h & i \end{vmatrix}$

then on applying $C_i \leftrightarrow R_i$

$$\Delta = \begin{vmatrix} a & d & g \\ b & e & h \\ c & f & i \end{vmatrix}$$

(ii) If any two rows (or columns) of a determinant are interchanged, then sign of the determinant changes.

Symbolically, this property is represented as $R_i \leftrightarrow R_j$ or $C_i \leftrightarrow C_j$

For example, if $\Delta = \begin{vmatrix} a & b & c \\ d & e & f \\ g & h & i \end{vmatrix}$ ....(i)

(1) on applying $R_1 \leftrightarrow R_2$ in eqn.(i)

$$\Delta = - \begin{vmatrix} d & e & f \\ a & b & c \\ g & h & i \end{vmatrix}$$

(2) on applying $C_1 \leftrightarrow C_3$ in eqn.(i)

$$\Delta = - \begin{vmatrix} c & b & a \\ f & e & d \\ i & h & g \end{vmatrix}$$

(iii) If any two rows (or columns) of a determinant are identical (all corresponding elements are same), then value of determinant is zero.

i.e, if $R_i = R_j$ or $C_i = C_j$

then $\Delta = 0$

For example,

(1) If $\Delta = \begin{vmatrix} 2 & 3 & -4 \\ 1 & 2 & 5 \\ 2 & 3 & -4 \end{vmatrix}$,

then $\Delta = 0$ $(\because R_1 = R_3)$

(2) If $\Delta = \begin{vmatrix} 3 & 3 & -4 \\ 2 & 2 & 5 \\ 1 & 1 & 4 \end{vmatrix}$,

then $\Delta = 0$ $\because C_1 = C_2$

(iv) If each element of a row (or a column) of a determinant is multiplied by a constant k, then its value gets multiplied by k.

Symbolically, this property is represented as $\mathbf{R}_i \to k\,\mathbf{R}_i$ or $\mathbf{C}_i \to k\,\mathbf{C}_i$

For example, if $\Delta = \begin{vmatrix} a & b & c \\ d & e & f \\ g & h & i \end{vmatrix}$ $\qquad$ ....(i)

(1) on applying $\mathbf{R}_2 \to -2\,\mathbf{R}_2$ in (i)

$$-2\,\Delta = \begin{vmatrix} a & b & c \\ -2d & -2e & -2f \\ g & h & i \end{vmatrix}$$

$$\Rightarrow \Delta = -\frac{1}{2}\begin{vmatrix} a & b & c \\ -2d & -2e & -2f \\ g & h & i \end{vmatrix}$$

(2) on applying $\mathbf{C}_1 \to 3\,\mathbf{C}_1$

$$3\,\Delta = \begin{vmatrix} 3a & b & c \\ 3d & e & f \\ 3g & h & i \end{vmatrix}$$

$$\Rightarrow \Delta = \frac{1}{3}\begin{vmatrix} 3a & b & c \\ 3d & e & f \\ 3g & h & i \end{vmatrix}$$

(v) If some or all elements of a row or column of a determinant are expressed as sum of two (or more) terms, then the determinant can be expressed as sum of two (or more) determinants.

For example,

(1) If $\Delta = \begin{vmatrix} a+x & b+y & c+z \\ d & e & f \\ g & h & i \end{vmatrix}$,

then $\quad \Delta = \begin{vmatrix} a & b & c \\ d & e & f \\ g & h & i \end{vmatrix} + \begin{vmatrix} x & y & z \\ d & e & f \\ g & h & i \end{vmatrix}$

(2) If $\Delta = \begin{vmatrix} a+l & b & c \\ d+m & e & f \\ g+n & h & i \end{vmatrix}$,

then $\Delta = \begin{vmatrix} a & b & c \\ d & e & f \\ g & h & i \end{vmatrix} + \begin{vmatrix} l & b & c \\ m & e & f \\ n & h & i \end{vmatrix}$

(vi) If we add each element of a row (or a column) of the given determinant, after multiplying them by a non-zero number k, to the corresponding elements of another row (or column), then the value of determinant remains unchanged.

Symbolically, this property is represented as

$$\mathbf{R}_i \to \mathbf{R}_i + k\mathbf{R}_j \qquad \text{or} \qquad \mathbf{C}_i \to \mathbf{C}_i + k\mathbf{C}_j$$

For example, if $\Delta = \begin{vmatrix} a & b & c \\ d & e & f \\ g & h & i \end{vmatrix}$ ....(i)

(1) on applying $\mathbf{R}_3 \to \mathbf{R}_3 + 5\mathbf{R}_2$

$$\Delta = \begin{vmatrix} a & b & c \\ d & e & f \\ g+5d & h+5e & i+5f \end{vmatrix}$$

(2) on applying $\mathbf{C}_2 \to \mathbf{C}_2 + (-3)\mathbf{C}_1$ in (i)

$$\Delta = \begin{vmatrix} a & b-3a & c \\ d & e-3d & f \\ g & h-3g & i \end{vmatrix}$$

Chapter-5   Continuity

1   Important Limits (studied earlier)

1.1   Formulae

(i) $\displaystyle \lim_{x \to a} \frac{x^n - a^n}{x - a} = n\,a^{n-1}$

(*for any rational number n and a being any positive number*)

- Also, $\displaystyle \lim_{x \to a} \frac{x - a}{x^n - a^n} = \frac{1}{na^{n-1}}$

(ii) $\displaystyle \lim_{x \to 0} \frac{\sin x}{x} = 1$

(*where angle x is in radians*)

- Also, $\displaystyle \lim_{x \to 0} \frac{x}{\sin x} = 1$

(iii) $\displaystyle \lim_{x \to 0} \frac{e^x - 1}{x} = 1$

- Also, $\displaystyle \lim_{x \to 0} \frac{x}{e^x - 1} = 1$

(iv) $\displaystyle \lim_{x \to 0} \frac{a^x - 1}{x} = \log_e a$

- Also, $\displaystyle \lim_{x \to 0} \frac{x}{a^x - 1} = \frac{1}{\log_e a}$

(v) $\displaystyle \lim_{x \to 0} \frac{\log_e |1+x|}{x} = 1$

- Also, $\displaystyle \lim_{x \to 0} \frac{x}{\log_e |1+x|} = 1$

(vi) $\displaystyle \lim_{x \to 0} \frac{\log_a |1+x|}{x} = \frac{1}{\log_e a}$

- Also, $\displaystyle \lim_{x \to 0} \frac{x}{\log_a |1+x|} = \log_e a$

---

*Asterisk (*) marked article (if any) is **not** in CBSE 2025-26 syllabus.*

2 Concept of Continuity of a function

We can say that a real function is continuous at a fixed point in its domain if we can draw the graph of the function *around* that point in one stroke from left to right without lifting the pen from the plane of the paper.

- If a real function f is not continuous at a point $x = c$ in its domain, then $x = c$ is known as its point of discontinuity.
- Also, a function is continuous if we can draw the graph of the function from left to right **in its domain** without lifting the pen from the plane of the paper.

Let's consider the cases where we have to lift our pen, and where we don't to draw the graph of a given function:

Case-1 (discontinuity)

If the function is **not defined** at point $x = c$, then we will have to lift the pen at $x = c$ while drawing its graph (as shown in adjoining figure).

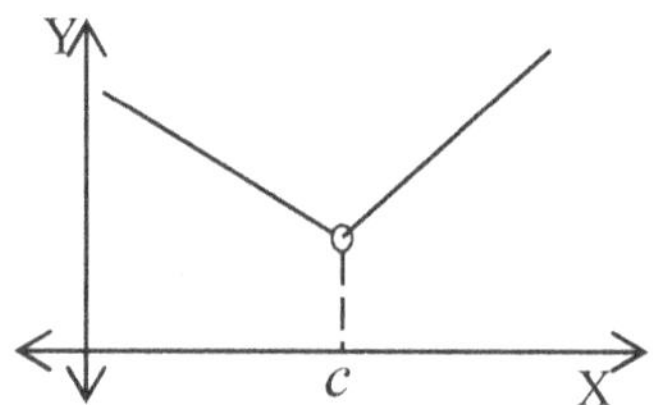

$\therefore$ *f(x)* is not continuous at $x = c$,
    if *f(c)* = not defined

- Whether $\boldsymbol{\lim\limits_{x \to c} f(x)}$ **exists or doesn't exist,** *f(x)* will not be continuous at $x = c$ if *f(c)* = not defined
- ***Note :*** If *f(c)* = not defined, then $x = c$ is not in its domain.

Example

Given function $\quad f(x) = \begin{cases} 2 + x & if\ x < 0 \\ 2 - x & if\ x > 0 \end{cases}$

Here, at $x = 0$ function is not defined, i.e., $f(0) =$ not defined.

$$\text{Now} \quad \text{LHL} = \lim_{x \to 0^-} f(x) = \lim_{x \to 0^-} 2 + x = 2$$

$$\text{and} \quad \text{RHL} = \lim_{x \to 0^+} f(x) = \lim_{x \to 0^+} 2 - x = 2$$

$$\Rightarrow \quad \text{LHL} = \text{RHL} = 2$$

$$\Rightarrow \quad \lim_{x \to 0} f(x) = 2 \quad (\text{i.e., } \lim_{x \to 0} f(x) \text{ exists })$$

Although $\lim\limits_{x \to 0} f(x)$ exists ,

but $f(0) =$ not defined

$\therefore \qquad$ *f(x)* is not continuous at $x = 0$

Case-2 (discontinuity)

If the function is **defined at point** $x = c$ and $\lim\limits_{x \to c} f(x)$ **does not exist** (i.e., at $x = c$, L.H.L $\neq$ R.H.L.) , then we will have to lift the pen at $x = c$ while drawing its graph. (*see* figure below)

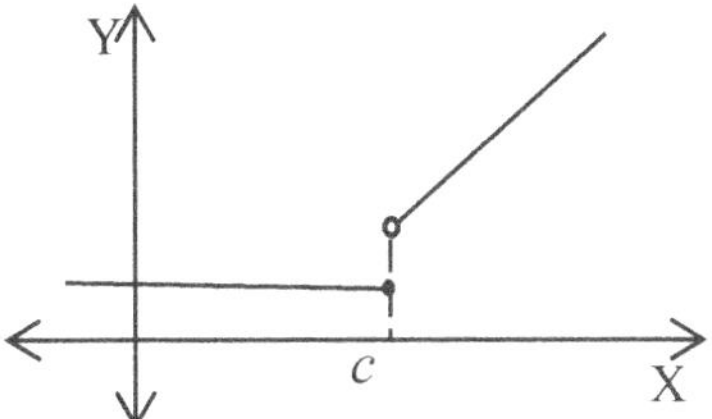

$\therefore$ *f(x)* is not continuous at $x = c$, if *f(c)* = defined, but

$$\lim_{x \to c^-} f(x) \neq \lim_{x \to c^+} f(x)$$

i.e., *f(x)* is not continuous at $x = c$ if **f(c) = defined, but**

$$\lim_{x \to c} f(x) \textbf{ does not exist.}$$

Example

Given function $f(x) = \begin{cases} 1 + x & if\ x > 1 \\ 1 & if\ x \leq 1 \end{cases}$

Here, at $x = 1$

$$\text{LHL} = \lim_{x \to 1^-} f(x) = 1$$

$$\text{and} \quad \text{RHL} = \lim_{x \to 1^+} f(x) = \lim_{x \to 1^+} 1 + x = 2$$

$$\Rightarrow \quad \lim_{x \to 1^-} f(x) \neq \lim_{x \to 1^+} f(x)$$

$$\Rightarrow \quad \lim_{x \to 1} f(x) \text{ doesn't exist.}$$

Now $f(1) = 1 \qquad$ (i.e., $f(1)$ is defined)

Although $f(1)$ is defined, but $\lim\limits_{x \to 1} f(x)$ doesn't exist.

So, *f(x)* is not continuous at $x = 1$

Case-3 (discontinuity)

If the function is **defined at point** $x = c$ and $\lim\limits_{x \to c} f(x)$ **exists** (i.e., at $x = c$, L.H.L = R.H.L.) but *f(c)* $\neq$ $\lim\limits_{x \to c} f(x)$, then it is not continuous at $x = c$ because we will have to lift the pen at $x = c$ while drawing its graph. (*see* figure below)

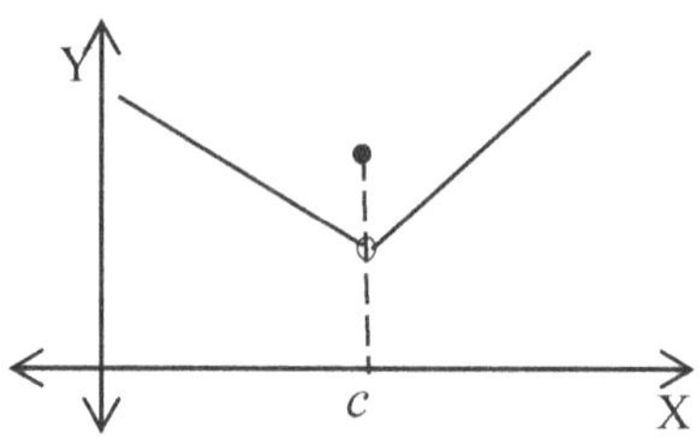

$\therefore$ *f(x)* is not continuous at $x = c$, if **f(c) = defined and also,**

$\lim\limits_{x \to c} f(x)$ **exists, but** **f(c) $\neq$** $\lim\limits_{x \to c} f(x)$

<u>Example</u>

Given function $f(x) = \begin{cases} 2 + x & if\ x < 0 \\ 1 & if\ x = 0 \\ 2 - x & if\ x > 0 \end{cases}$

Here, at $x = 0$

$$\text{LHL} = \lim\limits_{x \to 0^-} f(x) = \lim\limits_{x \to 0^-} 2 + x = 2$$

and $\quad$ $$\text{RHL} = \lim\limits_{x \to 0^+} f(x) = \lim\limits_{x \to 0^+} 2 - x = 2$$

$\Rightarrow \quad \text{LHL} = \text{RHL}$

$\Rightarrow \quad \lim\limits_{x \to 0} f(x) = 2 \quad$ (i.e., $\lim\limits_{x \to 0} f(x)$ exists)

Now $f(0) = 1 \qquad$ (i.e., $f(0)$ is defined)

Although $\lim\limits_{x \to 0} f(x)$ exists and $f(0)$ is defined,

but $\qquad \lim\limits_{x \to 0} f(x) \neq f(0)$

$\therefore \qquad$ *f(x)* is not continuous at $x = 0$

<u>Case-4 (continuity)</u>

If the function is **defined at point $x = c$ and** $\lim\limits_{x \to c} f(x)$ **exists** (i.e., at $x = c$, L.H.L = R.H.L.) **with** **f(c) =** $\lim\limits_{x \to c} f(x)$, then it is continuous at $x = c$ because we can draw its graph without lifting the pen at $x = c$.

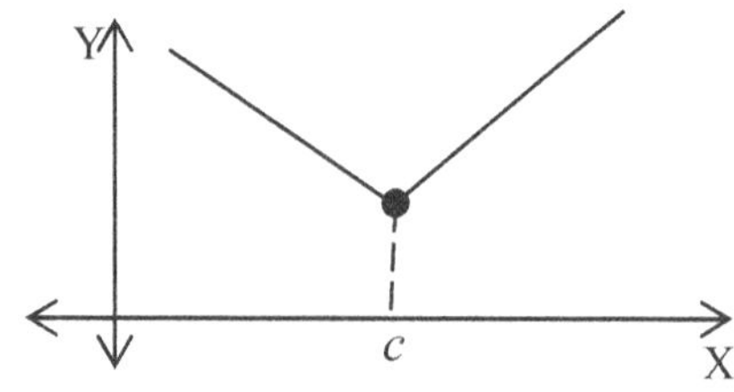

$\therefore$ If $\lim\limits_{x \to c^-} f(x) = l$ and $\lim\limits_{x \to c^+} f(x) = l$, then $\lim\limits_{x \to c} f(x) = l$

Also, if $f(c) = l$, then $\lim\limits_{x \to c} f(x) = f(c)$

So, $f(x)$ is continuous at $x = c$

<u>Example</u>

$$\text{Given function}\quad f(x) = \begin{cases} 2 + x & if \ x < 0 \\ 2 & if \ x = 0 \\ 2 - x & if \ x > 0 \end{cases}$$

Here, at $x = 0$

$$\text{LHL} = \lim\limits_{x \to 0^-} f(x) = \lim\limits_{x \to 0^-} 2 + x = 2$$

and $$\text{RHL} = \lim\limits_{x \to 0^+} f(x) = \lim\limits_{x \to 0^+} 2 - x = 2$$

$\Rightarrow$ LHL $=$ RHL

$\Rightarrow$ $\lim\limits_{x \to 0} f(x) = 2$ (i.e., $\lim\limits_{x \to 0} f(x)$ exists)

Now $f(0) = 2$ (i.e., $f(0)$ is defined)

We see that $\lim\limits_{x \to 0} f(x)$ exists and $f(0)$ is defined.

Also, $\lim\limits_{x \to 0} f(x) = f(0)$

$\therefore$ $f(x)$ is continuous at $x = 0$

2.1 Continuity of function (Definitions)

- *A real function f is continuous at point $x = c$ lying in its domain if*

$$\lim\limits_{x \to c} f(x) = f(c)$$

  i.e., $\lim\limits_{x \to c} f(x) = \lim\limits_{x \to c^+} f(x) = f(c)$

- *A real function f is said to be a continuous function if it is* **continuous at every point** *lying* **in its domain**.

- *If a real function f has its domain as a closed interval* $[a, b]$,

  then it is continuous at $x = a$ if

  $\lim\limits_{x \to a^+} f(x) = f(a)$ $[\because \lim\limits_{x \to a^-} f(x)$ does not make a sense$]$

  and it is continuous at $x = b$ if

  $\lim\limits_{x \to b^-} f(x) = f(b)$ $[\because \lim\limits_{x \to b^+} f(x)$ does not make a sense$]$

---

3 Continuity of some important functions

From the above mentioned definitions we can easily find the continuity of following functions, and remember them:

3.1 Constant function

Constant function $f(x) = k$ is continuous at every real number.

3.2 Identity function

Identity function $f(x) = x$ is continuous at every real number.

3.3 Polynomial function

Every polynomial function $f(x) = a_0 + a_1 x + a_2 x^2 + \ldots + a_n x^n$ (where n is non-negative integer) is continuous at every real number.

3.4 Modulus function

Modulus function $f(x) = |x|$ is continuous at every real number.

3.5 Sine function

Sine function $f(x) = \sin x$ is continuous at every real number.

3.6 Cosine function

Cosine function $f(x) = \cos x$ is continuous at every real number.

3.7 Tangent function

Tangent function $f(x) = \tan x$ is continuous at every point **in its domain**.

Note: At $x = $ odd multiple of $\dfrac{\pi}{2}$, this function is not defined, and hence odd multiples of $\dfrac{\pi}{2}$ do not lie in its domain.

3.8 Greatest Integer function

Greatest Integer function $f(x) = [x]$ is **discontinuous** at every **integer**.
It is continuous at every non integer.

3.9 Reciprocal function

Reciprocal function $f(x) = \dfrac{1}{x}$, $x \neq 0$ is continuous at every point **in its domain**.
Note: It is discontinuous at point $x = 0$, but it does not lie in its domain.

4   Algebra of Continuous Functions:

If two functions f and g both are continuous at x = c , then their sum, difference, and product are also continuous at x = c.
Their quotient is also continuous provided the quotient does not become zero at x = c.
i.e., if f and g both functions are continuous at x = c , then

(i) $f + g$ is also continuous at $x = c$

(ii) $f - g$ is also continuous at $x = c.$

(iii)$f . g$ is also continuous at $x = c.$

(iv) $\dfrac{f}{g}$ is also continuous at $x = c$ *provided* $g(c) \neq 0$

- We can say that sum, difference, and product of two continuous functions is a continuous function in their **common domain**.
- Quotient of two continuous functions is also continuous in their **common domain except at point(s) where denominator becomes zero**.

<u>**Example**</u>

Check the continuity of the function $f(x) = x^2 - 5 + \sin x$.

Solution:

Here we can express the given function as sum of two functions, one function as $g(x) = x^2 - 5$ and other as $h(x) = \sin x$ such that $f(x) = g(x) + h(x)$.

Now $g(x)$ is a polynomial function, and a polynomial function is continuous at every real number.

Also, $h(x)$ is a sine function, and sine function is also continuous at every real number.

We know that sum of two continuous function is continuous in their common domain.

$\therefore$ $f(x)$ is continuous at every real number.

Hence, $f(x)$ is a continuous function.

<u>**Example**</u>

Check the continuity of the function $f(x) = |x| \cos x$.

Solution:

Here we can express the given function as product of two functions, one function as $g(x) = |x|$ and other as $h(x) = \cos x$ such that $f(x) = g(x) . h(x)$

Now $g(x)$ is a modulus function, and a modulus function is continuous at every real number.

Also, $h(x)$ is a cosine function, and cosine function is also
continuous at every real number.
We know that product of two continuous function is continuous in
their common domain.
$\therefore$ $f(x)$ is continuous at every real number.
Hence, $f(x)$ is a continuous function.

Example

Check the continuity of the function $f(x) = \dfrac{x^2 - 5}{x + 1}$.

Solution:
Here we can express the given function as Quotient of two
functions, one function as $g(x) = x^2 - 5$ and other as $h(x) = x + 1$
such that $f(x) = \dfrac{g(x)}{h(x)}$.

Now $g(x)$ is a polynomial function, and a polynomial function is
continuous at every real number.
And $h(x)$ is also a polynomial function. So, it is also continuous
at every real number.
We know that quotient of two continuous function is continuous in
their common domain except at point(s) where denominator
becomes zero.
$\therefore$ $f(x)$ is continuous at every real number except when $h(x) = 0$
i.e., when $x + 1 = 0$ or we say that except at $x = -1$.
But at $x = -1$, $f(x)$ is not defined. So, $x = -1$ is not in the
domain of $f(x)$
Hence, $f(x)$ is a continuous function.

→ **Remember, the function is said to be continuous function if it
is continuous at every point in its domain.**

5   Continuity of Composite Functions

*If two functions f and g are such that f is continuous at $x = c$, and
g is continuous at $f(c)$, then their composite function (gof) is
continuous at $x = c$ provided gof is defined at $x = c$.*

Example

Check the continuity of the function $f(x) = \cos x^2$.

Solution:
Here we can express the given function as composite function of
two functions, one function as $g(x) = \cos x$ and other as $h(x) = x^2$
such that $goh(x) = g(h(x)) = g(x^2) = \cos x^2 = f(x)$
(*see* 'Composite Function' in the chapter - Relations and Functions)

Now $h(x)$ is a polynomial function, and a polynomial function is
continuous at every real number.

Also, $g(x)$ is a cosine function, and cosine function is also
continuous at every real number.

$\therefore$ g will be continuous at every value of $h(x)$.

Hence we can say that composite function goh is continuous at
every real number.

Since $goh(x) = f(x)$

$\therefore$ $f(x)$ is a continuous function.

Chapter-6   Derivatives

1   Concept of Derivatives and its Explanation:

Let f be a real function of x. We can write it as $y = f(x)$. If there is a change in x, then there will be a change in y. We write change in x as Δx and change in y as Δy.

When the value of x changes from x to $x + \Delta x$, the change in y per unit change in x will be $\dfrac{\Delta y}{\Delta x}$. But it will be over a range of value of x from x to $x + \Delta x$.

Now, if we want to find the rate at which y is changing with respect to x at a particular value of x (say, at $x = a$), then the change (Δx) in the value of x from a should be so small that change occurring in y can be considered just at $x = a$. i.e., we should find $\dfrac{\Delta y}{\Delta x}$ when Δx approaches to 0. We represent this situation as $\lim\limits_{\Delta x \to 0} \dfrac{\Delta y}{\Delta x}$ when $x = a$.

It is called the *derivative* of y with respect to x at $x = a$

- $\left.\dfrac{dy}{dx}\right|_{x=a}$ represents *derivative* of y with respect to x at $x = a$

- In general, *derivative* of y with respect to x, at any value of x, is represented as $\dfrac{dy}{dx}$

$$\therefore \; \frac{dy}{dx} = \lim_{\Delta x \to 0} \frac{\Delta y}{\Delta x}. \qquad \textbf{(wherever this limit exists)}$$

- $\dfrac{dy}{dx}$ represents rate of change of y with respect to x.

If we do not want to write the function $f(x)$ as y, then the whole concept explained above will be as follows:

(Here, for convenience, we can write Δx as h)

Let there is small change in value of x from a to $a + h$, where h approaches to 0.

It will change the value of $f(x)$ from $f(a)$ to $f(a + h)$.

So, change in the function f is $= f(a + h) - f(a)$

and at $x = a$, the change in f per unit change in x is given by

$$\lim_{h \to 0} \frac{f(a+h)-f(a)}{h}$$

This is the derivative of $f(x)$ at $x = a$, and is denoted by $f'(a)$. It means

- $f'(a) = \lim\limits_{h \to 0} \dfrac{f(a+h)-f(a)}{h}$. *(provided this limit exists)*

- In general, *derivative* of $f(x)$ with respect to x, at any value of x, is represented as $f'(x)$, and

$$f'(x) = \lim\limits_{h \to 0} \frac{f(x+h)-f(x)}{h} \quad \textbf{\textit{(wherever this limit exists)}}$$

- This is called *First Principle of Derivatives*.

- <u>Note</u> that we can use Δx instead of h in the above expression, and hence we can also write it as

$$f'(x) = \lim\limits_{\Delta x \to 0} \frac{f(x+\Delta x)-f(x)}{\Delta x} \quad \textbf{(wherever this limit exists)}$$

- $f'(x)$ denotes derivative with respect to x.

- We can write $f'(x)$ as $\dfrac{d}{dx}(f(x))$, and

$$\text{If } y = f(x), \text{ then } f'(x) = \frac{dy}{dx}.$$

- The process of finding derivative of a function is called as *differentiation*.

2 Differentiability

- From the above discussion, we know that a function f is differentiable at $x = a$ if the following limit exists:

$$\lim\limits_{\Delta x \to 0} \frac{f(a+\Delta x)-f(a)}{\Delta x} \quad \dots\dots\dots\dots(i)$$

It means this limit should result in same value whether Δx approaches to 0 from left side or from right side.

<u>**Left Hand Derivative (LHD)**</u>:

When Δx approaches to 0 from left side, the limit in (i) is known as *Left Hand Derivative* of f at $x = a$. We can find it as follows :

Putting $\Delta x = 0 - h$ in the above limit (i) where h is a negligibly small positive real number, we get

$$\textbf{LHD} = \lim\limits_{h \to 0} \frac{f(a-h)-f(a)}{-h}$$

(where h is a negligibly small +ve real number)

<u>**Right Hand Derivative (RHD):**</u>

When Δx approaches to 0 from right side, the limit in (i) is known as *Right Hand Derivative* of f at $x = a$. We can find it as follows:

Putting $\Delta x = 0 + h$ in the limit (i) where h is a negligibly small positive real number, we get

$$\mathbf{RHD} = \lim_{h \to 0} \frac{f(a+h)-f(a)}{h}$$

(where h is a negligibly small +ve real number)

- If **LHD = RHD** at $x = a$, then we say that f is differentiable at $x = a$ or $f'(a)$ exists, and

$$f'(a) = \mathbf{LHD} = \mathbf{RHD}$$

- If **LHD $\neq$ RHD** at $x = a$, then we say that f is not differentiable at $x = a$ or $f'(a)$ does not exist.

<u>**Example**</u>

Given the function $f(x) = |x - 2|$, check its differentiability at $x = 2$.

Solution:

We will first find $f(2)$, $f(2-h)$ & $f(2+h)$, and then LHD & RHD at $x = 2$ where h is a positive real number with $h \to 0$.

$$f(2) = |2-2| = 0$$
$$f(2-h) = |2-h-2|$$
$$= |-h|$$
$$= h \qquad (\because h \text{ is positive})$$
$$f(2+h) = |2+h-2|$$
$$= |h|$$
$$= h \qquad (\because h \text{ is positive})$$

Now,

$$\mathbf{LHD} = \lim_{h \to 0} \frac{f(2-h)-f(2)}{-h} = \lim_{h \to 0} \frac{h-0}{-h} = \lim_{h \to 0} \frac{h}{-h} = -1$$

$$\mathbf{RHD} = \lim_{h \to 0} \frac{f(2+h)-f(2)}{h} = \lim_{h \to 0} \frac{h-0}{h} = \lim_{h \to 0} \frac{h}{h} = 1$$

$$\because \mathbf{LHD} \neq \mathbf{RHD}$$

$$\therefore f(x) \text{ is } \mathbf{not\ differentiable} \text{ at } x = 2$$

<u>**Example**</u>
Given the function $f(x) = x^2$, check its differentiability at $x = 0$.
Solution:
We will first find $f(0)$, $f(0-h)$ & $f(0+h)$, and then
LHD & RHD at $x = 0$ where h is a positive real number with
$h \to 0$.

$$f(0) = 0^2 = 0$$
$$f(0 - h) = (-h)^2 = h^2$$
$$f(0 + h) = (h)^2 = h^2$$

Now,

$$\textbf{LHD} = \lim_{h \to 0} \frac{f(0-h) - f(0)}{-h}$$

$$= \lim_{h \to 0} \frac{h^2 - 0}{-h} = \lim_{h \to 0} \frac{h^2}{-h} = \lim_{h \to 0} (-h) = 0$$

$$\textbf{RHD} = \lim_{h \to 0} \frac{f(2+h) - f(2)}{h}$$

$$= \lim_{h \to 0} \frac{h - 0}{h} = \lim_{h \to 0} \frac{h^2}{h} = \lim_{h \to 0} h = 0$$

$\because$ **LHD** = **RHD**

$\therefore$ $f(x)$ is **differentiable** at $x = 0$

And $f'(0) = 0$ $\qquad$ ($\because$ LHD = RHD = 0 at $x = 0$)

Important:

- *If a function f is differentiable at a point $x = a$, then it is **also** continuous at that point.*
- *If a function f is continuous at a point $x = a$, then it is **not** necessarily differentiable at that point.*

3   Geometrical Meaning of Derivative

- **Geometrically, $\dfrac{dy}{dx}$ (or $f'(x)$) represents slope of tangent to the curve $y = f(x)$ at a point .**

<u>**Explanation**</u>
Consider the graph of a function $y = f(x)$, as shown in the figure
below.

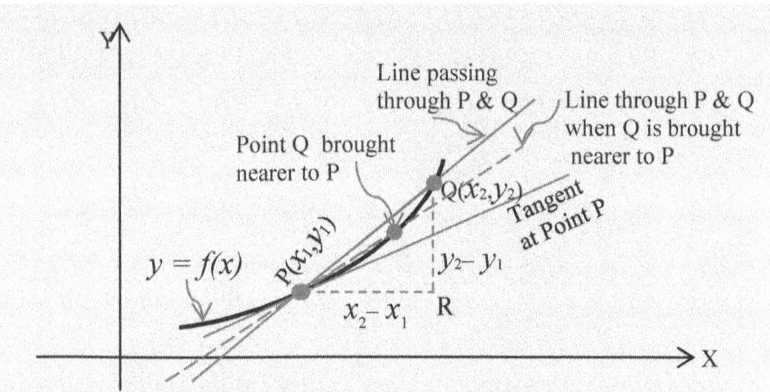

Two points P (x_1, y_1) and Q (x_2, y_2) are marked on the curve.

In the figure PR is parallel to x-axis, and QR is parallel to the y-axis.

From the right triangle PQR, we know that the slope of the line passing through PQ will be given by $tan \angle QPR$.

$\therefore$ Slope of PQ $= tan \angle QPR = \dfrac{QR}{PR} = \dfrac{y_2 - y_1}{x_2 - x_1}$

$\because$ $y_2 - y_1$ is change in y on moving from P to Q, which can be written as Δy,

and $x_2 - x_1$ is change in x on moving from P to Q, which can be written as Δx

$\therefore$ Slope of PQ $= \dfrac{\Delta y}{\Delta x}$

Let us bring point Q nearer to P.
We can easily observe that the line passing through P & Q will finally become tangent to the curve when Q coincides with P. And this is the case when $\Delta x \to 0$.

$\therefore$ Slope of tangent at point P is $= \displaystyle\lim_{\Delta x \to 0} \dfrac{\Delta y}{\Delta x}$

We know that it is the derivative of y with respect to x at point P

i.e., $\displaystyle\lim_{\Delta x \to 0} \dfrac{\Delta y}{\Delta x} = \dfrac{dy}{dx}$ or $f'(x)$

So, we conclude that

Geometrically, $\dfrac{dy}{dx}$ (or $f'(x)$) represents slope of tangent to the curve $y = f(x)$ at a point .

4 Differentiability of some important functions

From the above-mentioned conditions of differentiability (i.e., LHD=RHD), we can easily check the differentiability of some functions as follows:

4.1 Constant function

Constant function $f(x) = k$ is differentiable at every real number.

4.2 Identity function

Identity function $f(x) = x$ is differentiable at every real number.

4.3 Polynomial function

Every polynomial function $f(x) = a_0 + a_1 x + a_2 x^2 + \ldots + a_n x^n$

(where n is non-negative integer) is differentiable at every real number.

4.4 Modulus function

Modulus function $f(x) = |x|$ is **not differentiable at $x = 0$** but differentiable at every other real number.

4.5 Sine function

Sine function $f(x) = \sin x$ is differentiable at every real number.

4.6 Cosine function

Cosine function $f(x) = \cos x$ is differentiable at every real number.

4.7 Tangent function

Tangent function $f(x) = \tan x$ is differentiable at every point **in its domain.**

Note: At $x =$ odd multiple of $\dfrac{\pi}{2}$ this function is not differentiable, but odd multiples of $\dfrac{\pi}{2}$ do not lie in its domain.

4.8 Greatest Integer function

Greatest Integer function $f(x) = [x]$ is **not differentiable at any integer**.

- It is differentiable at every non integer.

4.9 Reciprocal function

Reciprocal function $f(x) = \dfrac{1}{x}$, $x \neq 0$ is differentiable at every point **in its domain**.

Note: It is not differentiable at point $x = 0$, but it does not lie in its domain.

Derivatives of some important functions are listed on next page, which can easily be obtained by using *first principle of derivative* and *concepts of limits.*

---

5 Derivatives of some important functions

5.1 Formulae

1) $\dfrac{d}{dx}\left(x^n\right) = n\,x^{n-1}$

$\longrightarrow \dfrac{d}{dx}\left(x\right) = 1$

$\longrightarrow \dfrac{d}{dx}(k) = 0$

$\longrightarrow \dfrac{d}{dx}\left(\dfrac{1}{x}\right) = -\dfrac{1}{x^2}$

2) $\dfrac{d}{dx}(\sin x) = \cos x$

3) $\dfrac{d}{dx}(\cos x) = -\sin x$

4) $\dfrac{d}{dx}(\tan\ x) = \sec^2 x$

5) $\dfrac{d}{dx}(\cot x) = -\operatorname{cosec}^2 x$

6) $\dfrac{d}{dx}(\sec x) = \sec x.\tan x$

7) $\dfrac{d}{dx}(\operatorname{cosec} x) = -\operatorname{cosec} x \cot x$

8) $\dfrac{d}{dx}\left(e^x\right) = e^x$

9) $\dfrac{d}{dx}\left(a^x\right) = a^x \log a$

10) $\dfrac{d}{dx}\left(\log x\right) = \dfrac{1}{x}$

11) $\dfrac{d}{dx}\left(\log_a x\right) = \dfrac{1}{x \log a}$

12) $\dfrac{d}{dx}\left(\sin^{-1}x\right) = \dfrac{1}{\sqrt{1-x^2}}$

13) $\dfrac{d}{dx}\left(\cos^{-1} x\right) = \dfrac{-1}{\sqrt{1-x^2}}$

14) $\dfrac{d}{dx}\left(\tan^{-1}x\right) = \dfrac{1}{1+x^2}$

15) $\dfrac{d}{dx}\left(\cot^{-1}x\right) = \dfrac{-1}{1+x^2}$

16) $\dfrac{d}{dx}\left(\sec^{-1}x\right) = \dfrac{1}{x\sqrt{x^2-1}}$

17) $\dfrac{d}{dx}\left(\operatorname{cosec}^{-1}x\right) = \dfrac{-1}{x\sqrt{x^2-1}}$

6 Algebra of Derivatives:

- If the derivatives of two functions $u = f(x)$ and $v = g(x)$ exist in their common domain, then derivatives of their sum and difference also exist in their common domains and are respectively equal to sum and difference of their derivatives.

- But the derivatives of their product and quotient are not the product and quotient of their derivatives.

  The rules to find derivatives of sum, difference, product, and quotient of 2 functions are as follows:

6.1 Sum or Difference Rule :

(i) $\quad \dfrac{d}{dx}[f(x) + g(x)] = \dfrac{d}{dx}f(x) + \dfrac{d}{dx}g(x)$

OR $\quad \dfrac{d}{dx}[u + v] = \dfrac{d}{dx}(u) + \dfrac{d}{dx}(v)$

(ii) $\quad \dfrac{d}{dx}[f(x) - g(x)] = \dfrac{d}{dx}f(x) - \dfrac{d}{dx}g(x)$

OR $\quad \dfrac{d}{dx}[u - v] = \dfrac{d}{dx}(u) - \dfrac{d}{dx}(v)$

<u>Example</u>

Find the derivative of $x^2 - \sin x$.

Solution:

Let $f(x) = x^2 - \sin x$

Differentiating both sides with respect to x

$$\dfrac{d}{dx}(f(x)) = \dfrac{d}{dx}(x^2 - \sin x)$$

$$f'(x) = \dfrac{d}{dx}(x^2) - \dfrac{d}{dx}(\sin x)$$

$$f'(x) = 2x - \cos x$$

(*see* 'Formulae' in 'Derivatives of some important functions'
in this chapter to find derivatives)

6.2 Product Rule :

$$\dfrac{d}{dx}[f(x).g(x)] = f(x)\dfrac{d}{dx}(g(x)) + g(x)\dfrac{d}{dx}(f(x))$$

OR

$$\dfrac{d}{dx}[u.v] = u\dfrac{d}{dx}(v) + v\dfrac{d}{dx}(u)$$

<u>Example</u>

Find the derivative of $x^2.\sin x$.

Solution:

Let $f(x) = x^2.\sin x$

Differentiating both sides with respect to x

$$\dfrac{d}{dx}(f(x)) = \dfrac{d}{dx}(x^2.\sin x)$$

$$f'(x) = x^2.\dfrac{d}{dx}(\sin x) + \sin x.\dfrac{d}{dx}(x^2)$$

$$f'(x) = x^2 \cos x + 2x \sin x$$

(*see* 'Formulae' in 'Derivatives of some important functions'
in this chapter to find derivatives)

---

*Asterisk (*) marked article (if any) is **not** in CBSE 2025-26 syllabus.*

6.3 Quotient Rule :

$$\frac{d}{dx}\left[\frac{f(x)}{g(x)}\right] = \frac{g(x)\frac{d}{dx}f(x) - f(x)\frac{d}{dx}g(x)}{[g(x)]^2}$$

OR

$$\frac{d}{dx}\left[\frac{u}{v}\right] = \frac{v\frac{d}{dx}(u) - u\frac{d}{dx}(v)}{v^2}$$

Example

Find the derivative of $\dfrac{x^2}{\sin x}$.

Solution:

Let $f(x) = \dfrac{x^2}{\sin x}$

Differentiating both sides with respect to x

$$\frac{d}{dx}(f(x)) = \frac{d}{dx}\left(\frac{x^2}{\sin x}\right)$$

$$f'(x) = \frac{\sin x.\frac{d}{dx}(x^2) - x^2\frac{d}{dx}(\sin x)}{\sin^2 x}$$

$$\Rightarrow f'(x) = \frac{\sin x.\,2x - x^2\cos x}{\sin^2 x}$$

(*see* 'Formulae' in 'Derivatives of some important functions'
in this chapter to find derivatives)

$$\Rightarrow f'(x) = \frac{2x\sin x - x^2\cos x}{\sin^2 x}$$

7 Derivative of Composite Functions (Chain Rule)

If a function f in x is a composite function of two or more
functions, then the derivative of f with respect to x is found by
chain rule as follows:

Suppose $f(x) = u \circ v \circ w\,(x)$

It means f is a composite function of the functions u, v and w such
that u is a function in v, v is a function in w and w is a function in x.

i.e., $u =$ in terms of v, $\quad v =$ in terms of w, $\quad w =$ in terms of x

we find $\quad\dfrac{du}{dv} = ?\qquad \dfrac{dv}{dw} = ?\qquad \dfrac{dw}{dx} = ?$

and then the derivative of $f(x)$ with respect to x is found by

$$f'(x) = \frac{du}{dv} \cdot \frac{dv}{dw} \cdot \frac{dw}{dx}$$

This chain can be extended to find the derivative of a composite function of any number of functions.

Example

Let $f(x) = \sqrt{\sin x^2}$

Here f is a composite function of the following functions:

$$u(v) = \sqrt{v}, \qquad v(w) = \sin w, \qquad w(x) = x^2$$

we can see that
$$u \circ v \circ w(x) = (u \circ v)(w(x)) = (u \circ v)(x^2)$$
$$= u(v(x^2)) = u(\sin x^2)$$
$$= \sqrt{\sin x^2}$$
$$= f(x)$$

Now $\dfrac{du}{dv} = \dfrac{1}{2\sqrt{v}}$, $\qquad \dfrac{dv}{dw} = \cos w$, and $\qquad \dfrac{dw}{dx} = 2x$

(*see* 'Formulae' in 'Derivatives of some important functions' in this chapter to find derivatives)

$$\therefore \ f'(x) = \frac{du}{dv} \cdot \frac{dv}{dw} \cdot \frac{dw}{dx}$$

$$= \frac{1}{2\sqrt{v}} \cdot \cos w \cdot 2x$$

$$= \frac{1}{2\sqrt{\sin x^2}} \cdot \cos x^2 \cdot 2x = \frac{x \cos x^2}{\sqrt{\sin x^2}}$$

→ **Alternatively, we can find its derivative as follows:**

$$f(x) = \sqrt{\sin x^2}$$

Differentiating both sides w.r.t. x

$$f'(x) = \frac{d}{dx}\left(\sqrt{\sin x^2}\right) = \frac{d}{dx}\left(\sin x^2\right)^{\frac{1}{2}}$$

We will apply the formula $\dfrac{d}{dx}(x^n) = n x^{n-1}$ in $\dfrac{d}{dx}(\sin x^2)^{\frac{1}{2}}$ and then multiply it with derivative of inner function $\sin x^2$.

$$\Rightarrow \quad f'(x) = \frac{1}{2(\sin x^2)^{\frac{1}{2}}} \ \frac{d}{dx}(\sin x^2)$$

Now apply the formula $\dfrac{d}{dx}(\sin x) = \cos x$ in $\dfrac{d}{dx}(\sin x^2)$, and then multiply it with derivative of inner function x^2.

$$\Rightarrow \quad f'(x) = \frac{1}{2\sqrt{\sin x^2}} \, \cos x^2 \, \frac{d}{dx}\left(x^2\right)$$

Again applying the formula $\frac{d}{dx}(x^n) = n\,x^{n-1}$ in $\frac{d}{dx}(x^2)$, we get

$$\Rightarrow \quad f'(x) = \frac{1}{2\sqrt{\sin x^2}} \, \cos x^2 \,.\, 2\,x$$

$$\Rightarrow \quad f'(x) = \frac{x\cos x^2}{\sqrt{\sin x^2}}$$

8   Derivative of implicit function

Implicit function is the function in which a variable y depends on other variable x, but this function is not written as $y = f(x)$ (i.e., **y is not expressed in terms of x**). Instead, an equation is written in x & y.

For example, $x - y = \pi$ is written as **implicit function** while the same function can be written as:

$$y = x - \pi \quad \text{which is } \textbf{explicit function}$$

- *To find $\dfrac{dy}{dx}$ from an implicit function of x & y, we simply differentiate both sides of it directly with respect to x.*

- **Remember :**
  After differentiating the term containing y, with respect to x, the term will have $\dfrac{dy}{dx}$ in the multiplication according to chain rule.

Example

To find $\dfrac{dy}{dx}$ in the implicit function $ax + by^2 = \cos y$, we differentiate both side with respect to x as follows:

$$\frac{d}{dx}(ax + by^2) = \frac{d}{dx}(\cos y)$$

$$\Rightarrow \quad \frac{d}{dx}(ax) + \frac{d}{dx}(by^2) = -\sin y\,\frac{dy}{dx}$$

(Using chain rule a term containing y, after differentiating w.r.t x, contains $\dfrac{dy}{dx}$)

$$\Rightarrow \quad a + 2by\,\frac{dy}{dx} = -\sin y\,\frac{dy}{dx}$$

$$\Rightarrow \qquad 2by\,\frac{dy}{dx} + \sin y\,\frac{dy}{dx} = -a$$

$$\Rightarrow \qquad (2by + \sin y)\,\frac{dy}{dx} = -a$$

$$\Rightarrow \qquad \frac{dy}{dx} = \frac{-a}{2by + \sin y}$$

9 Exponential Function

The exponential function $y = f(x)$ *is defined as a function* $f : \mathbf{R} \to \mathbf{R}$ *such that* $y = b^x$ *for base* $b > 0$ *, where* $\mathbf{R}$ *represents set of real numbers.*

- The value of x can be any real number (i.e., domain of exponential function is set of real number $\mathbf{R}$).
- The value of y can be only positive real number (i.e., range of exponential function is set of positive real number $\mathbf{R}^{+}$).
- *If the base of exponential is Euler's number e, then the exponential function is known as* **natural exponential function**.

  i.e., e^x is natural exponential function of x.
- *If the base of exponential is* $10,$ *then the exponential function is known as* **common exponential function**.

  i.e., 10^x is common exponential function of x.

9.1 Derivative of Exponential function

- $\dfrac{d}{dx}(a^x) = a^x \log_e a \qquad$ for any base $a > 0$

- $\dfrac{d}{dx}(e^x) = e^x \qquad\qquad$ natural exponential

These derivatives can be obtained easily by differentiating using first principle.

10 Logarithmic Function

The logarithmic function $y = f(x)$ *is defined as a function* $f : \mathbf{R}^{+} \to \mathbf{R}$ *such that* $y = \log_b x$ *if* $b^y = x$ *for* $b > 0$ *but* $b \neq 1$ *, where* $\mathbf{R}^{+}$ *represents set of positive real numbers, and* $\mathbf{R}$ *represents set of all real numbers .*

- $\log_b x$ is read as logarithm of x to the base b.
- $y = \log_b x$ is defined only for base $b > 0$ but $b \neq 1$.
- $y = \log_b x$ is defined only for $x > 0$ (i.e., for **positive** x).

  (Domain is set of positive real number $\mathbf{R}^{+}$).

- The value of y can be any real number (i.e., range of logarithmic function is set of real number **R**).
- *If the base of logarithm is Euler's number e, then the logarithmic function is known as* **natural logarithm**.

  i.e., $\log_e x$ is natural logarithm of x.

  Natural logarithm of x is usually, written as $\ln x$.
- *If the base of logarithm is* 10, *then the logarithmic function is known as* **common logarithm**.

  i.e., $\log_{10} x$ is common logarithm of x.

10.1 Properties of Logarithmic Function

- By definition: $\quad y = \log_b x \;\Rightarrow\; b^y = x$

  (i) Change of base : $\quad \log_b c = \dfrac{\log_a c}{\log_a b}$

  (ii) Logarithm of product : $\log_b mn = \log_b m + \log_b n$

  (iii) Logarithm of quotient : $\log_b \left(\dfrac{m}{n}\right) = \log_b m - \log_b n$

  (iv) Logarithm of exponent : $\log_b m^n = n \log_b m$

  (v) Logarithm of 1 : $\quad \log_b 1 = 0$

  (vi) Logarithm of b to the base b: $\log_b b = 1$

10.2 Derivative of Logarithmic function

- $\dfrac{d}{dx}\left(\log_a x\right) = \dfrac{1}{x \log_e a}\quad$ for any base $a > 0$ and $a \neq 1$

- $\dfrac{d}{dx}\left(\log_e x\right) = \dfrac{1}{x}\quad$ natural logarithm

These derivatives can be obtained easily by differentiating using first principle.

11 Logarithmic differentiation

Logarithmic differentiation is used to differentiate the following types of functions:

(i) $f(x) = [u(x)]^{v(x)}$ $\quad$ *(provided $f(x)$ and $u(x)$ are positive)*

  i.e., the functions having variable base raised to variable power.

(ii) $f(x) = \left[\dfrac{u_1(x).\, u_2(x).\,....\,.u_n(x)}{v_1(x).\, v_2(x).\,....\,.v_n(x)}\right]^n$

(provided every function present here is positive)

i.e., the function having several functions in multiplication and division.

- To differentiate these functions, we take natural *log* on both sides, and then apply the properties of logarithms before differentiating.

<u>Example</u>

Find $\dfrac{dy}{dx}$ *, if* $y = [sin\,(\log x)]^{cos\,x}$

Solution:

$y = [sin\,(\log x)]^{cos\,x}$

Taking log on both sides, we get

$\log y = \log\,[sin\,(\log x)]^{cos\,x}$

$\Rightarrow \log y = cos\,x\,\log\,[sin\,(\log x)]$

$$\dots\dots\,[\text{ using property: } \log_b m^n = n\,\log_b m\,]$$

Differentiating both sides with respect to x,

$\dfrac{d}{dx}(\log y) = \dfrac{d}{dx}\Big(cos\,x\,\log\,[sin\,(\log x)]\,\Big)$

$\Rightarrow \dfrac{1}{y}\dfrac{dy}{dx} = cos\,x\,\dfrac{d}{dx}\Big(\log\,[sin\,(\log x)]\Big) + \log\,[sin\,(\log x)]\,\dfrac{d}{dx}\Big(cos\,x\Big)$

$$\dots\dots\dots[\text{Using product rule of differentiation}]$$

$= cos\,x\,.\,\dfrac{1}{sin\,(\log x)}\,.[cos(\,\log x\,)].\dfrac{1}{x} + \log\,[sin(\log x)](-\,sin\,x)$

$$\dots\dots[\text{Using chain rule of differentiation}]$$

$\Rightarrow \dfrac{dy}{dx} = y\,.\left\{\dfrac{cos\,x\,.[cos\,(log\,x\,)]}{x\,.\,[sin\,(log\,x)]} - sin\,x\,.\,\log\,[sin(\log x)]\right\}$

$= [sin\,(\log x)]^{cos\,x}\,.\left\{\dfrac{cos\,x\,.\,cot\,(log\,x\,)}{x} - \right.$

$\left. sin\,x\,.\,\log\,[sin(\log x)]\right\}$

<u>Example</u>

Find $\dfrac{dy}{dx}$ *, if* $y = \sqrt{\dfrac{(x-3)\,(x^2+4)}{(\,3x^2+4x+5\,)}}$

Solution:

We can write, $\qquad y = \left[\dfrac{(x-3)\,(x^2+4)}{(3x^2+4x+5)}\right]^{\frac{1}{2}}$

Taking log on both sides, we get

$$\log y = \frac{1}{2}\log\left[\dfrac{(x-3)\,(x^2+4)}{(3x^2+4x+5)}\right]$$

$$\ldots\ldots\ [\text{using property: } log_b\, m^n = n\, log_b\, m\,]$$

$$\Rightarrow \log y = \frac{1}{2}\left\{\log\left[(x-3)\,(x^2+4)\right] - \log\left[(3x^2+4x+5)\right]\right\}$$

$$\ldots\ldots\ldots\left[\text{using property: } log_b\left(\dfrac{m}{n}\right) = log_b\, m - log_b\, n\,\right]$$

$$\Rightarrow \log y = \frac{1}{2}\log\left[(x-3)\,(x^2+4)\right] - \frac{1}{2}\log\left[(3x^2+4x+5)\right]$$

$$\Rightarrow \log y = \frac{1}{2}\log(x-3) + \frac{1}{2}\log(x^2+4)\,\frac{1}{2}\log(3x^2+4x+5)$$

$$\ldots\ldots\ldots\left[\text{using property: } log_b\, mn = log_b\, m + log_b\, n\,\right]$$

Differentiating both sides with respect to x :

$$\frac{d}{dx}(\log y) = \frac{d}{dx}\left[\frac{1}{2}\log(x-3)\right] + \frac{d}{dx}\left[\frac{1}{2}\log(x^2+4)\right]$$

$$- \frac{d}{dx}\left[\frac{1}{2}\log(3x^2+4x+5)\right]$$

$$\Rightarrow \frac{1}{y}\frac{dy}{dx} = \frac{1}{2(x-3)}\,(1-0) + \frac{1}{2(x^2+4)}\,(2x+0)$$

$$- \frac{1}{2(3x^2+4x+5)}\,(6x+4)$$

$$\ldots\ldots\ldots[\text{Using chain rule of differentiation}]$$

$$\Rightarrow \frac{dy}{dx} = y\cdot\left[\frac{1}{2(x-3)} + \frac{2x}{2(x^2+4)} - \frac{2(3x+2)}{2(3x^2+4x+5)}\right]$$

$$\Rightarrow \frac{dy}{dx} = \sqrt{\dfrac{(x-3)\,(x^2+4)}{(3x^2+4x+5)}}\cdot\left[\frac{1}{2(x-3)} + \frac{x}{(x^2+4)} - \frac{(3x+2)}{(3x^2+4x+5)}\right]$$

12 Derivatives of Functions in Parametric Forms

*When a relationship between 2 variables **x and y** of a function is established by expressing both variables **in terms of third variable**, then the function is said to be in parametric form. **The third variable is called as parameter**.*

- Parameter can be any variable like t, θ, ϕ etc.

  i.e. x and y expressed in the form $x = f(t)$ and $y = g(t)$ is parametric form and t is parameter.

12.1 Procedure to differentiate parametric function

To find $\dfrac{dy}{dx}$ from the parametric from $x = f(t)$ and $y = g(t)$, we proceed as follows:

Step-1 Differentiate both relations with respect to third variable.

$$x = f(t) \qquad \text{and} \qquad y = g(t)$$

$$\Rightarrow \qquad \frac{dx}{dt} = f'(t) \qquad \text{and} \qquad \frac{dy}{dt} = g'(t)$$

Step-2

$$\frac{dy}{dx} = \frac{\dfrac{dy}{dt}}{\dfrac{dx}{dt}} = \frac{g'(t)}{f'(t)} \qquad (\,provided\ f'(t) \neq 0\,)$$

<u>**Example**</u>

If $\quad x = sin\ t, \qquad y = cos\ 2t$

Here both x and y are expressed in terms of t

$\therefore t$ is parameter.

Differentiating both equations with respect to t :

$$\frac{dx}{dt} = cos\ t \quad \text{and} \quad \frac{dy}{dt} = -2sin\ 2t$$

$$\frac{dy}{dx} = \frac{\dfrac{dy}{dt}}{\dfrac{dx}{dt}} = \frac{-2sin\ 2t}{cos\ t}$$

$$= \frac{-4\ sin\ t\,.\,cos\ t}{cos\ t} \qquad \dots[\text{using: } sin2t = 2sint\,.\,cost\,]$$

$$= -4\ sin\ t$$

13 Second Order Derivative

Till now we have found derivative of y w.r.t. x as $\dfrac{dy}{dx}$. It is called *first order derivative* of y w.r.t. x.

('*with respect to*' in short is written as w.r.t.)

If $\dfrac{dy}{dx}$ is differentiable, then we can further differentiate $\dfrac{dy}{dx}$ w.r.t. x, and write it as $\dfrac{d^2y}{dx^2}$. It is called *second order derivative* of y w.r.t. x.

- $\dfrac{dy}{dx}$ is called as *first order derivative* of y w.r.t. x.

→ It is also written as y' or y_1

→ First order derivative of $f(x)$ is denoted by $f'(x)$

- $\dfrac{d^2y}{dx^2}$ is called as *second order derivative* of y w.r.t. x.

→ It is also written as y'' or y_2. It can also be written as D^2y.

→ Second order derivative of $f(x)$ is denoted by $f''(x)$.

13.1 Procedure to find second order derivative

To find second order derivative of $y = f(x)$ we proceed as follows:

Step-1 Differentiating both sides with respect to x, we get

$$\frac{d}{dx}(y) = f'(x)$$

$$\Rightarrow \quad \frac{dy}{dx} = f'(x)$$

Step-2 Again differentiating both sides with respect to x, we get

$$\frac{d}{dx}\left(\frac{dy}{dx}\right) = f''(x)$$

$$\Rightarrow \quad \frac{d^2y}{dx^2} = f''(x)$$

<u>Example</u>

If $\quad y = x^3 + e^x + \cos x$

Differentiating both sides with respect to x, we get

$$\frac{d}{dx}(y) = \frac{d}{dx}(x^3 + e^x + \cos x)$$

$$\Rightarrow \quad \frac{dy}{dx} = \frac{d}{dx}(x^3) + \frac{d}{dx}(e^x) + \frac{d}{dx}(\cos x)$$

$$\Rightarrow \quad \frac{dy}{dx} = 3x^2 + e^x - \sin x$$

Again differentiating both sides with respect to x, we get

$$\frac{d}{dx}\left(\frac{dy}{dx}\right) = \frac{d}{dx}(3x^2 + e^x - \sin x)$$

$$\Rightarrow \quad \frac{d^2y}{dx^2} = 6x + e^x - \cos x$$

14 *Rolle's Theorem

If a real function $f(x)$ is **continuous** *in the closed interval* $[a, b]$ *and* **differentiable** *in the open interval* (a, b) *such that* $f(a) = f(b)$

---

where a and b are real numbers, **then there exists** $c \in (a, b)$ **such that** $f'(c) = 0$.

14.1 *Procedure to verify Rolle's Theorem

Given: Function $f(x) = \ldots$ (in term of x) in the interval $[a, b]$.

Step-1 Checking the continuity of $f(x)$ in the interval $[a, b]$

→ If the given function is a polynomial, sine, cosine etc., we can directly say that $f(x)$ is continuous in the interval $[a, b]$ because these functions are always continuous at every real number, and proceed for step-2.

→ For other functions, we have to check whether there is any point of discontinuity in the interval $[a, b]$ or not.

→ If there is any point of discontinuity in the interval $[a, b]$, then we say that Rolle's theorem is not applicable.

→ If there is no point of discontinuity in the interval $[a, b]$, then we say that $f(x)$ is continuous in the interval $[a, b]$, and proceed for the step 2.

Step-2 Checking the differentiability of $f(x)$ in the interval (a, b)

Find $f'(x) = \ldots$ $------$eqn.(i)

→ If there exists any point in the interval (a,b) where $f'(x)$ is not defined, then we say that Rolle's theorem is not applicable.

→ If $f'(x)$ is defined at every point in the interval (a, b), then we say that $f(x)$ is differentiable in the interval (a,b) , and proceed for the step 3.

Step-3 Checking $f(a) = f(b)$

Find $f(a) = \ldots$ and $f(b) = \ldots$

→ If $f(a) \neq f(b)$, then we say that Rolle's theorem is not applicable.

→ If $f(a) = f(b)$, then we proceed for the step 4.

Step-4 Checking existence of $c \in (a, b)$ at which $f'(c) = 0$

Let for $x = c$, $f'(c) = 0$

→ Put $x = c$ in equation (i), and equate it with 0 to get the equation in terms of c

→ from this equation find the value(s) of $c = \ldots$

→ There will be at least one value of $c = \ldots$ such that $c \in (a, b)$.

We will say that Rolle 's Theorem is verified.

<u>**Example**</u>

Verify Rolle's theorem for the function $f(x) = x^2 + 2x - 8$ *in the interval* $[-4, 2]$

Step 1: Checking the continuity of in the interval $[-4, 2]$

$\because f(x)$ is a polynomial function,

$\therefore f(x)$ is continuous in the interval $[-4, 2]$

(polynomial functions are always continuous at every real number.)

Step 2: Checking the differentiability in the interval $(-4, 2)$

Now $f(x) = x^2 + 2x - 8$

Differentiating with respect to x

$$f'(x) = 2x + 2 \qquad ------ (i)$$

$\because f'(x)$ is defined at every point in the interval $(-4, 2)$

$\therefore f(x)$ is differentiable in the interval $(-4, 2)$.

Step 3: Checking $f(-4) = f(2)$

$$f(-4) = (-4)^2 + 2(-4) - 8 = 0$$

and $\quad f(2) = (2)^2 + 2(2) - 8 = 0$

$\Rightarrow \quad f(-4) = f(2)$

Step 4: Checking existence of $c \in (-4, 2)$ at which $f'(c) = 0$

Let for $x = c$, $f'(c) = 0$

Putting $x = c$ in equation (i), we get

$f'(c) = 2c + 2$

equate it with 0

$\therefore 2c + 2 = 0$

$\Rightarrow c = -1$

$\because c = -1 \in (-4, 2)$

$\therefore$ Rolle's theorem is verified.

<u>**Example**</u>

Check the applicability of Rolle's theorem for the function

$f(x) = x^{1/3}$ *in the interval* $[-4, 2]$.

Step 1: Checking the continuity of $f(x)$

Let $a \in [-4, 2]$

$$\lim_{x \to a} f(x) = \lim_{x \to a} x^{1/3} = a^{1/3}$$

Also, $f(a) = a^{1/3}$

$\because \lim_{x \to a} f(x) = f(a)$

$\therefore f(x)$ is continuous at all $a \in [-4, 2]$.

Step 2: Checking the differentiability of $f(x)$

Now $f(x) = x^{1/3}$

Differentiating with respect to x

$$f'(x) = \frac{1}{3\,x^{2/3}} \qquad ------(i)$$

$\because f'(x)$ is not defined at $0 \in [-4, 2]$

$\therefore f(x)$ is not differentiable in $[-4, 2]$

Hence, Rolle's theorem is not applicable for this function.

14.2 *Geometrical interpretation of Rolle's Theorem

Geometrically, according to Rolle's theorem if a function $f(x)$ is continuous in the closed interval $[a, b]$ and differentiable in the open interval (a, b) such that the values of the function at $x = a$ and $x = b$ are equal i.e., $f(a) = f(b)$, then **there exists at least one point $x = c \in (a, b)$ at which the tangent to the graph of $y = f(x)$ is parallel to x – axis (i.e., slope of tangent at it is 0)**. (see the figure below)

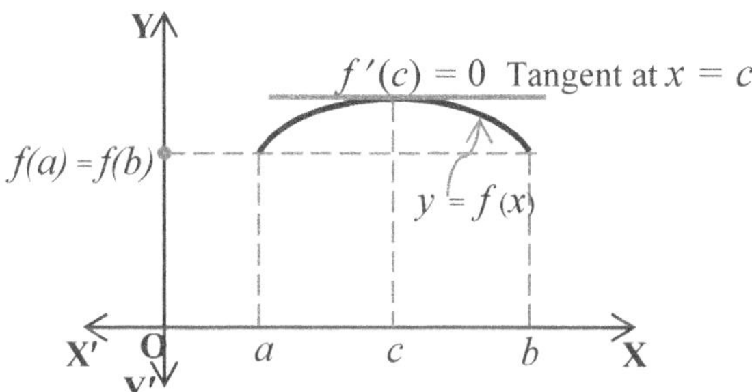

15 *Mean Value Theorem

*If a real function $f(x)$ is **continuous** in the closed interval $[a, b]$ and **differentiable** in the open interval (a, b) where a and b are real numbers*, then **there exists $c \in (a, b)$ such that**

$$f'(c) = \frac{f(b) - f(a)}{b - a}.$$

15.1 *Procedure to verify Mean Value Theorem

Given: Function $f(x) = \ldots.$ (in term of x) in the interval $[a, b]$.

(i) **Checking the continuity of $f(x)$ in the interval $[a, b]$**

→ If the given function is a polynomial, sine, cosine etc., we can directly say that $f(x)$ is continuous in the interval $[a, b]$ because these functions are always continuous at every real number, and proceed for step-2.

→ For other functions, we have to check whether there is any point of discontinuity in the interval $[a, b]$ or not.

→ If there is any point of discontinuity in the interval $[a, b]$, then we say that Mean Value theorem is not applicable.

→ If there is no point of discontinuity in the interval $[a, b]$, then we say that $f(x)$ is continuous in the interval $[a, b]$, and proceed for the step 2.

(ii) **Checking differentiability of $f(x)$ in the interval (a, b)**

   Find $f'(x) = \ldots\ldots$ $------$ eqn.(i)

→ If there exists any point in the interval (a,b) where $f'(x)$ is not defined, then we say that Mean Value theorem is not applicable.

→ If $f'(x)$ is defined at every point in the interval (a, b), then we say that $f(x)$ is differentiable in in the interval (a, b), and proceed for the step 3.

(iii) **Checking existence of $c \in (a, b)$ at which**

$$f'(c) = \frac{f(b) - f(a)}{b - a}$$

   Find $f(a) = \ldots..$ and $f(b) = \ldots..$

   Let for $x = c$, $f'(c) = \dfrac{f(b) - f(a)}{b - a}$

→ Put $x = c$ in equation (i) to get $f'(c)$, and equate it with $\dfrac{f(b) - f(a)}{b - a}$ to get the equation in terms of c

→ from this equation find the value(s) of $c = \ldots\ldots$

→ There will be at least one value of $c = \ldots$ such that $c \in (a, b)$

We say that Mean Value Theorem is verified.

<u>**Example**</u>

Verify Mean Value theorem for the function $f(x) = x^3 - 5x^2 - 3x$ in the interval $[1, 3]$.

Step 1: Checking the continuity in the interval $[1,3]$

   $\because f(x)$ is a polynomial function,

   $\therefore f(x)$ is continuous in the interval $[1,3]$

(polynomial functions are always continuous at every real number.)

Step 2: Checking the differentiability in the interval $(1,3)$

   Now $f(x) = x^3 - 5x^2 - 3x$

   Differentiating with respect to x

$$f'(x) = 3x^2 - 10x - 3 \quad ------ (i)$$

$\because f'(x)$ is defined at every point in the interval $(1, 3)$

$\therefore f(x)$ is differentiable in in the interval $(1, 3)$.

Step 3: Checking existence of $c \in (1,3)$ at which

$$f'(c) = \frac{f(3) - f(1)}{3 - 1}$$

Now $f(1) = 1^3 - 5(1)^2 - 3(1) = -7$

and $f(3) = 3^3 - 5(3)^2 - 3(3) = -27$

Putting $x = c$ in equation (i), we get

$$f'(c) = 3c^2 - 10c - 3$$

equate it with $\dfrac{f(3) - f(1)}{3 - 1}$

$$\therefore\ 3c^2 - 10c - 3 = \frac{-27 - (-7)}{3 - 1}$$

$$\Rightarrow 3c^2 - 10c - 3 = -10$$

$$\Rightarrow 3c^2 - 10c + 7 = 0$$

$$\Rightarrow (c - 1)(3c - 7) = 0$$

$$\Rightarrow c = 1 \text{ or } c = \frac{7}{3}$$

$$\because\ c = \frac{7}{3} \in (1, 3)$$

$\therefore$ Mean Value theorem is verified.

15.2 *Geometrical interpretation of Mean Value Theorem

Geometrically, according to Mean Value theorem if a function f(x) is continuous in the closed interval $[a, b]$ and differentiable in the open interval (a, b), then **there exists at least one point $x = c \in (a, b)$ at which the tangent to the graph of $y = f(x)$ is parallel to the chord joining the points at $x = a$ and $x = b$ (i.e., chord joining the points $(a, f(a))$ and $(b, f(b))$.**

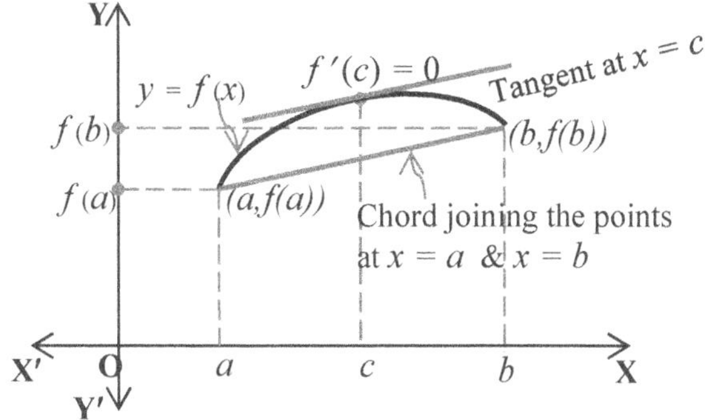

Chapter-7 Applications of Derivatives

1 Rate of change of Quantities

From the concept of derivatives as explained in the chapter 'Derivatives' we know that

- $\dfrac{dy}{dx}\Big|_{x=a}$ *represents change in y per unit change in x at x = a.*

  i.e., it represents rate of change of y with respect to x at x = a.

For a relation between x and y , we can find
(i) rate of change of y with respect to x, and
(ii) rate of change of y with respect to some third variable t.

(i) **Finding rate of change of y with respect to x at $x = a$:**

Step-1: Write the relationship between y and x under the given situation

Step-2: Differentiate the relation with respect to x to find $\dfrac{dy}{dx}$.

Step-3: Put $x = a$ in $\dfrac{dy}{dx}$ to find $\dfrac{dy}{dx}\Big|_{x=a}$

Example

A balloon, which always remains spherical has a variable radius. Find the rate at which its volume is increasing with the radius when the radius is 10 cm.

Solution:

Here, we consider two variables, r and V respectively for radius and volume of the balloon, and note down the given data and also, the quantity to find.

Let radius of balloon $= r$ and   Volume $=$ V

Given: - - -

To find: $\dfrac{dV}{dr}\Big|_{r=10} = ?$

Step-1: The relationship between V and r is
$$V = \frac{4}{3}\,\pi\,r^3$$

Step-2: Differentiating this relation with respect to r , we get
$$\frac{dV}{dr} = \frac{4}{3}\,\pi \times 3\,r^2 = 4\,\pi\,r^2$$

Step-3: Now putting $r = 10$, we get

$$\frac{dV}{dr}\bigg|_{r=10} = 4\pi \times 10^2 = 400\,\pi\ \text{cm}^3/\text{cm}$$

$\therefore$ The volume of balloon is increasing at the rate of $400\,\pi$ cm^3 per cm increase in its radius when the radius is 10 cm.

(ii) <u>**To find the rate of change of y with respect to t at $x = a$:**</u>

    Step-1: Write the relationship between y and x under the given situation

    Step-2: Differentiate the relation with respect to t to find $\dfrac{dy}{dt}$.

    There will be a term containing $\dfrac{dx}{dt}$

    Step-3: If the value of $\dfrac{dx}{dt}$ is known in the question, put its value. Otherwise, eliminate it somehow using the conditions mentioned in the question.

    Step-4: Put $x = a$ in the expression obtained above to find

$$\frac{dy}{dt}\bigg|_{x=a}$$

<u>**Example**</u>

An edge of a variable cube is increasing at the rate of 3 cm/s. How fast is the volume of the cube increasing when the edge is 10 cm long?

Solution:

Here, we consider two variables, l and V respectively for edge and volume of the cube, and note down the given data and the quantity to find.

Let edge of cube $= l$ and Volume $=$ V

Given: $\dfrac{dl}{dt} = 3\ cm/s$

To find: $\dfrac{dV}{dt}\bigg|_{l=10} = ?$

Step 1 : The relationship between V and l is
$$V = l^3$$

Step 2 : Differentiating this relation with respect to t, we get
$$\frac{dV}{dt} = 3\,l^2\,\frac{dl}{dt}$$

Step 3 : Put $\dfrac{dl}{dt} = 3$ ..... (given)
$$\frac{dV}{dt} = 3\,l^2 \times 3 = 9\,l^2$$

Step 4 : Now put $l = 10$ to get

$$\left.\frac{dV}{dt}\right|_{l=10} = 9 \times 10^2 = 900 \ cm^3/s$$

$\therefore$ The volume of cube is increasing at the rate of $900 \ cm^3$ per second when the edge is 10 cm.

2 *Approximation

Since $\dfrac{dy}{dx}$ represents change in y per unit change in x

$\therefore$ Approximate change in y, when there is small change in x, can be found by

- $$\Delta y = \left(\frac{dy}{dx}\right)\Delta x$$

  Here, Δx and Δy are changes in x and y respectively.

  <u>**Note:**</u> This will be an approximate change in y and not the exact change.

- Change in any quantity is denoted by putting the symbol Δ before the symbol of that quantity.

  e.g.

  If radius is r, then Δr denotes change in radius.

  If we denote the length by l, then Δl denotes change in length.

- Approximation can be used

  (i) to find approximate change in dependent variable (y) when there is small change in independent variable (x).

  (ii) to find the value of a function at such a point which is otherwise cumbersome.

  <u>**Example**</u>

  If the radius of a sphere is measured as 7 m with an error of 0.02 m, then find the approximate error in calculating its volume.

  Solution:

  Here, errors in radius and volume can be considered as changes in their values.

  Let radius of balloon $= r$ and   Volume $=$ V

  Given: $\Delta r = 0.02$ m when $r = 7$ m

  To find: $\Delta V = ?$

  Step-1: The relationship between V and r is

  $$V = \frac{4}{3}\pi r^3$$

  Step-2: Differentiating this relation with respect to r, we get

---

$$\frac{dV}{dr} = \frac{4}{3}\pi \times 3\,r^2 = 4\,\pi\,r^2$$

Step-3: Using approximation, we can find change in volume as

$$\Delta V = \left(\frac{dV}{dr}\right).\Delta r$$

$$\Rightarrow \qquad \Delta V = (4\,\pi\,r^2).\Delta r$$

Step-4: Now we are given $\Delta r = 0.02$ m when $r = 7$ m, so, we put these values to obtain:

$$\Delta V = 4\,\pi \times 7^2 \times 0.02$$

$$\Rightarrow \qquad \Delta V = 3.92\,\pi \ \text{m}^3$$

$\therefore$ Approximate error in volume is $3.92\,\pi\ \text{m}^3$.

Example

Find the approximate value of $\sqrt{24.5}$

Thinking:

Here, the function is *square root*, and we have to find its value at 24.5, which is slightly cumbersome. The number closest to 24.5, whose *square root*, we know, is 25, i.e., $\sqrt{25} = 5$.

So, we write 24.5 as $(25 - 0.5)$.

Solution:

Since $24.5 = 25 - 0.5$

We suppose, $x = 25$ and $\Delta x = -0.5$

$$\qquad\qquad\qquad \text{...(\textbf{take care of sign in the value of } } \Delta x)$$

Write the *square root* function as $y = \sqrt{x}$ $\quad\dots\dots$(i)

At $x = 25$, we have $y = \sqrt{25} = 5$

If Δx is change in x, approximate change Δy in y is found as

$$\Delta y = \left(\frac{dy}{dx}\right).\Delta x \qquad\qquad \dots\dots \text{(ii)}$$

Differentiating the function (i) w.r.t. x, we get

$$\frac{dy}{dx} = \frac{1}{2\sqrt{x}}$$

$\therefore$ eqn. (ii) becomes

$$\Delta y = \left(\frac{1}{2\sqrt{x}}\right).\Delta x$$

Putting value of x and Δx, we get

$$\Delta y = \left(\frac{1}{2\sqrt{25}}\right).(-0.5)$$

$$\Rightarrow \qquad \Delta y = \left(\frac{1}{10}\right).(-0.5) = -0.05 \ \dots \text{(iii)}$$

Now $\qquad y = \sqrt{x}$ $\qquad\qquad\dots \text{(iv)}$

$$\Rightarrow y + \Delta y = \sqrt{x + \Delta x} \qquad \ldots (v)$$

By subtracting equation (iv) from (v), we obtain

$$\Delta y = \sqrt{x + \Delta x} - \sqrt{x}$$

$$\Rightarrow \sqrt{x + \Delta x} - \sqrt{x} = -0.05 \ldots .(\text{as } \Delta y = -0.05 \text{ from eqn(iii)})$$

$$\Rightarrow \sqrt{25 - 0.5} - \sqrt{25} = -0.05$$

$$\Rightarrow \sqrt{24.5} = 5 - 0.05 = 4.95 \ (\text{approx.})$$

3   *Tangents and Normals

Here, we are given the equation of a curve and a point on the curve. We have to find the equations of tangent and normal at that point.

We know that slope of tangent at a point is given by $\left(\dfrac{dy}{dx}\right)$.

Therefore, we write as follows:

- **The slope of tangent at point** $(x_0, y_0) = \dfrac{dy}{dx}\Big|_{(x_0, y_0)}$

Now tangent and normal are perpendicular to each other, and product of slopes of two perpendicular lines is -1. Therefore, we have

- **The slope of normal at point** $(x_0, y_0) = \dfrac{-1}{\dfrac{dy}{dx}\Big|_{(x_0, y_0)}}$

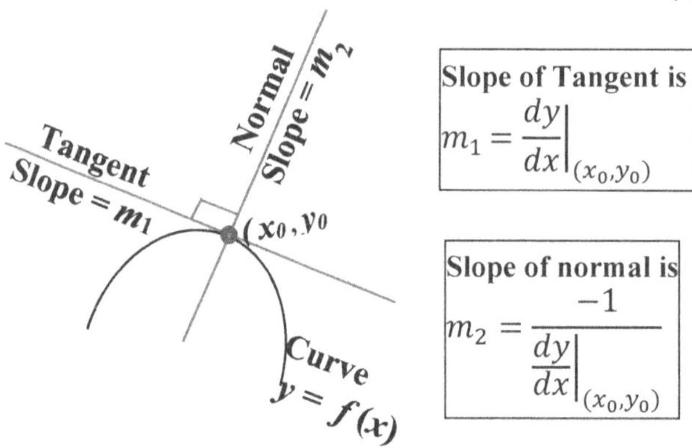

To solve different types of situations, we proceed as follows:

Situation-1

Given : (i) equation of curve is $y = f(x)$ $- - - - - -$ eqn.(i)

(The equation may be in implicit form)

(ii) a point on the curve is (x_0, y_0)

To find : Equations of Tangent and Normal at point (x_0, y_0)

Solution :

Step-1 Differentiate the given equation (i), and find $\dfrac{d\,y}{d\,x} = \,\text{-\,-\,-}$

Step-2 Put (x_0, y_0) in $\dfrac{dy}{dx}$ obtained above, and find $\dfrac{dy}{dx}\Big|_{(x_0, y_0)} = \text{-}$

This will be the slope of tangent at (x_0, y_0). So, we write it as:

The slope of tangent at point (x_0, y_0) is $m_1 = \dfrac{dy}{dx}\Big|_{(x_0, y_0)}$

$$= \text{-\,-\,-\,-\,-\,-}$$

Step-3 The slope of normal at point (x_0, y_0) is $m_2 = \dfrac{-1}{m_1}$

$$= \text{-\,-\,-\,-\,-\,-}$$

Step-4 Now the equation of tangent at point (x_0, y_0) is:

$$\dfrac{y - y_0}{x - x_0} = m_1$$

(see equation of straight line in slope-point form
done in class-XI)

Put the values of (x_0, y_0) and m_1 in the above equation to obtain the required equation of tangent.

Step-5 The equation of normal at point (x_0, y_0) is:

$$\dfrac{y - y_0}{x - x_0} = m_2$$

Put the values of (x_0, y_0) and m_2 in the above equation to obtain the required equation of normal.

Example

Find the equations of the tangent and normal to the curve,
$$y = x^4 - 6x^3 + 13x^2 - 10x + 5 \quad at\ point\ (0, 5).$$

Solution:

$$y = x^4 - 6x^3 + 13x^2 - 10x + 5 \qquad \ldots\ldots\ldots(i)$$

Step-1: $\dfrac{dy}{dx} = 4x^3 - 18x^2 + 26x - 10$

(Differentiating eqn (i) w.r.t. x)

Step-2: $\dfrac{dy}{dx}\Big|_{(0,5)} = -10$

(putting (0,5) in the eqn obtained in step-1.
Here, we have to put only $x = 0$
as y is absent on RHS)

$\therefore$ The slope of tangent at point $(0, 5)$ is $m_1 = \dfrac{dy}{dx}\bigg|_{(0,5)} = -10$

Step-3: The slope of normal at point $(0, 5)$ is $m_2 = \dfrac{-1}{m_1} = \dfrac{1}{10}$

Step-4: Now the equation of tangent at point $(0, 5)$ is:

$$\dfrac{y-5}{x-0} = m_1 \qquad \text{- - - -(eqn. of straight line using}$$
$$\text{slope-point form)}$$

$$\Rightarrow \quad \dfrac{y-5}{x-0} = -10$$

$$\Rightarrow \quad 10\,x + y - 5 = 0$$

This is the required equation of tangent at $(0,5)$.

Step-5: The equation of normal at point $(0, 5)$ is:

$$\dfrac{y-5}{x-0} = m_2 \qquad \text{- - - -(eqn. of straight line using}$$
$$\text{slope-point form)}$$

$$\Rightarrow \quad \dfrac{y-5}{x-0} = \dfrac{1}{10}$$

$$\Rightarrow \quad x - 10\,y + 50 = 0$$

This is the required equation of normal at $(0,5)$.

Situation-2

In some situations, we are given the equation of a curve but not the point on the curve. Instead, we are given some condition or other statement.

Using that condition, we can easily find the slope of the required tangent or the required normal.

Given : (i) equation of curve is $y = f(x)$ - - - - - - eqn.(i)

              (The equation may be in implicit form)

        (ii) a condition or statement to find the slope of the required tangent or the required normal.

To find : (i) Find the points of tangent or normal.

           (ii) Equations of Tangent and Normal at these points.

Solution :

Step-1 Suppose that (h, k) is a point on the curve where tangent or the normal is drawn.

Since, point (h, k) lies on the given curve, it has to satisfy the equation of the curve.

$\therefore$ Put (h, k) in this equation to obtain an equation in terms of h and k. We get an equation something like, as follows:

$$k = f(h) \qquad \textbf{(or it may be in implicit form)}$$

Step-2 By differentiating the equation of curve, we find the slope of tangent or normal in terms of h and k as follows:

Differentiate the given equation (i), and find $\dfrac{dy}{dx}$ = - - -

Put (h, k) in $\dfrac{d\,y}{d\,x}$, obtained above, and find $\dfrac{dy}{dx}\Big|_{(h,k)}$ = - -

(It will be in terms of h and k)

We have obtained slope of tangent, m_1 in terms of h and k.

- So, $\qquad m_1 = \dfrac{dy}{dx}\Big|_{(h,k)}$

- and the slope of normal at point (h, k) is $m_2 = \dfrac{-1}{m_1}$

$$= \text{ in terms of } h \text{ and } k$$

Step-3 Now, find the slope of the required tangent or the required normal from the given condition.

(How to find it, will depend on the given condition)

Step-4 Equate the slopes obtained in the steps 2 and 3.

We will get another equation in terms of h and k .

Step-5 Solve the 2 equations obtained in steps 1 and 4 , which are in terms of h and k to find out the values of h and k .

In this way, we get the point (h, k) on the curve where tangent or normal is drawn.

Step-6 Now put the values of h and k obtained in step 5 into the slopes m_1 and m_2 of step 2 .

Step-7 Now the equation of tangent at point (h, k) is:

$$\dfrac{y-k}{x-h} = m_1$$

Put the values of (h, k) and m_1 in the above equation to obtain the required equation of tangent.

The equation of normal at point (h, k) is:

$$\dfrac{y-k}{x-h} = m_2$$

Put the values of (h, k) and m_2 in the above equation to obtain the required equation of normal.

<u>**Example**</u>

Find a point on the curve $y = (x - 2)^2$ at which the tangent is parallel to the chord joining the points (2, 0) and (4, 4). Also find the equation of tangent.

Solution:

$$y = (x-2)^2 \qquad \ldots \ldots (i)$$

Step-1: Suppose that (h, k) is a point on the curve, where tangent is drawn.

$$\therefore k = (h-2)^2 \qquad \ldots \ldots (ii)$$

Step-2: Differentiating eqn. (i) w.r.t. x

$$\frac{dy}{dx} = 2(x-2)$$

$$\Rightarrow \quad \left.\frac{dy}{dx}\right|_{(h,k)} = 2(h-2)$$

$\therefore$ The slope of tangent at point (h, k) is $m_1 = 2(h-2)$

Step-3: Now, tangent is parallel to the chord joining $(2, 0)$ & $(4, 4)$, and slope of this chord $= \dfrac{4-0}{4-2} = 2$

(slope of line passing through 2 points (x_1, y_1) and (x_2, y_2) is given by $\dfrac{y_2 - y_1}{x_2 - x_1}$)

Step-4: Tangent is parallel to the chord.

$\therefore$ slope of tangent $=$ slope of the chord

$$\Rightarrow \quad 2(h-2) = 2$$
$$\Rightarrow \quad h = 3$$

Step-5: Using $h = 3$ in eqn.(ii), obtained in step-1,

$$k = (h-2)^2$$
$$\Rightarrow \quad k = (3-2)^2 = 1$$

$\therefore$ **the required point on the curve $(h, k) = (3, 1)$**

Step-6: Using $(h, k) = (3, 1)$ in the slope m_1, obtained in step-2,

we get $m_1 = 2$

(Here, we can also write directly, $m_1 =$ slope of chord $= 2$)

Step-7: Now the equation of tangent at point $(h, k) = (3, 1)$ is:

$$\frac{y-k}{x-h} = m_1$$

(equation of straight line using slope-point form)

$$\Rightarrow \quad \frac{y-3}{x-1} = 2$$

$$\Rightarrow \quad 2x - y + 1 = 0$$

This is the required equation of tangent.

4 Increasing and Decreasing Functions

A function can be any one of the following **Natures**:

(i) Strictly Increasing

(ii) Increasing

(iii) Strictly Decreasing

(iv) Decreasing

(v) Neither increasing Nor decreasing

4.1 Nature of the function from Graph

By drawing a graph of the given function $y = f(x)$, we can know the nature of the function as follows:

(i) On moving from left to right along the graph, if the height of the graph continuously increases, then the function is ***Strictly Increasing***. (*see* adjoining figure)

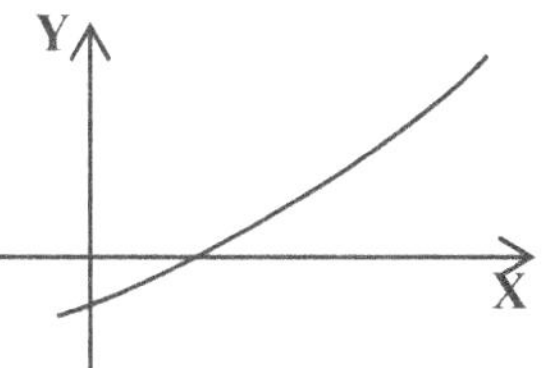

  • y –**coordinate** of points on the graph increases continuously from left to right in strictly increasing function.

(ii) On moving from left to right along the graph, if the height of the graph continuously increases except for some portions where the height becomes constant, then the function is ***Increasing***.

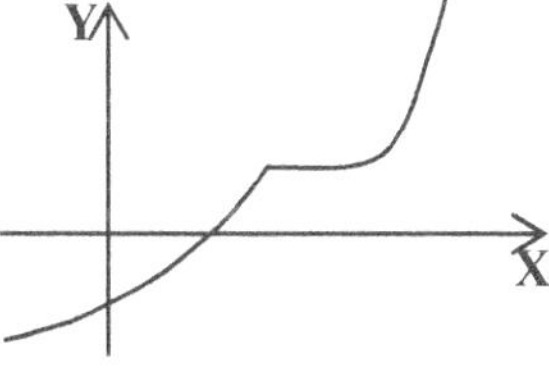

(iii) On moving from left to right along the graph, if the height of the graph continuously decreases, then the function is ***Strictly Decreasing***.

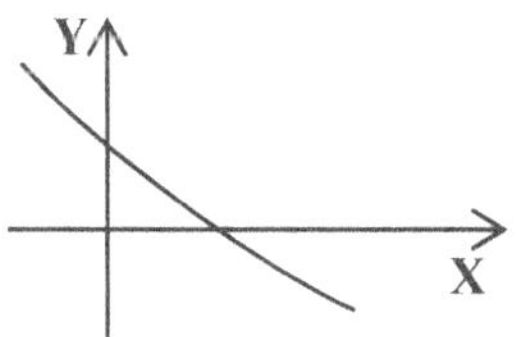

  • y –**coordinate** of points on the graph decreases continuously from left to right in strictly decreasing function.

(iv) On moving from left to right along the graph, if the height of the graph continuously decreases except for some portions where the height becomes constant, then the function is ***Decreasing***.

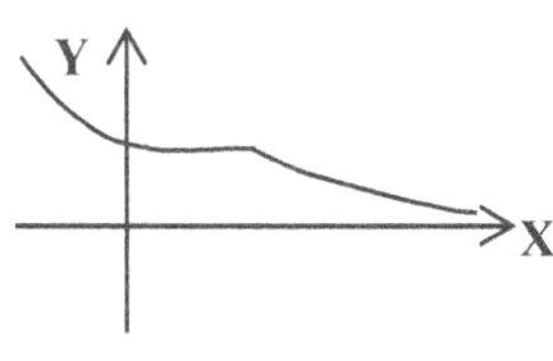

(v) On moving from left to right along the graph, if the height of the graph increases in some portion but decreases in some other portion, then the function is *Neither increasing nor decreasing.*

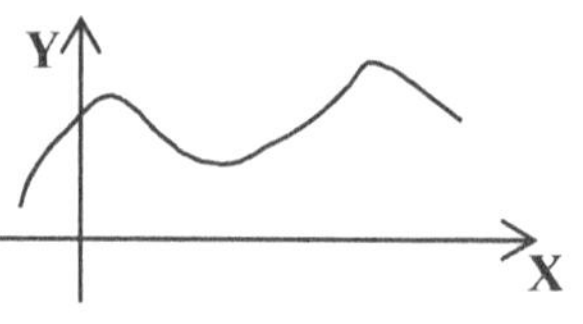

4.2 Nature of function <u>in an interval</u> (without using derivatives)

From the graphs of functions of different natures (discussed above), we can observe the followings:

For a real function f in an interval **I** in its domain (Interval **I** may be an open or a closed interval),

(i) if $x_2 > x_1 \Rightarrow f(x_2) > f(x_1)$ for all x_1, $x_2 \in$ **I**, then $f(x)$ is a strictly increasing function in **I** . (*see* figure below)

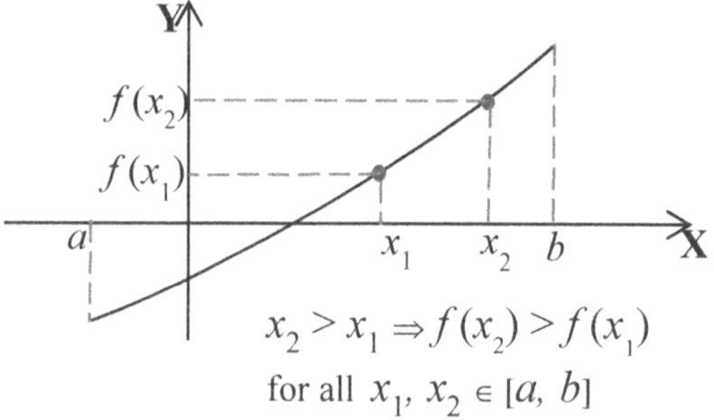

<u>**Example**</u>
Find the nature of function given by $f(x) = 3x - 4$ on set of real numbers **R.**

Solution:
Suppose x_1, $x_2 \in$ **R** such that $x_2 > x_1$.

$$f(x_1) = 3x_1 - 4 \qquad \text{and} \qquad f(x_2) = 3x_2 - 4$$

Now $x_2 > x_1 \Rightarrow 3x_2 > 3x_1$

$$\Rightarrow 3x_2 - 4 > 3x_1 - 4$$

$$\Rightarrow f(x_2) > f(x_1) \qquad \text{for all } x_1, x_2 \in \textbf{R}$$

Thus, $f(x)$ is **strictly increasing** in nature.

(ii) if $x_2 > x_1 \Rightarrow f(x_2) \geq f(x_1)$ for all x_1, $x_2 \in \mathbf{I}$, then $f(x)$ is an increasing function in $\mathbf{I}$. (*see* figure below)

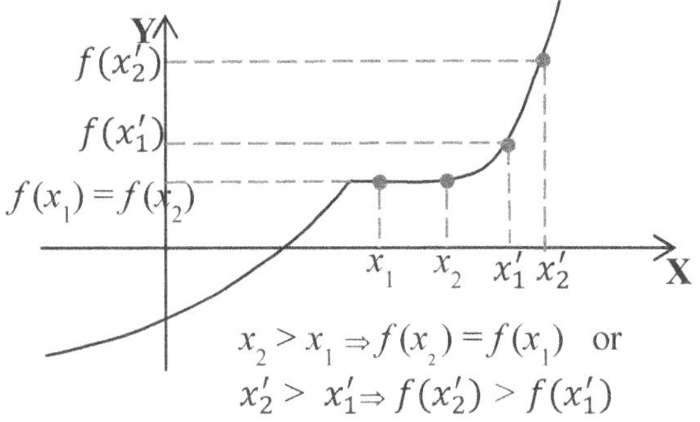

<u>Example</u>

Find the nature of function given by

$$f(x) = \begin{cases} 1 & if\ 0 \leq x \leq 5 \\ x - 4 & if\ x > 5 \end{cases} \quad on\ set\ of\ positive\ real\ numbers.$$

Solution:

Here, we can consider two cases, one for $x \in [\mathbf{0, 5}]$, and other for $x \in (\mathbf{5, \infty})$.

Case-1:

Suppose x_1, $x_2 \in [\mathbf{0, 5}]$ such that $x_2 > x_1$.

Now for $x \in [\mathbf{0, 5}]$, $f(x) = 1$, according to given function.

$\therefore \quad f(x_1) = 1 \quad$ and $\quad f(x_2) = 1$

$\therefore \quad x_2 > x_1 \Rightarrow f(x_2) = f(x_1)$

Case-2:

Suppose x_1, $x_2 \in (\mathbf{5, \infty})$ such that $x_2 > x_1$.

$\because$ for $x \in (\mathbf{5, \infty})$, $f(x) = x - 4$, according to given function.

$\therefore \quad f(x_1) = x_1 - 4 \quad$ and $\quad f(x_2) = x_2 - 4$

Now $x_2 > x_1 \Rightarrow x_2 - 4 > x_1 - 4$

$\Rightarrow f(x_2) > f(x_1)$

From case-1 and case-2, we can conclude that

$x_2 > x_1 \Rightarrow f(x_2) \geq f(x_1) \quad$ for all x_1, $x_2 \in (\mathbf{0, \infty})$

Thus, $f(x)$ is **increasing** in nature.

(iii) if $x_2 > x_1 \Rightarrow f(x_2) < f(x_1)$ for all $x_1, x_2 \in \mathbf{I}$, then $f(x)$ is a strictly decreasing function in $\mathbf{I}$. (*see* figure below)

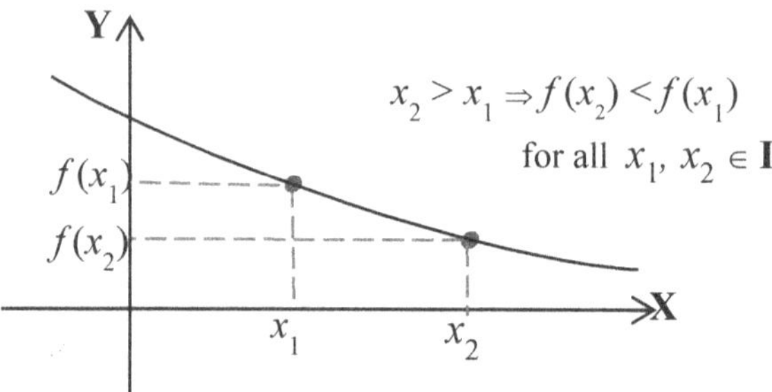

Example

Find the nature of function given by $f(x) = 4 - 3x$ on set of real numbers **R**.

Solution:

Suppose $x_1, x_2 \in \mathbf{R}$ such that $x_2 > x_1$.
$$f(x_1) = 4 - 3x_1 \quad \text{and} \quad f(x_2) = 4 - 3x_2$$

Now $x_2 > x_1 \Rightarrow 3x_2 > 3x_1$
$$\Rightarrow -3x_2 < -3x_1$$

$\qquad\qquad$ . . . (on multiplying by a $-$ ve number, sign of inequality gets reversed)

$$\Rightarrow 4 - 3x_2 < 4 - 3x_1$$
$$\Rightarrow f(x_2) < f(x_1) \qquad \text{for all } x_1, x_2 \in \mathbf{R}$$

Thus, $f(x)$ is **strictly decreasing** in nature.

(iv) if $x_2 > x_1 \Rightarrow f(x_2) \leq f(x_1)$ for all $x_1, x_2 \in \mathbf{I}$, then $f(x)$ is a decreasing function in $\mathbf{I}$.

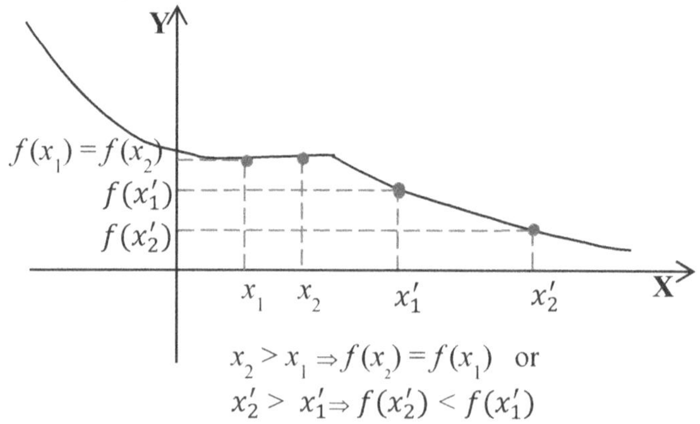

<u>**Example**</u>

Find the nature of function given by

$$f(x) = \begin{cases} 1 & \text{if } 0 \le x \le 3 \\ 4 - x & \text{if } x > 3 \end{cases} \quad \textit{on set of positive real numbers.}$$

Solution:

Here, we can consider two cases, one for $x \in [0, 3]$, and other for $x \in (3, \infty)$

Case-1:

Suppose $x_1, x_2 \in [0, 3]$ such that $x_2 > x_1$.

Now for $x \in [0, 3]$, $f(x) = 1$, according to given function.

$\Rightarrow \quad f(x_1) = 1 \quad$ and $\quad f(x_2) = 1$

$\therefore \quad x_2 > x_1 \Rightarrow f(x_2) = f(x_1)$

Case-2:

Suppose $x_1, x_2 \in (3, \infty)$ such that $x_2 > x_1$.

$\because$ for $x \in (3, \infty)$, $f(x) = 4 - x$, according to given function.

$\Rightarrow \quad f(x_1) = 4 - x_1 \quad$ and $\quad f(x_2) = 4 - x_2$

Now $x_2 > x_1 \Rightarrow -x_2 < -x_2$

$$\ldots \text{(on multiplying by a} - \text{ve number,}$$
$$\text{sign of inequality gets reversed)}$$

$$\Rightarrow \quad 4 - x_2 < 4 - x_1$$

$$\Rightarrow \quad f(x_2) < f(x_1)$$

From case-1 and case-2, we can conclude that

$$x_2 > x_1 \Rightarrow f(x_2) \le f(x_1) \quad \text{for all } x_1, x_2 \in (0, \infty)$$

Thus, $f(x)$ is **decreasing** in nature.

4.3 Nature of function <u>at a point</u> (without using derivatives)

Given a real function f at a point $x = x_0$, if there exists an interval I $= (x_0 - h, x_0 + h)$, where h > 0 [i.e. I is a small region around the point $x = x_0$] such that for $x_1, x_2 \in$ I, and

(i) $x_1 < x_2 \Rightarrow f(x_1) \le f(x_2)$ for all $x_1, x_2 \in$ I, then $f(x)$ is an increasing function at $x = x_0$

(ii) $x_1 < x_2 \Rightarrow f(x_1) < f(x_2)$ for all $x_1, x_2 \in$ I, then $f(x)$ is a strictly increasing function at $x = x_0$

(iii) $x_1 < x_2 \Rightarrow f(x_1) \ge f(x_2)$ for all $x_1, x_2 \in$ I, then $f(x)$ is an decreasing function at $x = x_0$

(iv) $x_1 < x_2 \Rightarrow f(x_1) > f(x_2)$ for all x_1, $x_2 \in$ I, then $f(x)$ is a strictly decreasing function at $x = x_0$

4.4 Nature of function in an interval (using derivatives)

- Before moving further, we recall the following points :
  → **Slope of tangent** to a curve $y = f(x)$ at any point is given by $\dfrac{dy}{dx}$ or $f'(x)$.
  → If a line makes **an acute angle with positive direction of X-axis,** then its slope is positive, and hence, $f'(x) > 0$.
  → If a line makes **an obtuse angle with positive direction of X-axis,** then its slope is negative, and hence, $f'(x) < 0$.
  → If a line is **parallel to X-axis, then** its slope is zero, and hence $f'(x) = 0$.

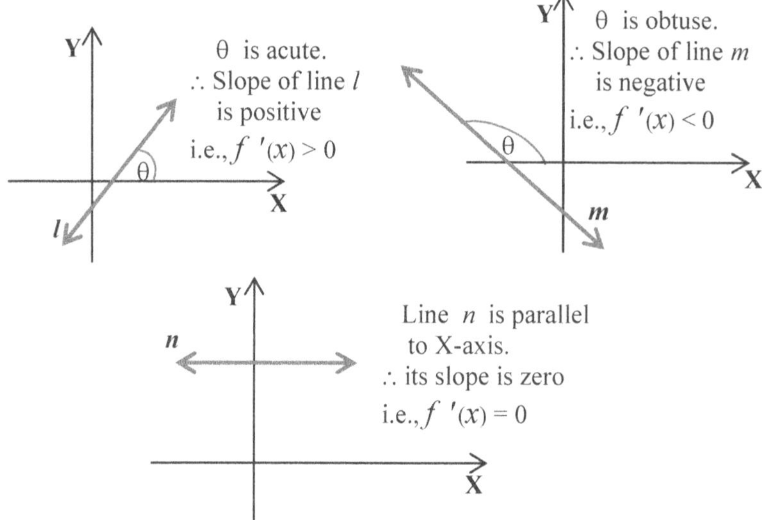

- Now from the graphs of functions of different natures discussed earlier, we observe that
  (i)   the slope of tangent is positive at every point for strictly increasing function.
  (ii) the slope of tangent is positive or equal to zero at every point for increasing function.
  (iii) the slope of tangent is negative at every point for strictly decreasing function.
  (iv) the slope of tangent is negative or equal to zero at every point for decreasing function.

- From the above discussion, we state the followings:

  If a function f be continuous on $[a, b]$ and differentiable on the open interval (a, b), then

  (i) f is strictly increasing in (a, b) if $f'(x) > 0$ for each $x \in (a, b)$. (see figure below)

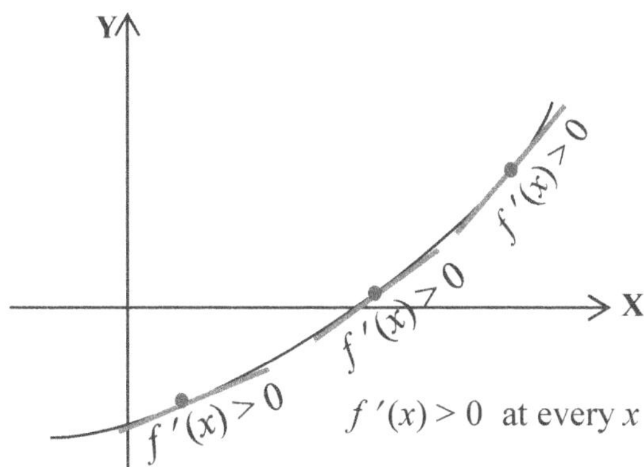

<u>Example</u>

Find the nature of function given by $f(x) = 3x - 4$ on set of real numbers **R**.

Solution:

$$f(x) = 3x - 4$$
$$\Rightarrow \quad f'(x) = 3 \quad \ldots \ldots \text{It is positive for every value } x$$
$$\Rightarrow \quad f'(x) > 0 \quad \quad \text{at every } x$$

Thus, $f(x)$ is **strictly increasing** in nature.

(ii) f is strictly decreasing in (a, b) if $f'(x) < 0$ for each $x \in (a, b)$. (see figure below)

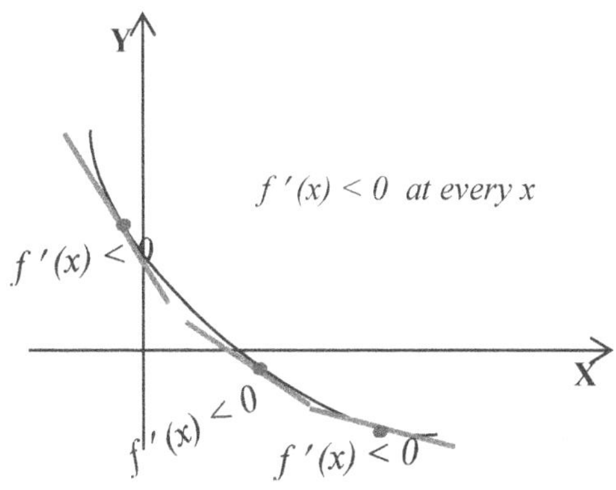

<u>**Example**</u>
Find the nature of function given by $f(x) = 4 - 3x$ *on set of real numbers* **R**.
Solution:

$$f(x) = 4 - 3x$$
$$\Rightarrow \quad f'(x) = -3 \quad \ldots\ldots \text{It is negative for every value } x$$
$$\Rightarrow \quad f'(x) < 0 \quad \text{at every } x$$

Thus, $f(x)$ is **strictly decreasing** in nature.

(iii) f is increasing in $[a, b]$ if $f'(x) \geq 0$ for each $x \in [a, b]$.
    (see figure below)

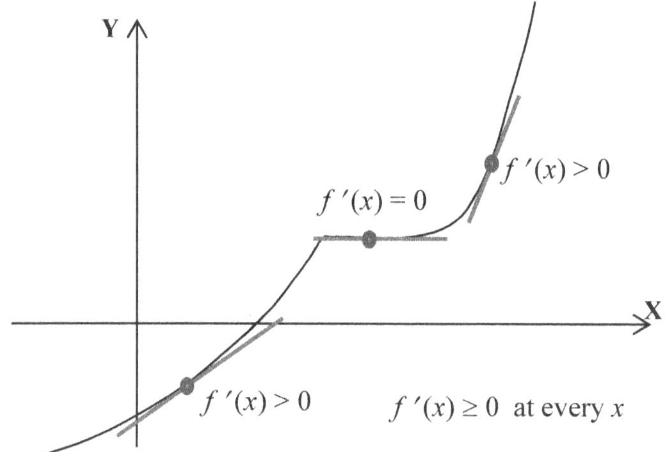

<u>**Example**</u>
Find the nature of function given by $f(x) = \sin x$ *in the interval* $[0, \frac{\pi}{2}]$.
Solution:

$$f(x) = \sin x$$
$$\Rightarrow \quad f'(x) = \cos x$$
$$\ldots\ldots\ldots (\text{It is positive for } 0 \leq x < \frac{\pi}{2} \text{ and}$$
$$\text{at } \frac{\pi}{2} \text{ , it is equal to 0})$$
$$\Rightarrow \quad f'(x) \geq 0 \quad \text{at every } x \in [0, \frac{\pi}{2}]$$

Thus, $f(x)$ is **increasing** in nature.

(iv) f is decreasing in $[a, b]$ if $f'(x) \leq 0$ for each $x \in [a, b]$.
    (see figure below)

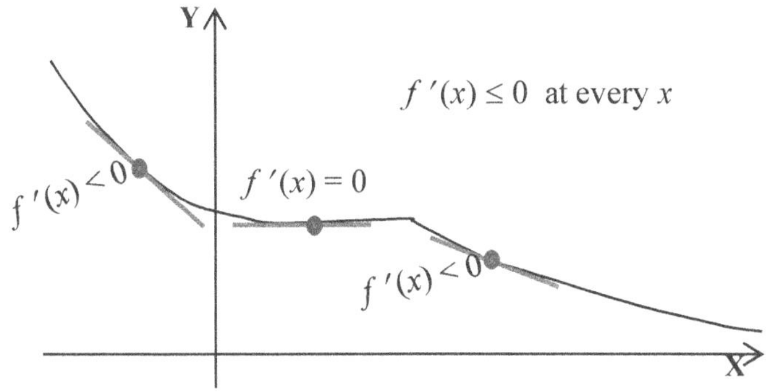

<u>**Example**</u>

Find the nature of function given by $f(x) = \cos x$ *in the interval* $[0, \frac{\pi}{2}]$.

Solution:

$$f(x) = \cos x$$
$$\Rightarrow \quad f'(x) = -\sin x$$

Now $\sin x \geq 0$ at every $x \in [0, \frac{\pi}{2}]$

$$\Rightarrow \quad -\sin x \leq 0$$
$$\Rightarrow \quad f'(x) \leq 0 \quad \text{at every } x \in [0, \frac{\pi}{2}]$$

Thus, $f(x)$ is **decreasing** in nature.

(v) f is a constant function in $[a, b]$ if $f'(x) = 0$ for each $x \in (a, b)$. (see figure below)

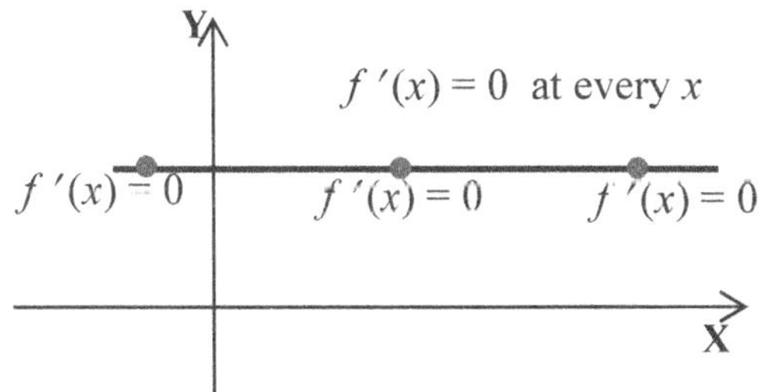

<u>**Example**</u>

Find the nature of function given by $f(x) = 5$ *on set of real numbers* **R.**

olution:

$$f(x) = 5$$
$$\Rightarrow \quad f'(x) = 0 \quad \text{for all } x \in \mathbf{R}$$

Thus, $f(x)$ is **constant function.**

4.5 Critical or Turning points

Critical points or turning points *are the points beyond which the function may change its nature from increasing to decreasing or vice-versa.*

- The curve of a continuous function will have some highs and lows as shown in figure below:

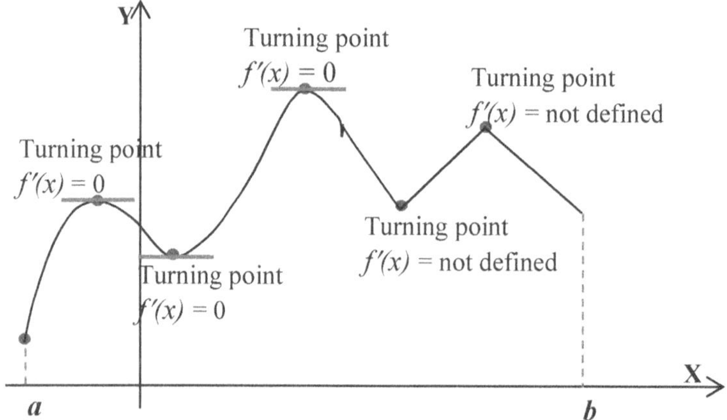

- From the above curve, we can observe that critical or turning points occur at points where slope of the tangent is zero or it is not defined.

  i.e, **Points where $f'(x) = 0$ or $f'(x) =$ not defined are Critical points or turning points.**

4.6 Point of inflexion

There may be a critical point where the function does not change its nature. That point is called as **point of inflexion.**

i.e, **Points where $f'(x) = 0$ or $f'(x) =$ not defined, but function does not change its nature beyond these points.** (See the figure below)

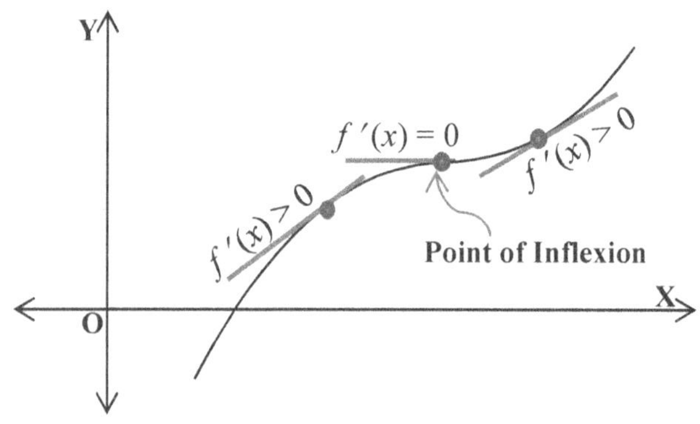

4.7 Finding intervals of increasing and decreasing

To find the intervals of increasing and decreasing for a function $f(x)$ in the given interval $\mathbf{I}$ (which may be a closed interval $[a,b]$ or an open interval (a, b)), we proceed as follows:

Step-1 Find $f'(x) = \ \text{-} \ \text{-} \ \text{-} \ \text{-} \ \text{-} \ \text{-}$

Step-2 Put $f'(x) = 0$, and find the values of x which lie in the interval $\mathbf{I}$.

Step-3 Find the values of x at which $f'(x)$ is not defined in the interval $\mathbf{I}$.

Step-4 List the values of x obtained in Steps 2 and 3 in increasing order.
These are known as critical points or turning points.
(These are the points beyond which the function may change its nature from increasing to decreasing or vice-versa)

Step-5 Put a before the first critical point and b after the last critical point (i.e., the extreme points).
If the critical points in increasing order are x_1, x_2, x_3, then sequence reads as a, x_1, x_2, x_3, b

Step-6 Now make intervals from this sequence, from one point to the next, and make a table as shown:

Intervals	Sign of $f'(x)$	Strictly ↑ or ↓
$[a, x_1)$		
(x_1, x_2)		
(x_2, x_3)		
$(x_3, b]$		

Step-7 Take any convenient value of x lying between (a, x_1), put it in $f'(x)$, and note the sign of $f'(x)$ for interval $[a, x_1)$ in the second column as $+$ or $-$.
Mark ↑ for $+$ and ↓ for $-$ in the 3ʳᵈ column.

Step-8 Repeat Step 7 for all the intervals listed in 1ˢᵗ column.

Step-9 (i) **For strictly increasing and strictly decreasing:**
→ Keep all the intervals open at critical points
→ Keep intervals closed at a and b if they are not critical points and if $f(x)$ is continuous at these points. Otherwise keep them open.

- If 3rd column has sign $\uparrow$ for an interval, then we write $f(x)$ is strictly increasing in that interval.
- If 3rd column has sign $\downarrow$ for an interval, then we write $f(x)$ is strictly decreasing in that interval.

(ii) For increasing and decreasing (not strictly):

→ Keep the intervals closed at a & b

→ Keep the intervals closed at those critical points, where $f(x)$ is continuous.

→ Intervals should remain open at points where $f(x)$ is not continuous.

- If 3rd column has sign $\uparrow$ for an interval, then we write $f(x)$ is increasing in that interval.
- If 3rd column has sign $\downarrow$ for an interval, then we write $f(x)$ is decreasing in that interval.

<u>**Example**</u>

Find the intervals in which the function f given by
$$f(x) = 2\,x^3 - 3\,x^2 - 36\,x + 7 \ is$$
(a) *strictly increasing*   (b) *strictly decreasing* .

Solution:

Step-1: $f(x) = 2\,x^3 - 3\,x^2 - 36\,x + 7$
$$f'(x) = 6\,x^2 - 6\,x - 36$$

Step-2: Put $f'(x) = 0$
$$\Rightarrow \quad 6\,x^2 - 6\,x - 36 = 0$$
$$\Rightarrow \quad 6\,(x^2 - x - 6) = 0$$
$$\Rightarrow \quad (x - 3)(x + 2) = 0$$
$$\Rightarrow \quad x = 3, \quad x = -2$$

Here the domain of the function is set of real numbers i.e., $(-\infty, \infty)$ and $3, -2 \in (-\infty, \infty)$.

Step-3: $f'(x)$ is defined at every real number.

i.e., there is no value of x at which $f'(x)$ is not defined.

Step-4: $\therefore$ all critical points in increasing order are -2 and 3

Step-5: We have to find the intervals between $(-\infty, \infty)$

$\therefore$ we write the numbers in increasing order as: $-\infty, -2, 3, \infty$

Step-6,7&8:

Now we make intervals from this sequence, and check the sign of $f'(x)$ in each of these intervals, and then make a table as shown:

Intervals	Sign of $f'(x)$	Strictly ↑ or ↓
$(-\infty, -2)$	$+$	↑
$(-2, 3)$	$-$	↓
$(3, \infty)$	$+$	↑

We can check sign of $f'(x) = 6x^2 - 6x - 36 = 6(x-3)(x+2)$

→ in the interval $(-\infty, -2)$, by putting any value between $-\infty$ and -2, e.g., on putting -3, we get 36, which is positive

→ in the interval $(-2, 3)$, by putting any value between -2 and 3, e.g. on putting 0, we get -36, which is negative

→ in the interval $(3, \infty)$, by putting any value between 3 and ∞, e.g. on putting 4, we get 36, which is positive

Step-9: (a) since we get positive sign in intervals $(-\infty, -2)$ and $(3, \infty)$

∴ we say that $f(x)$ is strictly increasing in the intervals $(-\infty, -2)$ and $(3, \infty)$.

Also, since $f(x)$ is defined at -2 & 3,

we say that $f(x)$ is increasing in the intervals $(-\infty, -2]$ and $[3, \infty)$.

(b) we get negative sign in the intervals $(-2, 3)$

∴ we say that $f(x)$ is strictly decreasing in the intervals $(-2, 3)$.

Also, since $f(x)$ is defined at -2 & 3,

we say that $f(x)$ is decreasing in the intervals $[-2, 3]$.

5 Maxima and Minima of a function

A function $y = f(x)$, in the given interval, can have the points of

(i) absolute maximum

(ii) absolute minimum

(iii) local maximum

(iv) local minimum

5.1 Maxima and Minima on the graph

By drawing a graph of the function $y = f(x)$ in the given interval (*see* figure below), we can find the points of maxima and minima as follows:

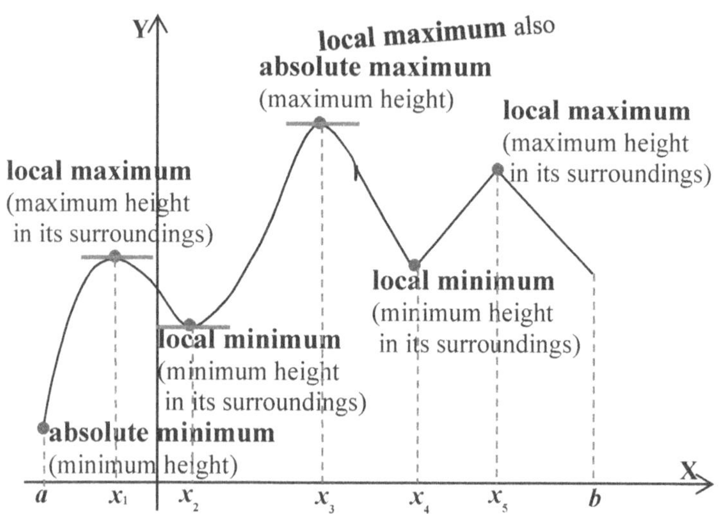

→ The point at which the graph attains its **maximum height** in the given interval is called as the point of **absolute maximum**.

It is at $x = x_3$ in the above graph.

→ The point at which the graph attains its **minimum height** in the given interval is called as the point of **absolute minimum**.

It is at $x = a$ in the above graph.

→ The point at which the graph has its **maximum height in a localised region** around it and on both side of it is called as the point of **local maximum**.

In the given graph, $x = x_1$, $x = x_3$ and $x = x_5$ are points of local maxima.

→ The point at which the graph has its **minimum height in a localised region** around it and on both side of it is called as the point of **local minimum**.

In the given graph, $x = a$, $x = x_2$ and $x = x_4$ are points of local minima.

5.2 Maxima and Minima (without derivative)

We know that graph will attain its maximum height when $f(x)$ has maximum value, and it will attain minimum height when value of $f(x)$ is minimum.

So, for a real function $f(x)$ in an interval **I** in its domain,

---

(i) $x = c$ is point of **absolute maximum** if $f(x)$ has maximum value at it in its domain, and the absolute maximum value is $f(c)$.

(ii) $x = c$ is point of **absolute minimum** if $f(x)$ has minimum value at it in its domain, and the absolute minimum value is $f(c)$.

(iii) $x = c$ is point of **local maximum** if $f(x)$ has maximum value at it in a small interval on both side of $x = c$ [i.e., in small interval $(c–h, c+h)$ where $h > 0$], and the local maximum value is $f(c)$.

(iv) $x = c$ is point of **local minimum** if $f(x)$ has minimum value at it in a small interval on both side of $x = c$ [i.e., in small interval $(c–h, c+h)$ where $h > 0$], and the local minimum value is $f(c)$.

5.3   To find Absolute Maximum and Minimum

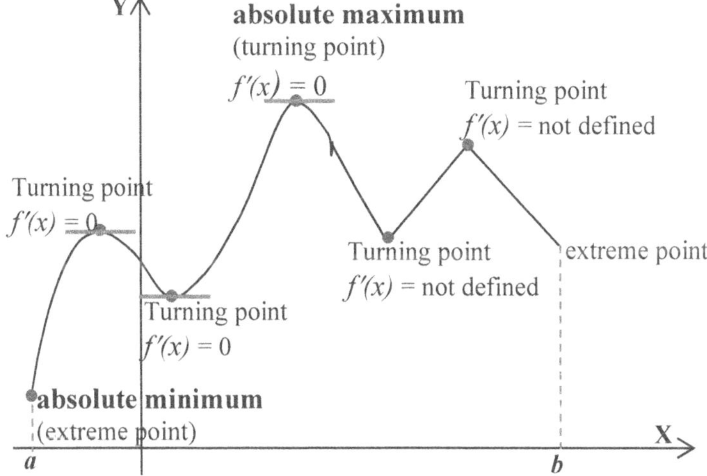

We can observe from the above graph that any continuous function $f(x)$ in the interval $[a, b]$ will have absolute maximum and absolute minimum at any of the **extreme points** (i.e. at a or b) or at any of the **turning points** (i.e., at points where $f'(x) = 0$ or $f'(x)$ = not defined).

So, to find absolute maxima and minima we proceed as follows:

Step-1 Find $f'(x) = - - - -$

Step-2 Put $f'(x) = 0$, and find the values of x which lie in the interval $[a, b]$

Step-3 Find the values of x at which $f'(x)$ is not defined in the interval $[a, b]$.

Step-4 The values of x obtained in Steps 1 and 2 are known as **critical points or turning points**.

Step-5 Find the value of $f(x)$ at all critical points and the 2 extreme points a & b.

If the critical points are x_1, x_2, x_3, *then* find

$$f(a) = - -, \quad f(x_1) = - -, \quad f(x_2) = - -, \quad f(x_3) = - -, \quad f(b) = - -$$

Step-6 Find which of the values in Step 5 is maximum and which one is minimum.

(If $f(x_1)$ is maximum and $f(b)$ is minimum, then we write

that $f(x)$ has absolute maximum at $x = x_1$ and

$f(x)$ has absolute minimum at $x = b$)

<u>Example</u>

Find absolute maximum and absolute minimum values of the function f given by $f(x) = x^3 - 6x^2 + 9x + 15$ *in the interval* $[-1, 4]$.

Solution:

Step-1: $\quad f(x) = x^3 - 6x^2 + 9x + 15$

$\qquad\qquad f'(x) = 3x^2 - 12x + 9$

Step-2: $\quad$ Put $\quad f'(x) = 0$

$\qquad\qquad \Rightarrow \qquad 3x^2 - 12x + 9 = 0$

$\qquad\qquad \Rightarrow \qquad 3(x^2 - 4x + 3) = 0$

$\qquad\qquad \Rightarrow \qquad (x - 3)(x - 1) = 0$

$\qquad\qquad \Rightarrow \qquad x = 3, \qquad\qquad x = 1$

$\qquad\qquad$ Here the domain the function is *the interval* $[-1, 4]$

$\qquad\qquad$ and $3, 1 \in [-1, 4]$

Step-3: $\quad f'(x)$ is defined at every real number

$\qquad\qquad\qquad\qquad\qquad$ (because it is a polynomial).

$\qquad\qquad$ i.e., there is no value of x at which $f'(x)$ is not defined.

Step-4: $\quad \therefore$ all critical points in increasing order are $\;1\;$ and 3

Step-5: $\quad$ We have to find the values in the intervals $[-1, 4]$

$\qquad\qquad$ So, we have to find the value of $f(x)$ at critical points 1 & 3, and also at extreme points -1 & 4 .

$\qquad\qquad$ Since $\quad f(x) = x^3 - 6x^2 + 9x + 15$

$\qquad\qquad \therefore \qquad f(1) = 19 \;\ldots\ldots$ **max**

$\qquad\qquad\qquad\quad f(3) = 15$

$\qquad\qquad\qquad\quad f(-1) = -1 \;\ldots\ldots$ **min**

$\qquad\qquad\qquad\quad f(4) = 19 \;\ldots\ldots$ **max**

Step-6: We find that $f(-1) = -1$ is the minimum value
and $f(1) = f(4) = 19$ is the maximum value
So, we say that:
$f(x)$ has absolute minimum at $x = -1$, and absolute minimum value is -1.
$f(x)$ has absolute maximum at two points $x = 1$ & 4, and absolute maximum value is 19.

5.4 To find Local Maximum / Minimum

A continuous function f(x) , in an interval **I** *, has local maximum and local minimum at* **turning points** *(i.e., at points where f ' (x) = 0 or f '(x) = not defined) as shown below.*

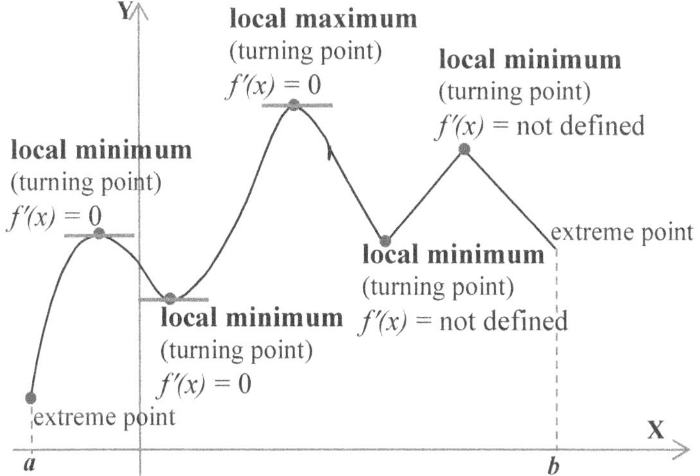

5.4.1 First Derivative Method

From the above figure, we can observe that

(i) If the slope of tangent just before a critical point is positive and just after it is negative, then that critical point is a point of local maximum.

(ii) If the slope of tangent just before a critical point is negative and just after it is positive, then that critical point is a point of local minimum.

(iii) If the slope of tangent just before a critical point and just after it doesn't change its sign, then that critical point is neither a point of local maximum nor a point of local minimum. It is a point of inflexion.

We know that **Slope of tangent is given by $f'(x)$**.
So, we proceed as follows:

Step-1 Find $f'(x) = - - - -$

Step-2 Put $f'(x) = 0$, and find the values of x which lie in the interval **I** .

Step-3 Find the values of x at which $f'(x)$ is not defined in the interval **I** .

Step-4 The values of x obtained in Steps 1 and 2 are known as Critical points.

Step-5 If the critical points are x_1 , x_2 , x_3, *then* check for each one of them as explained for $x = x_1$ below:

→ Take two values of x , first value slightly less than x_1 and second slightly greater than x_1 , and check the sign of $f'(x)$ on both.

Value of x	Sign of $f'(x)$
less than x_1	$+/-$
greater than x_1	$+/-$

→ If sign of $f'(x)$ changes from $-$ to $+$, then $x = x_1$ is a point of Local Minimum, and Local Minimum Value is $f(x_1)$

→ If sign of $f'(x)$ changes from $+$ to $-$, then $x = x_1$ is a point of Local Maximum, and Local Maximum Value is $f(x_1)$

→ If sign of $f'(x)$ does not change, then $x = x_1$ is neither a point of Local Minimum nor a point of Local Maximum. It is a ***point of Inflection***.

Step-6 Repeat the Step 5 for other critical points.

Example

Find the local maxima and local minima of the function f given by
$$f(x) = \tfrac{1}{4}x^4 + \tfrac{2}{3}x^3 - \tfrac{1}{2}x^2 - 2x.\ \textit{Also find the local maximum and}$$
minimum values.

Solution:

Step-1: $\quad f(x) = \tfrac{1}{4}x^4 + \tfrac{2}{3}x^3 - \tfrac{1}{2}x^2 - 2x$

$\qquad\qquad f'(x) = x^3 + 2x^2 - x - 2$

Step-2: $\quad$ Put $\quad f'(x) = 0$

$\qquad\qquad \Rightarrow \quad x^3 + 2x^2 - x - 2 = 0$

$\qquad\qquad \Rightarrow \quad x^2(x+2) - (x+2) = 0$

$$\Rightarrow \qquad (x+2)(x^2-1) = 0$$
$$\Rightarrow \qquad (x+2)(x-1)(x+1) = 0$$
$$\Rightarrow \qquad x = -2,\, x = 1, \qquad x = -1$$

Step-3: $f'(x)$ is defined at every real number

(because it is a polynomial).

i.e., there is no value of x at which $f'(x)$ is not defined.

Step-4: $\therefore$ all critical points in increasing order are $-2, -1$ and 1.

Step-5: We have to check for local maxima and minima for each of these critical points.

(i) For $x = -2$

Take two values of x, first value slightly less than -2 and second slightly greater than -2, and check the sign of $f'(x)$ on both.

We can take -2.1 and -1.9 respectively.

Value of x	Sign of $f'(x)$
-2.1 (less than -2)	$-$
-1.9 (greater than -2)	$+$

It means sign of $f'(x)$ changes from $-$ to $+$ when we move from left to right on x-axis.

$\therefore$ **$x = -2$ is point of local minima**

and local minimum value is $f(-2) = \dfrac{2}{3}$

(ii) For $x = -1$

Take two values of x, first value slightly less than -1 and second slightly greater than -1, and check the sign of $f'(x)$ on both.

We can take -1.1 and -0.9 respectively.

Value of x	Sign of $f'(x)$
-1.1 (less than -1)	$+$
-0.9 (greater than -1)	$-$

It means sign of $f'(x)$ changes from $+$ to $-$ when we move from left to right on x-axis.

$\therefore$ **$x = -1$ is point of local maxima**

and local maximum value is $f(-1) = \dfrac{13}{12}$

(iii) For $x = 1$

Take two values of x, first value slightly less than 1 and second slightly greater than 1, and check the sign of $f'(x)$ on both.

We can take 0.9 and 1.1 respectively.

Value of x	Sign of $f'(x)$
0.9 (less than -1)	$-$
1.1 (greater than -1)	$+$

It means sign of $f'(x)$ changes from $-$ to $+$ when we move from left to right on x-axis.

$\therefore$ **$x = 1$ is point of local minima**

and local minimum value is $f(1) = -\dfrac{19}{12}$

<u>**Example**</u>

Find the local maxima and local minima of the function f given by
$$f(x) = 12\,x^{\frac{4}{3}} - 6\,x^{\frac{1}{3}}, \quad x \in [-1,1]. \text{ Also find the local maximum}$$
and minimum values.

Solution:

Step-1: $f(x) = 12\,x^{\frac{4}{3}} - 6\,x^{\frac{1}{3}}$

$$f'(x) = 16\,x^{\frac{1}{3}} - 2\,x^{-\frac{2}{3}}$$

$$= 16\,x^{\frac{1}{3}} - \frac{2}{x^{\frac{2}{3}}}$$

$$= \frac{16\,x - 2}{x^{\frac{2}{3}}} = \frac{2\,(8\,x - 1)}{x^{\frac{2}{3}}}$$

Step-2: Put $\quad f'(x) = 0$

$$\Rightarrow \quad \frac{2\,(8\,x - 1)}{x^{\frac{2}{3}}} = 0$$

$$\Rightarrow \quad x = \frac{1}{8}$$

Step-3: Here we see that $f'(x)$ is not defined at $x = 0$.

Step-4: $\therefore$ all critical points are 0 and $\dfrac{1}{8}$.

Step-5: We have to check for local maxima and minima for each of these critical points.

(i) For $x = 0$

$$f'(x) = \frac{2\,(8\,x - 1)}{x^{\frac{2}{3}}} = \frac{2\,(8\,x - 1)}{\left(x^2\right)^{\frac{1}{3}}}$$

We observe that denominator will remain always positive for any value of $x \neq 0$. We have to just check sign of numerator.

Take two values of x, first value slightly less than 0 and second slightly greater than 0 , and check the sign of $f'(x)$ on both.

We can take -0.1 and 0.1 respectively (their cube root can be be found easily).

Value of x	Sign of $f'(x)$
-0.1 (less than 0)	$-$
0.1 (greater than 0)	$-$

It means sign of $f'(x)$ doesn't change when we move from left to right on x-axis.

∴ $x = 0$ is neither point of local minima nor local maxima.

It is point of inflexion

(ii) For $x = \dfrac{1}{8}$

$$f'(x) = \frac{2\,(8\,x - 1)}{x^{\frac{2}{3}}} \;=\; \frac{2\,(8\,x - 1)}{\left(x^2\right)^{\frac{1}{3}}}$$

Take two values of x, first value slightly less than $\dfrac{1}{8}$ and second slightly greater than $\dfrac{1}{8}$, and check the sign of $f'(x)$ on both.

We can take $\dfrac{1}{9}$ and $\dfrac{1}{7}$ respectively.

Value of x	Sign of $f'(x)$
$\dfrac{1}{9}$ (less than $\dfrac{1}{8}$)	$-$
$\dfrac{1}{7}$ (greater than $\dfrac{1}{8}$)	$+$

It means sign of $f'(x)$ changes from $-$ to $+$ when we move from left to right on x-axis.

∴ $x = \dfrac{1}{8}$ is point of local minima

and local minimum value is

$$f\left(\tfrac{1}{8}\right) = 12\left(\tfrac{1}{8}\right)^{\frac{4}{3}} - 6\left(\tfrac{1}{8}\right)^{\frac{1}{3}} = -\frac{9}{4}$$

5.4.2 Second Derivative Method :

For a continuous function $f(x)$ in an interval **I** (open $(a,\ b)$ or closed $[a,\ b]$)

Step-1 Find $f'(x) = - - - - -$

Step-2 Put $f'(x) = 0$, and find the values of x which lie in the interval **I**.

Step-3 Find the values of x at which $f'(x)$ is not defined in the interval **I**.

Step-4 Values of x obtained, in step-2 and 3, are at critical points.

Step-5 Find $f''(x) = - - - -$

Step-6 If the values of x obtained in Step 2 are x_1, x_2, x_3, *then*
find the following:

$$f''(x_1) = - -, \qquad f''(x_2) = - -, \qquad f''(x_3) = - -,$$

Note the sign of $f''(x_1), \ f''(x_2), \ f''(x_3)$

Step-7

(i) If $f''(x_1)$ is $-$ ve, then $x = x_1$ is a point of Local Maximum and Local Maximum Value is $f(x_1)$

(ii) If $f''(x_1)$ is $+$ ve, then $x = x_1$ is a point of Local Minimum, and Local Minimum Value is $f(x_1)$

(iii) If $f''(x_1) = 0$, then **second derivative method fails** at $x = x_1$, and we have to **use First Derivative Method.**

→ Similarly we conclude for other values of x (which are obtained in step 2).

→ For the values of x (which are obtained in step 3) at which $f'(x)$ is **not defined**, the **second derivative method fails**, and we have to **use First Derivative Method.**

<u>**Example**</u>

Find the local maxima and local minima of the function f given by $f(x) = \frac{1}{4}x^4 + \frac{2}{3}x^3 - \frac{1}{2}x^2 - 2x$. Also find the local maximum and minimum values.

Solution:

Step-1: $f(x) = \frac{1}{4}x^4 + \frac{2}{3}x^3 - \frac{1}{2}x^2 - 2x$

$\qquad\qquad f'(x) = x^3 + 2x^2 - x - 2$

Step-2: Put $f'(x) = 0$

$\qquad \Rightarrow \quad x^3 + 2x^2 - x - 2 = 0$

$\qquad \Rightarrow \quad x^2(x+2) - (x+2) = 0$

$\qquad \Rightarrow \quad (x+2)(x^2 - 1) = 0$

$\qquad \Rightarrow \quad (x+2)(x-1)(x+1) = 0$

$\qquad \Rightarrow \quad x = -2, x = 1, \qquad\quad x = -1$

Step-3: $f'(x)$ is defined at every real number

$\qquad\qquad\qquad\qquad\qquad$ (because it is a polynomial).

$\qquad$ i.e., there is no value of x at which $f'(x)$ is **not defined.**

Step-4: $\therefore$ all critical points in increasing order are $-2, -1$ and 1

Step-5: Now $f'(x) = x^3 + 2x^2 - x - 2$

$\Rightarrow \quad f''(x) = 3x^2 + 4x - 1$

Step-6: We have to find value of $f''(x)$ at all critical points.

$f''(-2) = 3(-2)^2 + 4(-2) - 1 = 3 \ > 0$

$f''(-1) = 3(-1)^2 + 4(-1) - 1 = -2 \ <0$

$f''(1) = 3(1)^2 + 4(1) - 1 \ = 6 \quad > 0$

Step-7:

$\rightarrow$ Since $f''(-2)$ is $+$ve

$\therefore \ x = -2$ is point of local minima,

and local minimum value is $f(-2) = \dfrac{2}{3}$

$\rightarrow$ Since $f''(-1)$ is $-$ve

$\therefore \ x = -1$ is point of local maxima,

and local maximum value is $f(-1) = \dfrac{13}{12}$

$\rightarrow$ Since $f''(1)$ is $+$ve

$\therefore \ x = 1$ is point of local minima,

and local minimum value is $f(1) = -\dfrac{19}{12}$

5.5 Word Problems on maxima and minima

To solve the word problems on maxima and minima, we proceed as follows:

Step-1 Write down the formula or relation of the quantity (like volume, area, cost etc.), which is to be maximised or minimised.

For example, if curved surface area of right circular cylinder is to be maximised, we write its relation , $S = 2\pi r h$. This is the function to be maximised.

Step-2 If the function written in step-1 has two or more variables, find the relation(s) among them from the given situation or from the figure or it may, already, be given in the problem.

Step-3 From the relation found in step-2, express one variable in terms of the other, and put it in the function written in step-1. It will change the function in one variable only. *For example*, expression of curved surface area of right circular cylinder is in terms of radius and height. If both are variables, then we have to find the relation between r and h from the given situation (*see* in example later).

And express r in terms of h or h in terms of r. It will change the area in terms only r or only h.

Step-4 Now we have got the function in one variable, which is to be maximised or minimised. So, we follow the steps of maxima and minima using 1st derivative or 2nd derivative methods.

Example

Of all the closed right circular cylinder , of a given volume , prove that the surface area is minimum when height is double its radius.

Solution:

Let

$$r \; = \; radius\ of\ cylinder$$
$$h \; = \; height\ of\ cylinder$$
$$S \; = \; total\ surface\ area\ of\ cylinder$$

$\left. \right\}$ *variables*

V = volume of cylinder

(V is constant because it is given)

Step-1: We have to minimise the surface area of closed right circular cylinder, and its formula is:

$$S = 2\pi rh + 2\pi r^2 \qquad \ldots (i)$$

Step-2: In the above expression of surface area, there are two variables r and h .

We can obtain the relationship between r and h by writing formula of volume, which is constant.

(because it is mentioned as given in the question)

$$V = \pi r^2 h \qquad \ldots (ii)$$

(We say that it is relation between r and h only as V is constant)

Step-3: We must eliminate either r or h from eqn(i) using eqn(ii).

Since it is easier to put h in term of r in eqn(i), we find h in terms of r from (ii), and put in (i).

$$\therefore \quad h = \frac{V}{\pi r^2} \qquad \ldots (iii)$$

Eqn(i) becomes

$$S = 2\pi r \left(\frac{V}{\pi r^2} \right) + 2\pi r^2$$

$$\Rightarrow \quad S = \left(\frac{2V}{r} \right) + 2\pi r^2 \qquad \ldots (iv)$$

Step-4: This is a function of r and is to be minimised. We can write it as :

$$S(r) = \left(\frac{2V}{r}\right) + 2\pi r^2$$

We can proceed as in maxima/minima by 2nd derivative method.

Differentiating w.r.t. 'r', we get

$$S'(r) = \frac{-2V}{r^2} + 4\pi r \qquad \ldots\ldots (v)$$

Put $S'(r) = 0$ to find critical point

$$\Rightarrow \quad \frac{-2V}{r^2} + 4\pi r = 0$$

$$\Rightarrow \quad 4\pi r = \frac{2V}{r^2}$$

$$\Rightarrow \quad r^3 = \frac{V}{2\pi}$$

$$\Rightarrow \quad r = \left(\frac{V}{2\pi}\right)^{\frac{1}{3}} \qquad \ldots\ldots (vi)$$

$$\text{(This is the critical point for } S(r))$$

We note that $S'(r)$ is not defined at $r = 0$, and it should also be a critical point. But radius $= 0$ is not possible. So, we reject this as critical point.

Now differentiating $S'(r)$ of eqn(v) w.r.t. 'r', we get

$$S''(r) = \frac{4V}{r^3} + 4\pi$$

$$\Rightarrow \quad S''\left(\left(\frac{V}{2\pi}\right)^{\frac{1}{3}}\right) = \frac{4V}{\left(\left(\frac{V}{2\pi}\right)^{\frac{1}{3}}\right)^3} + 4\pi$$

$$\Rightarrow \quad S''\left(\left(\frac{V}{2\pi}\right)^{\frac{1}{3}}\right) = \frac{4V}{\left(\frac{V}{2\pi}\right)} + 4\pi = 8\pi > 0$$

Since $S''\left(\left(\frac{V}{2\pi}\right)^{\frac{1}{3}}\right) > 0$

$$\therefore \quad S(r) \text{ is minimum at } r = \left(\frac{V}{2\pi}\right)^{\frac{1}{3}}$$

Putting $r = \left(\dfrac{V}{2\pi}\right)^{\frac{1}{3}}$ in eqn(iii) , we can get h when surface is minimum.

$$h = \frac{V}{\pi\left(\left(\dfrac{V}{2\pi}\right)^{\frac{1}{3}}\right)^2} = 2\left(\dfrac{V}{2\pi}\right)^{\frac{1}{3}} = 2r$$

Thus, surface area of a closed right circular cylinder, of given volume, is minimum when its height is double of its radius.

5.5.1 Maxima and Minima in Inscribed/circumscribed figures

Here, we will find relations between variables for some important inscribed or circumscribed figures.

1) <u>Cylinder in cone</u>

If a right circular cylinder is to be inscribed in a right circular cone, then every dimension of cone (radius, height and slant height) is constant while radius and height of cylinder are variables.

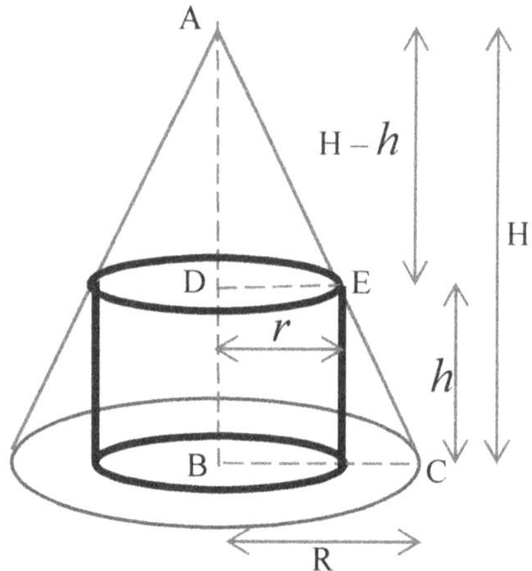

Let   Radius of base of cone = R (constant)
Height of cone   = H (constant)
Radius of cylinder = r (variable)
Height of cylinder = h (variable)

Here, axis of inscribed cylinder and the axis of outer cone both will coincide as shown in the above figure.
In the figure, we have

DE = r (Radius of cylinder), BC = R (Radius of cone)

BD = h (Height of cylinder), AB = H (Height of cone)

$\Rightarrow$ AD = AB – BD = H – h

Now $\triangle$ ADE ~ $\triangle$ ABC   . .(by AA similarity criterion)

$\Rightarrow \quad \dfrac{AD}{AB} = \dfrac{DE}{BC} = \dfrac{AE}{AC}$

. . . (Corresponding sides of similar triangles are in proportion)

Take $\dfrac{AD}{AB} = \dfrac{DE}{BC}$ from the above relation.

$\Rightarrow \quad \dfrac{H-h}{H} = \dfrac{r}{R}$

$\Rightarrow \quad r = \dfrac{R}{H}(H - h) \qquad$ or $\qquad h = H - \dfrac{H}{R}r$

Using these relations, we can convert r in terms of h or h in terms of r.

2) <u>Cylinder in sphere</u>

If a right circular cylinder is to be inscribed in a sphere, then the radius of sphere is constant while radius and height of cylinder are variables.

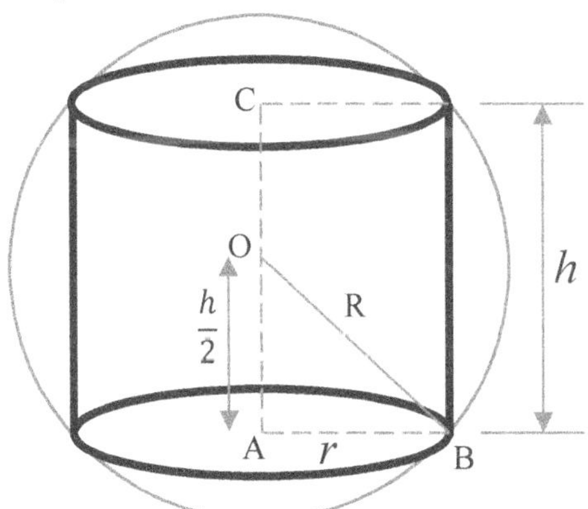

Let   Radius of sphere = R (constant)

radius of cylinder = r (variable)

Height of cylinder = h (variable)

Here, the centre of sphere will lie on the axis of cylinder at its mid-point O as shown in the figure.

In the figure,

AB = r (Radius of cylinder),

OB = R (Radius of sphere)

$AC = h$ (Height of cylinder) , $OA = \dfrac{h}{2}$

Using Pythagoras theorem in ΔOAB

$$OB^2 = OA^2 + AB^2$$

$$\Rightarrow \quad R^2 = (h/2)^2 + r^2$$

$$\Rightarrow \quad r^2 = R^2 - \dfrac{h^2}{4} \quad \text{or} \quad h^2 = 4\,(R^2 - r^2)$$

Using these relations, we can convert r in terms of h or h in terms of r.

3) <u>Cone in sphere</u>

If a right circular cone is to be inscribed in a sphere, then the radius of sphere is constant while all dimensions of cone (radius of base, height and slant height) are variables.

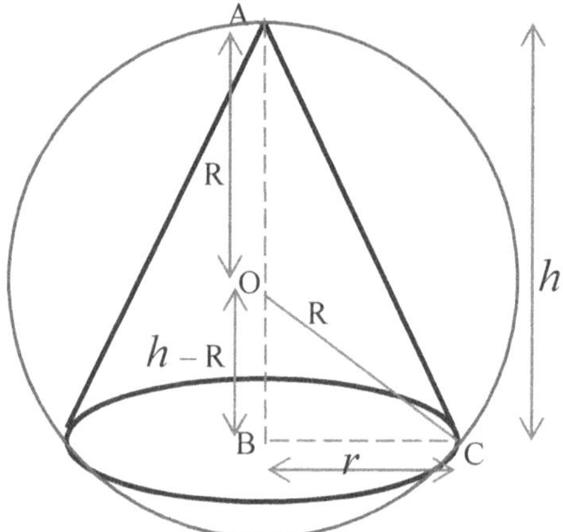

Let   Radius of sphere = R (constant)

        Radius of cone $= r$ (variable)

        Height of cone $= h$ (variable)

Here, the centre of sphere will lie on the axis of cone **but not at its mid-point** O as shown in the figure.

In the figure,

$BC = r$ (Radius of base of cone),

$OA = OC =$ R (Radius of sphere)

$AB = h$ (Height of cone) ,

$OB = AB - OA = h - R$

Using Pythagoras theorem in ΔOBC

$$OC^2 = OB^2 + BC^2$$

$$\Rightarrow \quad R^2 = (h - R)^2 + r^2$$
$$\Rightarrow \quad r^2 = 2Rh - h^2 \quad \text{or} \quad h = \sqrt{(R^2 - r^2)} + R$$

Using these relations, we can convert r in terms of h or h in terms of r.

4) **<u>Rectangle in Circle</u>**

If a rectangle is to be inscribed in a circle, then the radius of circle is constant while dimensions of rectangle (length and breadth) are variables.

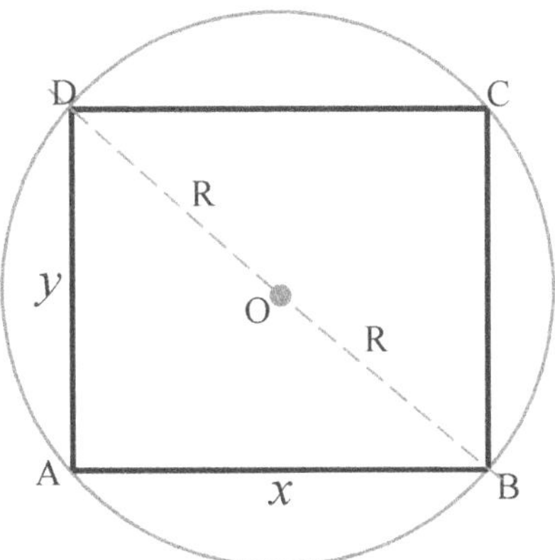

Let   Radius of circle = R (constant)

       Length of rectangle = x (variable)

       Breadth of rectangle = y (variable)

Here, the centre, O of circle will lie on the diagonals of rectangle.

∴ Diagonals of rectangle are diameters of circle as shown in the figure.

In the figure,

AB = x (length of rectangle),

OB = OD = R (Radius of circle)

AD = y (breadth of rectangle) ,

BD = 2R (diameter of circle)

Using Pythagoras theorem in $\triangle$ABD
$$BD^2 = AB^2 + AD^2$$
($\because \angle A = 90°$, each angle of rectangle is right angle)
$$\Rightarrow \quad (2R)^2 = x^2 + y^2$$
$$\Rightarrow \quad 4R^2 = x^2 + y^2$$

Using this relation, we can convert x in terms of y or y in terms of x.